W9-BIN-450

Human Resource Management
Essential Perspectives
third edition

Robert L. Mathis
University of Nebraska at Omaha

John H. Jackson
University of Wyoming

THOMSON
—TM
SOUTH-WESTERN

Australia · Canada · Mexico · Singapore · Spain · United Kingdom · United States

THOMSON

SOUTH-WESTERN ™

Human Resource Management: Essential Perspectives, 3/e
Robert L. Mathis and John H. Jackson

VP/Editorial Director:
Jack W. Calhoun

VP/Editor-in-Chief:
Michael P. Roche

Executive Editor:
John Szilagyi

Sr. Developmental Editor:
Mardell Toomey

Marketing Manager:
Jacque Carrillo

Production Editor:
Margaret M. Bril

Media Developmental Editor:
Kristen Meere

Media Production Editor:
Karen Schaffer

Manufacturing Coordinator:
Diane Lohman

Production House:
Trejo Production

Printer:
Webcom
Toronto, Ontario M1W 2S7

Design Project Manager:
Justin Klefeker

Internal Designer:
Justin Klefeker

Cover Designer:
Justin Klefeker

Cover Images:
© Photodisc

COPYRIGHT © 2005
by South-Western, part of
the Thomson Corporation.
South-Western, Thomson,
and the Thomson logo are
trademarks used herein under
license.

Printed in Canada
2 3 4 5 07 06 05 04

ISBN: 0-324-20217-2

Library of Congress Control
Number:
2003114607

ALL RIGHTS RESERVED.

No part of this work covered
by the copyright hereon may
be reproduced or used in any
form or by any means—graphic,
electronic, or mechanical,
including photocopying, recording, taping, Web distribution
or information storage and
retrieval systems—without
the written permission of the
publisher.

For permission to use material
from this text or product,
contact us by
Tel (800) 730-2214
Fax (800) 730-2215
http://www.thomsonrights.com

For more information
contact South-Western,
5191 Natorp Boulevard,
Mason, Ohio 45040.
Or you can visit our Internet
site at:
http://www.swlearning.com

Foundations of Strategic Management, 3e

Jeffrey S. Harrison and Caron H. St. John

0-324-25917-4 Available January 2004

Foundations of Strategic Management provides a concise and balanced introduction to the important theories and views in the field of strategy. The authors present an up-to-date look at the most critical topics in strategy today and use examples from cutting-edge firms to help learners begin to understand and develop decision-making and analysis techniques that are relevant in all types of organizations. Its brevity allows instructors to tailor their courses by incorporating additional readings and cases of their choosing.

A Primer for Management

Michael P. Dumler and Steven J. Skinnner

0-324-27111-5 Available January 2004

A *Primer for Management* is a concise introduction to the functions of management. It charts the links between management's essential concepts and their applicability to today's organizations, but its real strength lies in the way that it distills the big ideas. All the important concepts that instructors try to communicate to their students—how to build, plan, organize, lead, control, and sustain organizations—are covered in this brief and streamlined text. Its brevity allows instructors to tailor their courses by incorporating additional readings and cases of their choosing.

About the Authors

DR. ROBERT L. MATHIS

Dr. Robert Mathis is a Professor of Management at the University of Nebraska at Omaha (UNO). Born and raised in Texas, he received a BBA and MBA from Texas Tech University and a Ph.D. in management and organization from the University of Colorado. At UNO he received the university's "Excellence in Teaching" award.

Dr. Mathis has co-authored several books and published numerous articles covering a variety of topics over the last twenty-five years. On the professional level, Dr. Mathis has held numerous national offices in the Society for Human Resource Management and in other professional organizations, including the Academy of Management. He also served as President of the Human Resource Certification Institute (HRCI) and is certified as a Senior Professional in Human Resources (SPHR) by HRCI.

He has had extensive consulting experiences with organizations of all sizes in a variety of areas. Firms assisted have been in telecommunications, telemarketing, financial, manufacturing, retail, health care, and utility industries. He has extensive specialized consulting experience in establishing or revising compensation plans for small and medium-sized firms. Internationally, Dr. Mathis has consulting and training experience with organizations in Australia, Lithuania, Romania, Moldova, and Taiwan.

DR. JOHN H. JACKSON

Dr. John H. Jackson is a Professor of Management at the University of Wyoming. Born in Alaska, he received his BBA and MBA from Texas Tech University. He then worked in the telecommunications industry in human resources management for several years. After leaving that industry, he completed his doctoral studies at the University of Colorado and received his Ph.D. in management and organization.

During his academic career, Dr. Jackson has authored six other college texts and more than fifty articles and papers, including those appearing in *Academy of Management Review, Journal of Management, Human Resources Management,* and *Human Resource Planning.* He has consulted with a variety of organizations on HR and management development matters and served as an expert witness in a number of HR-related cases.

At the University of Wyoming he served three terms as department head in the Department of Management and Marketing. Dr. Jackson received the university's highest teaching award and worked with two-way interactive television for MBA students. He designed one of the first classes in the nation on Business, Environment, and Natural Resources. Two Wyoming state governors have appointed him to the Wyoming Business Council and the Workforce Development Council. Dr. Jackson is also president of Silverwood Ranches, Inc.

Preface

The importance of human resources issue for managers and organizations is evident every day. As indicated by frequent headlines and news media reports on downsizing, workforce shortages, sexual harassment, union activity, and other topics, the management of human resources is growing in importance in the United States and the world. Many individuals are affected by HR issues; consequently, they will benefit by becoming more knowledgeable about HR management. Those interested in the field of HR management must understand more about the nature of various HR activities. Every manager's HR actions can have major consequences for organizations. This book has been prepared to provide an essential overview of HR management for students, HR practitioners, and others in organizations.

A need exists for an overview of HR management that both HR practitioners and students can use. The positive reception of the previous editions of *Human Resource Management: Essential Perspectives* proved this need. Consequently, we are pleased to provide an updated version. In addition, this book presents information in a way that is useful to various industry groups and professional organizations. Finally, this condensed view of HR management also addresses the tremendous interest in U.S. practices of HR management in other countries, making it a valuable resource for managers worldwide.

As authors, it is our belief that this book will be a useful and interesting resource for those desiring a concise discussion of the important issues and practices in HR management. It is our hope that it will contribute to more effective management of human resources in organizations.

Robert L. Mathis, Ph.D., SPHR
John H. Jackson, Ph.D.

Table of Contents

Human Resource Management

Essential Perspectives

Chapter 1

Basics of Human Resource Management

For many organizations, talented employees are the cornerstone of a competitive advantage. If the organization competes based on new ideas, outstanding customer service, or quick, accurate decisions, having excellent employees is critical.[1] Of course, not every organization must compete on the basis of having the best employees, but even for those that do not, employees are a major source of performance, problems, growth, resistance, and lawsuits.

NATURE OF HUMAN RESOURCE MANAGEMENT

Human Resource (HR) management is a field that has evolved a great deal since its beginnings about 1900. It began as a primarily clerical operation concerned with payroll, employee records, and arranging community visits. The social legislation of the 1960s and 1970s forced dramatic changes. "Personnel departments," as they were called, became concerned with the legal ramifications of policies and procedures affecting employees. In the 1990s, globalization, competition, mergers, and acquisitions forced Human Resource departments to become more concerned with costs, planning, and the implications of various HR (human resources) strategies for both organizations and their employees.

HR in Small and Large Organizations

Not every organization is able to have an HR department. In a company with an owner and 10 employees, the owner usually takes care of HR issues. However, despite the obvious differences between large and small organizations, the same HR issues must be managed. At about 80–100 employees, organizations typically need to designate a person to specialize in HR management. Others are added only as the company gets much larger. The specific HR activities that must be done in any organization regardless of its size are discussed in the next section.

HR Activities

HR management is composed of several groups of interlinked activities taking place within the context of the organization, represented by the inner rings in Figure 1.1. Additionally, all managers with HR responsibilities must consider external environmental forces—legal, political, economic, social, cultural, and technological—when addressing these activities.

▶ *HR Planning and Analysis.* Through *HR planning,* managers attempt to anticipate forces that will influence the future supply of and demand for employees. Having adequate *human resource information systems (HRIS)* to provide accurate and timely information for HR planning is crucial. The importance of human resources in organizational competitiveness must be addressed as well.

▶ *Equal Employment Opportunity.* Compliance with equal employment opportunity (EEO) laws and regulations affects all other HR activities and is integral to \ HR management. For instance, strategic HR plans must ensure sufficient availability of a *diversity* of individuals to meet *affirmative action* requirements.

▶ *Staffing.* The aim of staffing is to provide an adequate supply of qualified individuals to fill the jobs in an organization. By studying what workers do, *job analysis* is the foundation for the staffing function. Then *job descriptions* and *job specifications* can be prepared to be used when *recruiting* applicants for job openings. The *selection* process is concerned with choosing qualified individuals to fill jobs in the organization.

▶ *HR Development.* Beginning with the *orientation* of new employees, HR development also includes *job-skill training.* As jobs evolve and change, ongoing *retraining* is necessary to accommodate technological changes. Encouraging *development* of all employees, including supervisors and managers, is necessary to prepare organizations for future challenges. *Career planning* identifies paths and activities for individual employees as they develop within the organization.

▶ *Compensation and Benefits.* Compensation rewards people for performing organizational work through *pay, incentives,* and *benefits.* Employers must develop and refine their basic *wage and salary* systems. Also, *incentive programs* such as gainsharing and productivity rewards are growing in usage. The rapid increase in the costs of *benefits,* especially health-care benefits, will continue to be a major issue.

▶ *Health, Safety, and Security.* Ensuring the physical and mental health and safety of employees is vital. The Occupational Safety and Health Act of 1970 (OSHA) has made organizations more responsive to *health and safety* concerns. Additionally, workplace *security* has grown in importance in response to the increasing number of acts of workplace violence.

FIGURE 1.1 HR Management Activities

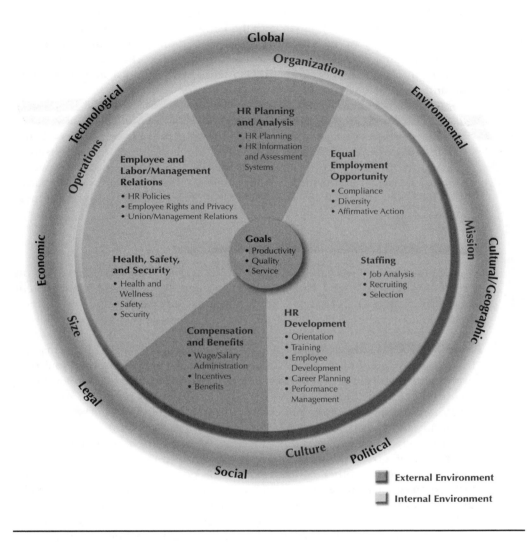

► *Employee and Labor/Management Relations.* The relationship between managers and their employees must be handled effectively if both the employees and the organization are to prosper together. Whether or not some of the employees are represented by a union, *employee rights* must be addressed. It is important to develop, communicate, and update HR *policies and procedures* so that managers and employees alike know what is expected.

GLOBALIZATION OF BUSINESS AND HR

Throughout the world in developed, industrialized countries such as those in the European Union (EU), Japan, and the United States, population growth has slowed significantly. In those areas an aging population and declining birth rates have contributed to slower growth in the number of workers and consumers. However, the population in China, India, Africa, Latin America, and other countries and regions continues to grow significantly.

To take advantage of this growth, firms throughout the world have established operations, formed joint ventures, or merged with firms in these countries. The prospect of billions of new consumers and employees in the faster-growing countries is driving global investments and operations. Consumer demands for products from other countries is also driving globalization. As examples, German and Japanese cars, French cosmetics, U.S. fast food, Mexican beer, and Korean electronics are all available globally and desired by consumers in many countries.

Factors Affecting Global HR Management

Managing human resources in different cultures, economies, and legal systems presents some challenges. However, when done well, global HR management pays dividends. Doing business globally requires consideration of four general factors.

Legal and Political Factors. The nature and stability of political systems vary from country to country. Firms in the United States are accustomed to a relatively stable political system, and the same is true in many of the other developed countries in Europe. Although presidents, prime ministers, premiers, governors, senators, and representatives may change, the well-established legal systems offer continuity and consistency on which global firms can depend.

However, many other nations function under turbulent legal and political systems. Some governments regularly are overthrown by military coups. Dictators and despots in other countries use their power to require international firms to buy goods and services from host-country firms owned or controlled by the rulers or the rulers' families. In some parts of the world, the number of political parties and factions causes constant change in governments. In other countries, one-party rule or a ruling "political elite" has led to pervasive corruption.

Economic Factors. Economic factors are linked to political, legal, and cultural issues, and different countries have different economic systems. Some even still operate with a modified version of communism, which has essentially failed. For example, in China communism is the official doctrine. But as the government attempts to move to a more mixed model, it is using the capitalist tools of unemployment and layoffs to reduce government enterprises bloated with too many workers.

In addition, nations with weak economies may not be able to invest in maintaining and upgrading the necessary elements of their infrastructures, such as roads, electric power, schools, and telecommunications. The absence of good infrastructures may make it more difficult to convince managers from the United States, EU countries, or Japan to take assignments overseas.

Cultural Factors. Cultural forces represent another important concern affecting international HR management. **Culture** is composed of the societal forces affecting the values, beliefs, and actions of a distinct group of people. Cultural differences certainly exist between nations, but significant cultural differences exist within countries also. One only has to look at the conflicts caused by religion or ethnicity in Central Europe and other parts of the world to see the importance of culture in international organizations.

U.S. WORKFORCE AVAILABILITY AND QUALITY

In some industries and areas in the United States today, workforce availability and quality concerns exist due to an inadequate supply of workers with the skills needed to perform the jobs being added. Also, industries and companies repeatedly report shortages of some types of qualified, experienced workers. Consequently, HR professionals face greater pressures to retain, recruit, and train workers.

Even though more Americans are graduating from high school (84% over age 25 have high school diplomas) and from college (almost 26% over age 25 now have college degrees), employers are often concerned about the preparation and specific skills of new graduates.[2] Comparisons of international test results show that U.S. children perform slightly above average in math and science, but *well behind* some other directly competitive nations.[3] Also, graduates with degrees in computers, engineering and health sciences remain in short supply relative to the demand for them that is expected over the next five years.

Growth in Contingent Workforce

In the past, temporary workers were used for vacation relief, maternity leave, or workload peaks. Today "contingent workers" (temporary workers, independent contractors, leased employees, and part-timers) represent more than 20% of the workforce. Many employers operate with a core group of regular employees with critical skills and then expand and contract the workforce through the use of contingent workers.[4]

One reason for use of contingent workers is the possible reduction in legal liability for employers. As more and more employment-related lawsuits are filed, some employers have become more wary about adding regular employees. Instead, by using contract workers supplied by others, employers face fewer employment legal issues regarding selection, discrimination, benefits, discipline, and termination.

Demographics and Diversity

The U.S. workforce has been changing dramatically. It is more diverse racially, women are in the labor force in much greater numbers than ever before, and the average age of the workforce is now considerably older than before. As a result of these demographic shifts, HR management in organizations has had to adapt to a more varied labor force both externally and internally. For example, at Trident Manufacturing in Webster, New York, 14 different languages are spoken on the shop floor.[5] Major changes in the demographics and diversity of the workforce include the following:

▶ Minority racial and ethnic persons account for a growing percentage of the overall labor force, with the percentage of Latinos equal to or exceeding the number of African Americans. Immigrants will continue to expand this growth.

▶ A growing number of individuals characterize themselves as "multiracial," suggesting that the American "melting pot" is blurring racial/ethnic identities.

▶ Women constitute a growing percentage of the U.S. workforce, and a majority of women with younger children are employed. A large percentage of the 3.67 million new moms are in the workforce.

▶ The average age of the U.S. population and workforce is increasing, and a large number of those workers will be retiring from full-time employment in the next five to ten years.

▶ A significant number of individuals have disabilities, but they also represent a pool of highly motivated and capable individuals.

Balancing Work and Family

For many workers in the United States, balancing the demands of family and work is a significant challenge. Although this balancing has always been a concern, the increased number of working women and dual-career couples has resulted in greater tensions for many workers.

The decline of the traditional family and the increasing numbers of dual-career couples and working single parents place more stress on employees to balance family and work. To respond to pressures faced by employees, many employers have instituted various "family friendly" initiatives. Although important to both males and females, the reality is that family care for children and elderly relatives still is carried primarily by women. Thus, actions taken by employers to enable women to balance work and family responsibilities can be beneficial for both employee retention and organizational productivity.

Organizational Restructuring

To respond to these changes, many organizations have restructured by: (1) eliminating layers of managers, (2) closing facilities, (3) merging with other organizations, and (4) outplacing workers. A common transformation has been to flatten organizations by removing several layers of management in order to improve productivity, quality, and service while also reducing costs. As a result, jobs are redesigned and people affected. One of the challenges that HR management faces with organizational restructuring is dealing with such human consequences of change as a survivor's mentality for those who remain, unfulfilled cost savings estimates, loss of loyalty, and many people looking for new jobs.

Mergers and acquisitions frequently fail to achieve their planned financial and strategic objectives. Many possible reasons explain why attempted M&As fail, and several of those reasons are in the HR arena.[6] Unanticipated consequences of restructuring after an M&A often cause the need for more organizational restructuring later and a longer time frame for normal operations to resume.

HR MANAGEMENT ROLES

HR management professionals and their responsibilities, approaches, and credibility with upper management vary from organization to organization. In some, HR is a full, contributing partner to the mission and strategies of organizations. In such firms senior executives would not even consider a merger without consulting HR on the issues previously mentioned. However, in other organizations HR remains more of a clerical and administrative operation limited primarily to doing payroll and benefits work. Figure 1.2 shows the different roles for HR Management, and these roles are discussed next.

FIGURE 1.2 Different Roles for HR Management

- **Strategic**: As business contributor
- **Operational**: Manages most HR activities
- **Employee Advocate**: Serves as "morale officer"
- **Administrative**: Focuses extensively on clerical administration

Administrative Role for HR

At the most basic level, the necessary HR activities in a company are handled by operating managers or "outsourced" under contract to specialized vendors. At this level HR management is mostly a clerical and administrative support operation. The organization may not even hire any employees directly, but "lease" them for a fee from an employee leasing firm that hires, pays, provides benefits, and dismisses them when necessary.

Employee Advocate Role for HR

Traditionally, HR has been viewed as the "employee advocate" in organizations. As the voice for employee concerns, HR professionals traditionally have been seen as "company morale officers" who do not understand the business realities of the organizations and do not contribute measurably to the strategic success of the business. Some have even suggested dismantling HR departments totally because they contribute little to the productivity and growth of organizations.

Despite this view, someone must be the "champion" for employees and employee issues. HR professionals spend considerable time on HR "crisis management" dealing with employee problems that are both work- and nonwork-related.

Operational Role for HR

Typically the operational role requires HR professionals to identify and implement needed programs and policies in the organization in cooperation with operating managers. This role traditionally includes many of the HR activities mentioned earlier in the chapter. HR implements plans suggested by or developed in conjunction with other managers, as well as those identified by HR professionals. Even though priorities may change as labor markets and the economy change, in the operational role HR managers devote time to a variety of basic HR concerns.

The operational HR role emphasizes support for the organization through adept handling of HR problems and issues. However, HR may not be heavily involved in strategic decision making in the organization.

Strategic Role for HR

For HR to play a strategic role it must focus on the longer-term implications of HR issues. How changing workforce demographics and workforce shortages will affect the organization, and what means will be used to address the shortages over time, are examples of the strategic role. A strategic role for HR is important, but it requires a high level of professional and business knowledge.

The importance of the strategic role has been the subject of extensive discussions recently in the field, and those discussions emphasize the need for HR management to become a greater strategic contributor to the success of organizations. Even organizations that are not-for-profit, such as governmental or social service entities, must manage their human resources in a "business-oriented" manner. The research and writings of a number of scholars stress the role of HR as a *strategic business partner.*

ETHICS AND HR

As the issues faced in HR management increase in number and complexity, so do the pressures and challenges of acting ethically. Ethical issues pose fundamental questions about fairness, justice, truthfulness, and social responsibility. Concerns arise about the ethical standards used by managers and employees, particularly those in business organizations. It appears that the concerns are well-founded, based on many of the "scandals" involving Enron, MCI, Citibank, and others during the past five years.

What Is Ethical Behavior?

Ethics deals with what "ought" to be done. For the HR professional it is the way in which the manager *ought* to act relative to a given human resource issue. However, determining specific actions is not always easy. Just complying with the laws does not guarantee ethical behavior. Laws and regulations cannot cover every situation HR professionals and employees will face. Instead, people must be guided by values and personal behavior "codes," including the following:

▶ Does the behavior or result meet all applicable *laws, regulations, and government codes?*
▶ Does the behavior or result achieved meet all *organizational standards* of ethical behavior?
▶ Does the behavior or result achieved *meet professional standards* of ethical behavior?

HR MANAGEMENT COMPETENCIES AND CAREERS

As HR management becomes more and more complex, greater demands are placed on individuals who make the HR field their career specialty. Although most readers of this book will not become HR managers, it is useful to know about the competencies required for effective HR management.

A wide variety of jobs can be performed in HR departments. As a firm grows large enough to need someone to focus primarily on HR activities, the role of the **HR generalist** emerges—that is, a person who has responsibility for performing a variety of HR activities. Further growth leads to adding **HR specialists** who have in-depth knowledge and expertise in a limited area. Intensive knowledge of an activity such as benefits, testing, training, or affirmative action compliance typifies the work of HR specialists.

Changes in the HR field are leading to changes in the competencies and capabilities of individuals concentrating on HR management. The development of broader competencies by HR professionals will ensure that HR management plays a strategic role in organizations. The following sets of capabilities are important for HR professionals:

▶ Knowledge of business and organization
▶ Influence and change management
▶ Specific HR knowledge and expertise

Professional Certification

One of the characteristics of a professional field is having a means to certify the knowledge and competence of members of the profession. The CPA for accountants and the CLU for life insurance underwriters are well-known examples. The most well-known certification program for HR generalists is administered by the Human Resource Certification Institute (HRCI), which is affiliated with the Society for Human Resource Management (SHRM). More than 12,000 HR professionals take the HRCI each year. The HRCI test specifications are available in Appendix A.

Increasingly, employers hiring or promoting HR professionals are requesting certification as a "plus." HR professionals feel that HR certification gives them more credibility with corporate peers and senior managers. Certification by HRCI is available at two levels, Professional in Human Resources (PHR) and Senior Professional in Human Resources (SPHR).

HR AS AN ORGANIZATIONAL CORE COMPETENCY

Certainly, many organizations have voiced the idea that their human resources differentiate them from their competitors. Organizations as widely diverse as FedEx, Nordstrom's Department Stores, and Dell Computers have focused on human resources as having special strategic value for the organization.

Some ways that human resources can become a core competency as appropriate are through attracting and retaining employees with unique professional and technical capabilities, investing in training and development of those employees, and compensating them in ways that retain and keep them competitive with their counterparts in other organizations. For example, smaller community-oriented banks have picked up numerous small- and medium-sized commercial loan customers because they have emphasized that "you can talk to the same person," rather than having to call an automated service center in another state.

Organizational Strategies Based on Human Resources

Recognition has been growing that, under certain conditions, human resources contribute to a competitive advantage for organizations. People can be an organizational core competency when they have special capabilities to make decisions and be innovative in ways that competitors cannot easily imitate.[7] Having those capabilities requires selection, training, and retention of good employees. An employee group without those special abilities would *not* be as strong a basis for competitive advantage.

The shared values and beliefs of a workforce make up the **organizational culture**. For people to be a core competency managers must consider the culture of the organization because otherwise excellent strategies can be negated by a culture incompatible with those strategies. Further, the culture of the organization, as viewed by the people in it, affects attraction and retention of competent employees. Numerous examples can be given of key technical, professional, and administrative employees leaving firms because of corporate cultures that seem to devalue people and create barriers to the use of individual capabilities.[8]

Organizations and Productivity

Productivity at the organizational level ultimately affects profitability and competitiveness in a for-profit organization, and total costs in a not-for-profit organization. Perhaps none of the resources used for productivity in organizations are so closely scrutinized as the human resources. Many of the activities undertaken in an HR system are designed to affect individual or organizational productivity. Pay, appraisal systems, training, selection, job design, and compensation are HR activities directly concerned with productivity.

A useful way to measure organizational HR productivity is by considering **unit labor cost**, which is computed by dividing the average cost of workers by their average levels of output. Using unit labor costs, one can see that a company paying relatively high wages still can be economically competitive if it can also achieve an offsetting high productivity level. Low unit labor costs can be a basis for a strategy focusing on human resources.

U.S. firms have been on a decade-long crusade to improve organizational productivity. Much of the productivity improvement efforts focused on their workforces. The early stages included downsizing, re-engineering jobs, increasing computer usage, and working employees harder and longer. These approaches have been useful in some firms. Some ideas for the next round in productivity improvements include:

▶ *Outsourcing:* Contract with someone else to perform activities previously done by employees of the organization. For instance, if UPS can deliver products at a lower cost than a manufacturing company can ship them internally, then the firm could outsource shipping to UPS.

▶ *Making workers more efficient by using capital equipment:* Typically, the more spent on equipment per worker, the greater the output per worker.

▶ *Completely replacing workers with equipment:* Certain jobs are not done as well by humans. The jobs may be mindless, physically difficult, or require extreme precision. For example, a ditch usually is better dug by one person operating a backhoe than by several workers with shovels.

▶ *Helping workers work better:* Replace outmoded processes, methods, and rules. Also, find better ways of training people to work more efficiently.

▶ *Redesigning the work:* Some work can be redesigned to make it faster, easier, and possibly even more rewarding to employees. Such changes generally improve productivity.

Linking HR Planning and Strategy for Competitive Advantage

Many think that organizations decide on strategies and then HR planning is done to supply the right number and kinds of employees. However, the relationship should go deeper. Figure 1.3 shows the relationship among the variables that determine the HR plans an organization will adopt. Because business strategies affect HR plans, consideration of HR issues should be part of the initial input to the strategy formulation process. For example, it may be important to identify competitive advantage opportunities that fit the existing employees or assess strategic alternatives given the current capabilities of organizational human resources. HR professionals should be doing environmental scanning to know and pinpoint which skills are available and which are not. HR professionals also should be able to estimate lead times for adjusting to labor shortages or surpluses, because HR will be involved in implementing any strategies that affect people.[9]

FIGURE 1.3   Factors That Determine HR Plans

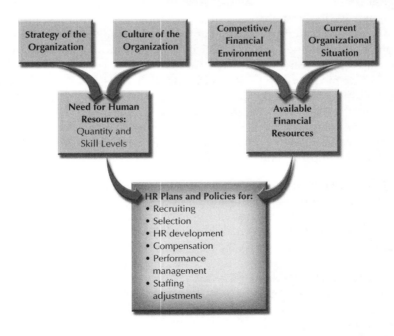

HUMAN RESOURCE PLANNING

The competitive organizational strategy of the firm derived with input from HR becomes the basis for **human resource (HR) planning**, which is the process of analyzing and identifying the need for and availability of human resources so that the organization can meet its objectives. This section discusses HR planning responsibilities, the importance of HR planning even in small businesses, and the HR planning process.

Developing the HR Plan

The HR plan is guided by longer-term organizational plans. For example, in planning for human resources, an organization must consider the allocation of people to jobs over long periods of time, not just for the next month or even the next year. This level of planning requires knowledge of strategic expansions or reductions in operations and any technological changes that may affect the organization. On the basis of such analyses, plans can be made for shifting employees within the organization, laying off or otherwise cutting back the number of employees, retraining present employees, or increasing the number of employees in certain areas. Factors to consider include the current employees' knowledge, skills, and abilities in the organization and the expected vacancies resulting from retirements, promotions, transfers, or discharge.

The most telling evidence of successful HR planning is an organization in which the human resources are consistently aligned with the needs of the business over a period of time. If HR planning is done well, the following benefits should result:

▶ Upper management has a better view of the human resource dimensions of business decisions.
▶ HR costs may be lower because management can anticipate imbalances before they become expensive or unmanageable.
▶ More time is available to locate talent because needs are anticipated and identified before the actual staffing is required.
▶ Better opportunities exist to include members of protected groups in future growth plans to increase organizational diversity.
▶ Development of managers can be better planned.

Scanning the Environment

At the heart of HR planning is the knowledge gained from **environmental scanning**, which is the process of studying the environment of the organization to pinpoint opportunities and threats. The external environment especially affects HR planning because each organization must draw from the same labor market that supplies all other employers. Indeed, one measure of organizational effectiveness is the ability of an organization to compete for a sufficient supply of human resources with the appropriate capabilities. To get a feel for the impact of environmental changes on businesses consider the following:

- The government has deregulated major sectors of the economy.
- During the past decade uncertainty in energy prices has brought new pressures on firms having major transportation/energy expenses.
- The globalization of markets and sources of supply has increased competition in many industries
- The composition of the workforce, along with its values, age, and working approaches, have changed.

Assessing the Organizational Workforce

Analyzing the jobs that will need to be done and the skills of people currently available to do them is the next part of HR planning. The needs of the organization must be compared against the labor supply available inside the organization.

The starting point for evaluating internal strengths and weaknesses is an audit of the jobs currently being done in the organization. This comprehensive analysis of all current jobs provides a basis for forecasting what jobs will need to be done in the future. Much of the data to answer these questions should be available from existing staffing and organizational databases. The following questions are addressed during the internal assessment:

- What jobs exist now?
- How many individuals are performing each job?
- What are the reporting relationships of jobs?
- How essential is each job?
- What jobs will be needed to implement future organizational strategies?
- What are the characteristics of anticipated jobs?

Forecasting HR Supply and Demand

The information gathered from external environmental scanning and assessment of internal strengths and weaknesses is used to predict or *forecast* HR supply and demand in light of organizational objectives and strategies. **Forecasting** uses information from the past and present to identify expected future conditions. Projections for the future are, of course, subject to error. Changes in the conditions on which the projections are based might even completely invalidate them, which is the chance forecasters take. Usually, though, experienced people are able to forecast with enough accuracy to benefit organizational long-range planning.

The demand for employees can be calculated on an organization-wide basis or calculated based on the needs of individual units in the organization. For example, to forecast that the firm needs 125 new employees next year might mean less than to forecast that it needs 25 new people in sales and customer service, 45 in production, 20 in accounting, 5 in HR, and 30 in the warehouse. This unit breakdown obviously allows HR planners to better pinpoint the specific skills needed than the aggregate method does.

Once human resources needs are forecasted, then their availability must be identified. Forecasting the availability of human resources considers both *external* and *internal* supplies. Although the internal supply may be easier to calculate, it is important to calculate the external supply as accurately as possible.

MANAGING HUMAN RESOURCE SURPLUS OR SHORTAGE

Planning is of little value if no subsequent action is taken. The action taken depends on the likelihood of a human resources surplus or shortage. A surplus of workers can be managed within an HR plan in a variety of ways. But regardless of the means, the actions are difficult because workforce reductions ultimately are necessary.

Workforce Reductions and the WARN Act

In this era of mergers, acquisitions, and downsizing, many workers have been laid off or had their jobs eliminated due to closing of selected offices, plants, and operations. To provide employees with sufficient notice, a federal law was passed, the Worker Adjustment and Retraining Notification (WARN) Act. This act requires employers to give a 60-day notice before a layoff or facility closing involving more than 50 people. However, part-time employees working fewer than 20 hours per week do not count toward the 50 employees. Also, seasonal employees do not have to receive WARN notification. The WARN Act also imposes stiff fines on employers who do not follow the required process and give proper notice.

Workforce Realignment

It has been called "downsizing," "rightsizing," "reduction in force" (RIF), and many other terms, but it almost always means cutting employees. "Layoffs" come in response to shortfall in demand for products, while "downsizing" involves job reductions based on a desire to operate more efficiently even when demand is strong. Downsizing is a structural change that negates rehiring laid-off workers. However, sometimes workers who are laid off (but not as part of downsizing) may get their jobs back when demand picks up.

The outcome of downsizing is a bit clearer after a decade of many examples and studies. Downsizing has worked for some firms, but it doesn't generate additional revenue. It only generates lower costs in the short term. But when companies cannibalize the human resources they need to grow and innovate, disruption usually follows for some time.

Senior executives still see layoffs as their first line defense against an economic downturn, but some research suggests downsizing can hurt productivity by leaving "surviving" employees overburdened and demoralized. Loss of employees may mean a loss of informal knowledge of how to handle specific problems and issues or respond to specific customers or suppliers. However focusing on trimming underperforming units or employees as part of a plan based on sound organizational strategies may make sense. Such a plan often includes cutting capital spending.

ASSESSING HR EFFECTIVENESS

A long-standing myth perpetuates the notion that one cannot really measure what the HR function does. That myth has hurt HR departments in some cases, because it suggests that any value added by HR efforts is somehow "mystical" or "magical." That notion is, of course, untrue; HR—like marketing, legal, or finance—must be evaluated based on the value it adds to the organization. Even though defining and measuring HR effectiveness is not as straightforward as with some areas, it is part of HR planning.

To demonstrate to the rest of the organization that the HR unit is a partner with a positive influence on the bottom line of the business, HR professionals must be prepared to measure the results of HR activities. Then the HR unit must communicate that information to the rest of the organization. Measurement is a key to demonstrating the success of the HR activities. Data to evaluate performance can come from several sources. Some of those sources are already available in most organizations, but some data may have to be collected from existing HR records, an HR audit, or HR research.

HR Performance and Benchmarking

When information on HR performance has been gathered, it must be compared to a *standard,* which is a model or measure against which something is compared to determine its performance level. For example, it is meaningless to know that the firm's turnover rate is 75% if the turnover rates at comparable organizations are unknown. One approach to assessing HR effectiveness is **benchmarking**, which compares specific measures of performance against data on those measures in other "best practices" organizations. HR professionals interested in benchmarking try to locate organizations that do certain activities particularly well and thus become the "benchmarks." Some common benchmarked performance measures in HR management are:

- ▶ Total compensation as a percentage of net income before taxes
- ▶ Percent of management positions filled internally
- ▶ Dollar sales per employee
- ▶ Benefits as a percentage of payroll costs

Human Resource Information Systems (HRIS)

Computers have simplified the task of analyzing vast amounts of data, and they can be invaluable aids in HR management, from payroll processing to record retention. With computer hardware, software, and databases, organizations can keep records and information better, as well as retrieve them with greater ease. A **human resource information system (HRIS)** is an integrated system that provides information used in HR decision making.

Purposes of an HRIS. An HRIS serves two major purposes in organizations. One relates to administrative and operational efficiency, the other to effectiveness. The first purpose of an HRIS is to improve the efficiency with which data on employees and HR activities are compiled. Many HR activities can be performed more efficiently and with less paperwork if automated, and better information is available.

The second purpose of an HRIS is more strategic and related to HR planning. Having accessible data enables HR planning and managerial decision making to be based to a greater degree on information rather than relying on managerial perceptions and intuition.

Uses of an HRIS. An HRIS has many uses in an organization. The most basic is the automation of payroll benefit activities. With an HRIS, employees' time records are entered into the system, and the appropriate deductions and other individual adjustments are reflected in the final paychecks. As a result of HRIS development and implementation in many organizations, several payroll functions are being transferred from accounting departments to HR departments. Another common use of HRIS is EEO/Affirmative Action tracking.

NOTES

1. Robert Wiseman, "Book Review of Rewarding Excellence, by Edward E. Lawler III," *Academy of Management Review,* 25 (2001), 135–138.
2. "Census: Americans Graduating at Record Rates," *Omaha World Herald,* December 19, 2000, 8.
3. June Kronholz, "U.S. Students Backslide on International Retest," *The Wall Street Journal,* December 6, 2000, B2.
4. Michelle Conlin, "And Now, the Just-in-Time Employee," *Business Week,* August 28, 2000, 169.
5. "Trident Precision Manufacturing Inc.," *Workindex.Com,* available at *http://www.workindex.com/PMR/PMR-0104-3.asp.*
6. Mitchell L. Marks and Philip H. Mirvis, "Making Mergers and Acquisitions Work: Strategic and Psychological Preparation," *Academy of Management Executive,* May 2001, 80–94.
7. Michael A. Hitt et al., "Direct and Moderating Effects of Human Capital on Strategy and Performance in Professional Service Firms," *Academy of Management Journal,* 44 (2001), 13.
8. Daniel M. Cable et al., "The Source and Accuracy of Job Applicants' Beliefs About Organizational Culture," *Academy of Management Journal,* 43 (2000), 1076–1086.
9. Charles Greer, Strategic *Human Resource Management,* 2nd ed. (Upper Saddle River, NJ: Prentice Hall, 2001).

INTERNET RESEARCH

U.S. Bureau of Labor Statistics This Web site contains data on workforce composition and trends from the U.S. Department of Labor, Bureau of Labor Statistics. **http://stats.bls.gov/sahome.html**

Saratoga Institute This organization is well-known for its HR benchmarking data and studies. **http://www.saratogainstitute.com**

SUGGESTED READINGS

Jac Fitz-Enz and Barbara Davison, *How to Measure Human Resources Management*, 3rd ed, McGraw-Hill, 2002.

Linda Gravett, *HRM Ethics*, Atomic Dog Publishing, 2003.

Linda Holbeche, *Aligning Human Resources and Business Strategy*, Butterworth-Heinemann, 2001.

Alfred J. Walker, *Web-Based Human Resources*, McGraw-Hill, 2001.

Chapter 2

Individual Performance and Retention

In most organizations the performance of individual employees is a major determinant of organizational success. Just as individuals in an organization can be a competitive advantage, they can also be a liability. When few employees know how to do their jobs, when people are constantly leaving the organization, and when employees work ineffectively, the human resources are a competitive problem that puts the organization at a disadvantage. Individual performance, motivation, and employee retention are key for organizations to maximize the effectiveness of individual human resources.

INDIVIDUAL EMPLOYEE PERFORMANCE

Many factors affect the performance of individual employees—their abilities, efforts expended, and the organizational support they receive. The HR unit in an organization exists in part to analyze and address these areas.

Individual Performance Factors

The three major factors that affect how a given individual performs are illustrated in Figure 2.1. The factors are: (1) individual ability to do the work, (2) effort level expended, and (3) organizational support. The relationship of these factors is widely acknowledged in management literature as:

$$\text{Individual Performance } (P) = \text{Ability } (A) \times \text{Effort } (E) \times \text{Support } (S)$$

Individual performance is enhanced to the degree that all three components are present with an individual employee. However, performance is diminished if any of these factors is reduced or absent.

FIGURE 2.1   Components of Individual Performance

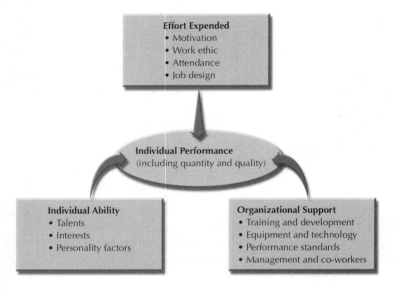

Individual Motivation

Motivation is the desire within a person causing that person to act. People usually act for one reason: to reach a goal. Thus, motivation is a goal-directed drive, and it seldom occurs in a void. The words *need, want, desire,* and *drive* are all similar to *motive,* from which the word *motivation* is derived. Understanding motivation is important because performance, reaction to compensation, and other HR concerns are affected by and influence motivation. Approaches to understanding motivation vary because different theorists have developed their own views and models.

Management Implications for Motivating Individual Performance

Motivation is complex and individualized, but managerial strategies and tactics must be somewhat uniform in order to address equity and expectations of individuals. Managers must determine whether inadequate individual behavior is due to low effort-performance ties (ability), low performance-reward linkages (inconsistent reward policies), or low value (low desire for the rewards).

In the case of low effort-performance, managers may try training to improve the relationship and thus encourage high performance. In the case of low performance-reward links, managers must look to the methods by which they appraise and reward performance.

Finally, managers must investigate the desirability of the rewards given for performance. Even if skills and rewards for performance are both high, the employee may not value the rewards. The rewards must be based on what the employees value, not what the managers value.

Many organizations spend considerable money to "motivate" their employees using a wide range of tactics. For example, firms have motivational speakers to inspire employees, with some of the "motivational coaches" as they are called, commanding as much as $50,000 per speech. Other employers give T-shirts, mugs, books, and videos to employees as motivators. Such efforts are estimated to cost in excess of $3 billion per year, not including sales motivation rewards.[1] However, the effectiveness of these expenditures can be questioned, particularly given the short-term nature of many of these programs and rewards.

INDIVIDUAL/ORGANIZATIONAL RELATIONSHIPS

Various surveys have found that only about half of the workers in U.S. organizations are relatively satisfied with their jobs, a decline of 10% from five years previously. The biggest decline occurred with workers 45–54 years old. Even more concerning is that just 24% said they were committed to stay at least two years at their current employer. Also about one-fifth of employees in some surveys are so dissatisfied with their jobs that they negatively affect other employees.[2] Because the long-term economic health of most organizations depends on the efforts of employees with the appropriate capabilities and motivation to perform their jobs well, organizations that are successful over time demonstrate that individual relationships do matter and should be managed effectively.

The Psychological Contract

One concept that has been useful in discussing employees' relationships with organizations is that of a **psychological contract**, which refers to the unwritten expectations employees and employers have about the nature of their work relationships. Because the psychological contract is individual and subjective in nature, it focuses on expectations about "fairness" that may not be defined clearly by employees.

Both tangible items (such as wages, benefits, employee productivity, and attendance) and intangible items (such as loyalty, fair treatment, and job security) are encompassed by psychological contracts between employers and employees. Many employers may attempt to detail their expectations through employee handbooks and policy manuals, but those materials are only part of the total "contractual" relationship.

Rather than just paying employees to follow orders and put in time, increasingly employers are expecting employees to utilize their knowledge, skills, and abilities to accomplish organizational results. An effective psychological contract recognizes the following components:

Employers provide:	**Employees contribute:**
▸ Competitive compensation and benefits	▸ Continuous skill improvement and increased productivity
▸ Career development opportunities	▸ Reasonable time with organization
▸ Flexibility to balance work and home life	▸ Extra effort when needed

Loyalty

Employees *do* believe in the ideas behind the concept of psychological contracts and hope their employers will honor that side of the "agreement." Many employees still want security and stability, interesting work, a supervisor they respect, and competitive pay and benefits. If these elements are not provided, employees may feel a diminished need to contribute to organizational performance. When organizations merge, lay off large numbers of employees, outsource work, and use large numbers of temporary and part-time workers, employees see fewer reasons to give their loyalty to employers in return for this loss of job security. This decline is evident in such firms as AT&T and Lucent, where significant staff cutbacks and declines in stock prices have demoralized many of the remaining staff members.[3] More employers are finding that turnover of key people occurs more frequently when employee loyalty is low, which in turn emphasizes the importance of a loyal and committed workforce.

JOB SATISFACTION AND ORGANIZATIONAL COMMITMENT

In its most basic sense, **job satisfaction** is a positive emotional state resulting from evaluating one's job experiences. Job *dis*satisfaction occurs when one's expectations are not met. For example, if an employee expects clean and safe working conditions on the job, then the employee is likely to be dissatisfied if the workplace is dirty and dangerous.

No simple formula can predict an individual employee's job satisfaction. Furthermore, the relationship between productivity and job satisfaction is not entirely clear. The critical factor is what employees expect from their jobs and what they receive as rewards from their jobs. Even though job satisfaction itself is important, perhaps the "bottom line" is the impact that job satisfaction has on organizational commitment, which affects employee turnover and organizational performance.[4]

Absenteeism

Absenteeism is expensive, with total employer productivity losses due to absenteeism exceeding $12 billion annually. Being absent from work may seem like a small matter to an employee. But if a manager needs 12 people in a unit to get the work done, and four of the 12 are absent most of the time, the unit's work will probably not get done, or additional workers will have to be hired.

Types of Absenteeism. Employees can be absent from work for several reasons. Clearly, some absenteeism is inevitable. Because illness, death in the family, and other personal reasons for absences are unavoidable and understandable, many employers have sick-leave policies that allow employees a certain number of paid absent days per year for these types of *involuntary* absenteeism. However, much absenteeism is avoidable, or *voluntary* absenteeism. Often, a relatively small number of individuals in the workplace are responsible for a disproportionate share of the total absenteeism in an organization. One study found that 41% of employees had 0–2 days of unscheduled absences, 43% of employees had 3–8 days, and 13% of employees had 9 or more days per year.[5]

Controlling Absenteeism. Controlling voluntary absenteeism is easier if managers understand its causes more clearly. However, a variety of approaches can be used to reduce voluntary absenteeism. Organizational policies on absenteeism should be stated clearly in an employee handbook and stressed by supervisors and managers. The policies and rules an organization uses to govern absenteeism may provide a clue to the effectiveness of its absenteeism control efforts. Absenteeism control options fall into several categories:

▶ *Disciplinary approach:* Many employers use a disciplinary approach. People who are absent the first time receive an oral warning, but subsequent absences bring written warnings, suspension, and finally dismissal.

▶ *Positive reinforcement:* Positive reinforcement includes such methods as giving employees cash, recognition, time off, or other rewards for meeting attendance standards. Offering rewards for good attendance, giving bonuses for missing fewer than a certain number of days, and "buying back" unused sick leave are all positive methods of reducing absenteeism.

▶ *Combination approach:* Combination approaches ideally reward desired behaviors and punish undesired behaviors. This "carrot and stick" approach uses policies and discipline to punish offenders and develops various programs and rewards for employees with outstanding attendance.

▶ *"No fault" absenteeism:* Here, the reasons for absences do not matter, but the employees must manage their time rather than having managers make decisions about excused and unexcused absences. Once absenteeism exceeds normal limits, then disciplinary action up to and including termination of employment can occur. The advantages of the "no fault" approach are that all employees can be covered by it, and supervisors and HR staff do not have to judge whether absences count as excused or unexcused. Therefore, the employees manage their own attendance except where extreme abuses occur.

▶ *Paid time-off (PTO) programs:* Some employers have a **paid time-off (PTO) program** in which vacation time, holidays, and sick leave for each employee are combined into a PTO account. Employees use days from their accounts at their discretion for illness, personal time, or vacation. If employees run out of days in their accounts, then they are not paid for any additional days missed. The PTO programs generally have reduced absenteeism, particularly one-day absences, but overall time away from work often increases because employees use all of "their" time off by taking unused days as vacation days.

Turnover

Like absenteeism, turnover is related to job satisfaction and organizational commitment. Turnover occurs when employees leave an organization and have to be replaced.

Many organizations have found that turnover is a costly problem, as documented by a number of studies. One study found that 45% of surveyed employers estimate annual turnover cost to exceed $10,000 per person. In the hotel/hospitality industry the average turnover cost of $4,100 per leaving employee costs a typical hotel $631,400 annually.[6] In many service industries the turnover rates and these turnover costs are very high. In the retail industry turnover of part-time workers averages 124% per year and 74% for full-time workers. In supermarkets the typical stay for an employee is only 97 days. Costing billions to the nation's grocers and other retailers, the costs per full-time employee leaving are estimated to be between $6,900 and $10,500, depending upon the type of retailer.[7] For higher-level executives and professionals, turnover costs can run as much as two times annual salary.

Types of Turnover. Turnover is classified in a number of different ways. Each of the following classifications can be used and are not mutually exclusive.

▸ **Involuntary Turnover**
Terminations for poor performance or work rule violations

▸ **Voluntary Turnover**
Employee leaves by choice

Involuntary turnover is triggered by organizational policies, work rules, and performance standards that are not met by employees. Voluntary turnover can be caused by many factors, including career opportunities, pay, supervision, geography, and personal/family reasons. Voluntary turnover also appears to increase with the size of the organization, most likely due to the larger firms having more employees who may move, the more impersonal nature of organizations, and the "organizational bureaucracy" that is present in these organizations.

▸ **Functional Turnover**
Lower-performing or disruptive employees leave

▸ **Dysfunctional Turnover**
Key individuals and high performers leave at critical times

Not all turnover is negative for organizations because some workforce losses are desirable, especially if those workers who leave are lower-performing, less reliable individuals, or those who are disruptive to co-workers. Unfortunately for organizations, dysfunctional turnover occurs when key individuals leave, often at crucial work times. For example, a software project leader left in the midst of a system upgrade to take a promotion at another firm in the city, causing the system upgrade timeline to slip by two months due to the difficulty of replacing the project leader.

▶ **Uncontrollable Turnover**	▶ **Controllable Turnover**
Occurs for reasons outside the impact of the employer	Occurs due to factors that could be influenced by the employer

Many reasons employees quit cannot be controlled by the organization and include: (1) the employee moving out of the geographic area, (2) the employee deciding to stay home for family reasons, (3) transfer of the employee's spouse, or (4) a student employee graduating from college. But, it is the controllable turnover that must be addressed, and organizations are better able to retain employees if they deal with the concerns of employees that are leading to turnover.

RETENTION OF HUMAN RESOURCES

As a practical matter, every individual who is retained means one less person to recruit, select, and train. Also, organizational and individual performance is enhanced by the continuity of employees who know their jobs, co-workers, organizational services and products, and the firm's customers.

Changes in economic conditions, along with the collapse of the dot.com employment bubble and slowing of the growth of technology firms, led some to speculate that the emphasis on retention was a temporary concern. However, an updated McKinsey & Company survey found that 90% of those firms surveyed said it is more difficult to retain talented individuals than it was several years before.[8] Therefore, it is imperative that organizations and managers recognize that retention must be a continuing HR emphasis and a significant responsibility for all supervisors and managers.

Determinants of retention include organizational, career opportunities, rewards components, and job/work relationships. Both employers and employees recognize that some common areas affect employee retention. If certain organizational components are being provided, then other factors may affect retention. Surveys of employees consistently show that career opportunities and rewards are the two most important determinants of retention. Finally, job design/work factors and fair and supportive employee relationships with others inside the organization contribute to retention. How each set of components in Figure 2.2 affects employee retention is covered next.

Organizational Components

A number of organizational components influence individuals in their decisions to stay or leave their employers. Organizations with positive, distinctive cultures and values experience less turnover.

FIGURE 2.2 Retention Determinants

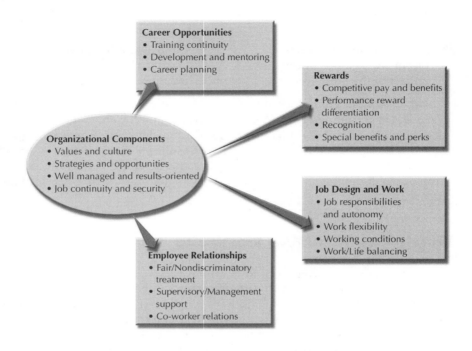

Organizational Culture and Values. **Organizational culture** is a pattern of shared values and beliefs that provides organizational members meaning and rules for behavior. Numerous examples can be given of key technical, professional, and administrative employees leaving firms because of corporate cultures that seem to devalue people and create barriers to the use of individual capabilities. In contrast, creating a culture that values people highly enables some corporations to successfully attract and retain employees.

One key organizational value that affects employee retention is *trust.* Employees who believe that they can trust managers, co-workers, and the organizational justice systems are much less willing to leave their current employers.

Organizational Strategies, Opportunities, and Management. Other organizational components that affect employee retention are related to the strategies, opportunities, and management of the organization. In some organizations external events are seen as threatening, whereas others see changes as challenges requiring responses. The latter approach can be a source of competitive advantage, especially if an organization is in a growing, dynamic industry.

Job Continuity and Security. Many individuals have seen a decline in job security over the past decade. All of the downsizings, layoffs, mergers and acquisitions, and organizational restructurings have affected employee loyalty and retention. Also as co-workers experience layoffs and job reductions, anxiety levels of the remaining employees rise. Consequently, employees start thinking about leaving before they too get cut. On the other hand, organizations where job continuity and security are high tend to have higher retention rates.

Organizational Career Opportunities

Surveys of workers in all types of jobs consistently indicate that organizational career development efforts can significantly affect employee retention. A Workforce Commitment Survey conducted annually by AON Consulting found that *opportunities for personal growth* lead the reasons why individuals took their current jobs and why they stay there, which ranks ahead of compensation and work/family balance.[9] This factor is even more essential for technical professionals and those under age 30, for whom opportunities to develop skills and obtain promotions rank above compensation as a retention concern.

Career Development and Planning. Organizations address career opportunities and development in a number of ways. Tuition aid programs typically offered as benefits by many employers allow employees to pursue additional educational and training opportunities, which may contribute to higher retention rates. However, just offering such a program is not sufficient. Organizations must also identify ways to use the employees' new knowledge and capabilities inside the organization.

Organizations also increase employee retention by having formal career planning efforts. Employees and their managers mutually discuss career opportunities within organizations and what career development activities will enhance employees' future growth.

Rewards and Retention

The tangible rewards that people receive for working come in the form of pay, incentives, and benefits. Numerous surveys and experiences of HR professionals reveal that one key to retention is to have *competitive compensation practices.* Many managers believe that money is the prime retention factor, 89% in one survey, and many employees cite better pay or higher compensation as a reason for leaving one employer for another.[10] However, the reality is a bit more complex.

Pay and benefits must be competitive, which means they must be "close" to what other employers are providing and what individuals believe to be consistent with their capabilities, experience, and performance. If compensation is not close, often defined as within 10% of the "market," then turnover is likely to be higher, especially true for individuals making lower rates of pay, such as those with less than $25,000 to $30,000 annual income. Simply put, their living costs and financial requirements mean that if these lower-paid workers can get $1 per hour more or get employer-paid family benefit coverage elsewhere, they are more likely to move. However, for more highly paid individuals, especially those paid $60,000 and higher, their retention is affected by having compensation relatively competitive. At that level, other considerations are more likely to enter into the decision to stay or leave. In fact, money may be why some people leave a job, but other factors may be why many stay.

Competitive Benefits. Another compensation issue affecting employee retention is having competitive benefits programs. Health insurance, 401(k) retirement, tuition assistance, and many other benefits commonly offered by competing employers is vital.

Employers also are learning that having some *benefits flexibility* aids retention. When employees choose how much and what benefits they will have from a "cafeteria" of choices, given a set sum of money available from the employer, the employees can tailor the benefits to their needs. By giving employees greater choice, employees feel more "individual" and "in control," thus reducing their desire to move to another employer.

Special Benefits and Perks. A number of employers use a wide range of special benefits and perks to attract and retain employees. By offering these special benefits and perks, employers hope to reduce the time employees spend after work on personal chores and to be seen as more desirable employers where individuals will remain for longer stays.

Performance and Compensation. Many individuals expect their rewards to be differentiated from others based on performance. For instance, if an employee receives about the same pay increase and overall pay as others who have lower productivity, more absenteeism, and work fewer hours, then the result may be a feeling of "unfairness." This may prompt the individual to look for another job where compensation recognizes performance differences. The results of a survey on rewards at work found that individuals are more satisfied with the actual levels of their pay than the processes used to determine pay. For this reason, the performance management system and performance appraisal processes in organizations must be linked to compensation increases.

To achieve greater performance links to organizational and individual performance, a growing number of private-sector firms are using variable pay and incentives programs. These programs in the form of cash bonuses or lump sum payments are one mechanism used to reward extra performance.

Recognition. Employee recognition as a form of reward can be both tangible and intangible. Recognition also can be intangible and psychological in nature. Feedback from managers and supervisors that acknowledges extra effort and performance of individuals provides recognition, even though monetary rewards are not given.

Job Design and Work

A fundamental factor affecting employee retention is the nature of the jobs and work done. Once individuals have been placed into jobs, several job/work factors affect retention. Because individuals spend significant time at work, they expect to work with modern equipment and technology and have good *working conditions*, given the nature of the work. Such factors as space, lighting, temperature, noise, layout, and other physical and environmental factors affect retention of employees.

Additionally, workers want a *safe work environment* where risks of accidents and injuries have been addressed. This is especially true for employers in such industries as manufacturing, agriculture, utilities, and transportation with higher safety risks than in many service industries and office environments.

Work Flexibility. Flexibility in work schedules and how work is done has grown in importance. Flexible HR policies such as casual dress can also be useful as retention aids. Work flexibility is particularly vital in the wake of increased workload pressures increased due to organizational restructurings and "rightsizing." It is crucial that employers wishing to retain employees monitor the workloads placed on employees. If these demands become too great, then employees are more likely to change jobs to reduce their workloads.

One way employers provide work flexibility is through *work scheduling alternatives.* These alternatives include telecommuting, whereby employees can work from home or other locations, and arrangements such as flextime and compressed workweeks (4 days/10 hours, 3 days/12 hours, etc.).

Work/Life Balancing. One of the greatest benefits of work flexibility is that it meshes well with work/family efforts by employers. The changing demographics of the U.S. workforce is prompting many individuals to work harder at balancing work responsibilities, family needs, and personal life demands. With more single-parent families, dual-career couples with children, and workers' responsibilities for elderly relatives, balancing work and family roles may sometimes be incompatible.

Work/life programs offered by employers can include a wide range of items. Some include work/job options, such as flexible work scheduling, job sharing, or telecommuting. Other components include flexible benefits, on-site fitness centers, child-care or elder-care assistance, and sick-leave policies. The purpose of these offerings is to convey that employers recognize the challenges employees face when balancing work/life demands.

Employee Relationships

A final set of factors found to affect retention is based on the relationships among employees in organizations. Such areas as the reasonableness of HR policies, the fairness of disciplinary actions, and the means used to decide work assignments and opportunities all affect employee retention. If individuals feel that policies are unreasonably restrictive or applied inconsistently, then they may be more likely to look at jobs offered at other employers.

Other concerns that affect employee retention are *supervisory/management support* and *co-worker relations.* Many individuals build close relationships with co-workers. A supervisor builds positive relationships and aids retention by being fair and nondiscriminatory, allowing work flexibility and work/family balancing, giving employee feedback that recognizes employee efforts and performance, and supporting career planning and development for employees.

THE RETENTION MANAGEMENT PROCESS

In addition to identifying the determinants of retention, it is important that HR professionals and their organizations have processes in place to manage retention of employees. Left to chance or infrequent attention, employee retention is not as likely to be successful, which makes using the retention management process outlined in Figure 2.3 important.

Retention Measurement and Assessment

To ensure that appropriate actions are taken to enhance retention and reduce turnover, management decisions require data and analyses rather than subjective impressions, anecdotes of selected individual situations, or panic reactions to the loss of a few key people. Therefore, having several different types of measures and analyses is important.

Measuring Turnover. The turnover rate for an organization can be computed in different ways. The following formula from the U.S. Department of Labor is widely used; in it *separation* means leaving the organization.

$$\frac{\text{Number of employee separations during the month} \times 100}{\text{Total number of employees at midmonth}}$$

Common turnover figures range from almost zero to more than 100% per year, with turnover rates varying among industries. Often a part of human resource information systems, turnover data can be gathered and analyzed in a number of ways, including the following:

- Jobs and job levels
- Departments, units, and location
- Reason for leaving
- Length of service

- Demographic characteristics
- Education and training
- Knowledge, skills, and abilities
- Performance ratings/levels

Costs of Turnover. Determining turnover costs can be relatively simple or very complex, depending upon the nature of the efforts and data used. More

FIGURE 2.3   The Retention Management Process

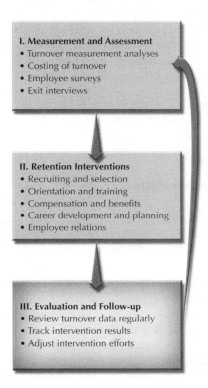

detailed and sophisticated turnover costing models consider a number of factors. Some of the most common areas considered include the following:[11]

▶ *Hiring costs:* Includes recruiting and advertising expenses, search fees, HR interviewer and staff time and salaries, employee referral fees, relocation and moving costs, supervisor and managerial time and salaries, employment testing costs, reference checking time, pre-employment medical expenses, etc.

▶ *Training costs:* Includes paid orientation time, training staff time and salaries, costs of training materials, supervisors' and managers' time and salaries, co-worker "coaching" time and salaries, etc.

▶ *Productivity costs:* Includes lost productivity due to "break-in" time of new employees, loss of customer contacts, unfamiliarity with organizational products and services, more time to use organizational resources and systems, etc.

▶ *Separation costs:* Includes HR staff and supervisor time and salaries to prevent separations, exit interview time, unemployment expenses, legal fees for separations challenged, etc.

Employee Surveys. Employee surveys can be used to diagnose specific problem areas, identify employee needs or preferences, and reveal areas in which HR activities are well received or are viewed negatively. For example, questionnaires may be sent to employees to collect ideas for revising a performance appraisal system or to determine how satisfied employees are with their benefits programs. Regardless of the topic of the survey, obtaining employee input provides managers and HR professionals with data on the "retention climate" in an organization.

Exit Interviews. One widely used type of interview is the **exit interview**, in which individuals are asked to identify reasons for leaving the organization. One survey of employers found that 87% of them conduct exit interviews, and more than half use the information gathered to make changes to aid retention.[12]

Retention Interventions

Based on what the measurement and assessment data reveal, a variety of HR interventions can be undertaken to improve retention. Turnover can be controlled and reduced in several ways. During the *recruiting* process, the job should be outlined and a *realistic job preview* presented, so that the reality of the job matches the expectations of the new employee. By ensuring that the expectations of potential employees match what the organization is likely to offer, voluntary turnover may be reduced.

Another way to eliminate turnover is to improve the *selection process* in order to better match applicants to jobs. By fine-tuning the selection process and hiring people who will not have disciplinary or performance problems or whose work histories suggest higher turnover potential, employers can reduce turnover. Once selected, individuals who receive effective *orientation and training* are less likely to leave.

Other HR factors are important as well. *Compensation* is important because a competitive, fair, and equitable pay system can help reduce turnover. Inadequate benefits also may lead to voluntary turnover, especially if other employers offer significantly higher compensation levels for similar jobs. *Career development and planning* can help an organization keep employees. If individuals believe they have few opportunities for career development advancement, they are more likely to leave the organization. *Employee relations,* including fair/nondiscriminatory treatment and enforcement of HR policies, can enhance retention also.

Evaluation and Follow-Up

Once retention intervention efforts have been implemented, it is important that they be evaluated and appropriate follow-up and adjustments made. Regular *review of turnover data* can identify when turnover increases or decreases among different employees classified by length of service, education, department, gender, or other factors.

Tracking intervention results also should be part of evaluation efforts. Some firms may use pilot programs to see how turnover is affected before extending changes to the entire organization.

NOTES

1. Del Jones, "Firms Spend Billions to Fire Up Workers—With Little Luck," *USA Today,* May 10, 2001, 1A.

2. Shari Caudron, "The Myth of Job Happiness," *Workforce,* April 2001, 32–36; and "Jobs: A Labor of Love? Not in U.S.," *Omaha World-Herald,* September 3, 2001, 3D.

3. Andrew Backover, "Loyalty Costs Employees of Struggling AT&T, Lucent," *USA Today,* February 2, 2001, 1B.

4. Daniel J. Koys, "The Effects of Employee Satisfaction, Organizational Citizenship Behavior, and Turnover on Organizational Effectiveness," *Personnel Psychology,* 54 (2001), 101–114.

5. CCH Absenteeism Survey, *CCH Human Resource Management,* November 1, 2000.

6. Carla Joinson, "Capturing Turnover Costs," *HR Magazine,* July 2000, 107–109.

7. "Employee Turnover," *The Economist,* July 15, 2000, 64–65; and "Turnover Costs," *The Wall Street Journal,* August 29, 2000, B12.

8. Elizabeth Axelrod, Helen Handfield-Jones, and Timothy Welsh, "War for Talent, Part Two," *The McKinsey Quarterly,* 2001, available at *http://www.mckinsey.com.*

9. *United States @Work,* AON Consulting, 2000, available at *http://www.aon.com.*

10. Hara Marks, "Money—That's Not What They Want," *HR-eSource,* May 7, 2001.

11. Wayne F. Cascio, *Costing Human Resources* (Cincinnati: South-Western Publishing, 2000), 73–75.

12. *SHRM Retention Practices Survey* (Alexandria, VA: Society for Human Resource Management, 2000), 10.

INTERNET RESEARCH

Employee Retention Strategies.Com The Internet has an abundance of information about retention. This Web site offers newsletters and articles on improving employee retention. **http://www.employeeretentionstrategies.com**

KeepEmployees.Com This Web site assists organizations by providing tools and services in the area of retention management. **http://www.keepemployees.com/**

SUGGESTED READINGS

Lisa M. Aldisert, *Valuing People,* Dearborn Trade Publishing, 2002.

Roger E. Herman and Joyce L. Gioia, *Workforce Stability,* Oakhill Press, 2000.

Jack S. Phillips, *Retaining Your Best Employees,* ASTD/SHRM, 2002.

Bruce Tulgan, *Winning the Talent Wars,* W.W. Norton, 2001.

Chapter 3

Equal Employment

The diversity of the U.S. workforce has led to increasing emphasis on opportunity and equity for employees from differing backgrounds. Also, employers of all sizes in various industries have incurred significant costs for violating federal, state, and local laws and regulations prohibiting illegal employment-related discrimination. This chapter discusses management of diversity and reviews what employers should do to comply with Equal Employment Opportunity (EEO) laws, regulations, and requirements.

DIVERSITY, EQUAL EMPLOYMENT, AND AFFIRMATIVE ACTION

The changing composition of the workforce in the United States and other countries is evident in the diversity in the workforce. The concept of **diversity** recognizes the differences among people.

Figure 3.1 shows that diversity management is the broadest level at which organizations have taken initiatives and made efforts that value all people equally, regardless of their differences. Organizations can also address diversity issues in more restricted ways: equal employment opportunity and affirmative action. Each of these levels are discussed next. As organizations and managers have more diverse individuals in the workplace, they are finding that diversity is a strategic HR consideration.

Managing Diversity

Diversity can be seen in demographic differences in the workforce. The U.S. workforce is more diverse racially, women are in the labor force in much greater numbers than ever before, and the average age of the workforce is now considerably older than before. As a result of these and other demographic shifts, HR

FIGURE 3.1   Diversity Management, Equal Employment Opportunity, and Affirmative Action

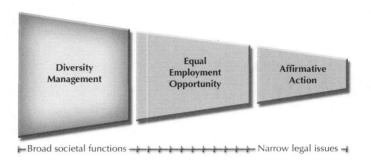

management in organizations has had to adapt to a more diverse labor force both externally and internally.

Organizations can approach the management of diversity from several different perspectives. The continuum can run from resistance to creation of an inclusive diversity culture. The increasing diversity of the workforce available, combined with growing shortages of workers in many occupations and industries, has forced more employers to recognize that diversity must be addressed. A number of organizations have found that because they serve a diverse set of customers, there are significant business reasons for having a diverse workforce. The employees have greater cultural understanding of how products and services can be viewed and accepted by different groups.

Diversity Management Programs and Training. A wide variety of programs and activities have been used in organizations as part of diversity management efforts. Once management accountability for diversity results has been established, then a number of different activities can be implemented as part of a diversity management program, including diversity training.

Approaches to diversity training vary, but often include at least three components. *Legal awareness* is the first and most common component of diversity training. Here the training focuses on the legal implications of discrimination. A limited approach to diversity training stops with these legal "do's and don'ts."

By introducing *cultural awareness,* employers hope to build greater understanding of the differences among people. Cultural awareness training may help all participants to see and accept the differences in people with widely varying cultural backgrounds.

The third component of diversity training—*sensitivity training*—is more difficult. The aim here is to "sensitize" people to the differences among them and how their words and behaviors are seen by others. Some diversity training includes exercises containing examples of harassment and other behaviors.

Effectiveness of Diversity Training. Mixed reviews about the effectiveness of diversity training suggest two common concerns, as follows:

1. Diversity training tends to draw attention to differences, building walls rather than breaking them down.
2. Much of the content in diversity training is viewed as "politically correct," which blames majority individuals, particularly white males, for past wrongs.

Some argue that diversity training more often than not has failed, pointing out that it does not reduce discrimination and harassment complaints. Rather than reducing conflict, in a number of firms it has produced divisive effects and not taught the behaviors needed for employees to relate better in a diverse workplace.

This last point, focusing on behaviors, seems to hold the most promise for making diversity training more effective. Teaching appropriate behaviors and skills in relationships with others is more likely to produce satisfactory results than focusing just on attitudes and beliefs among diverse employees.

Equal Employment Opportunity

Equal employment opportunity (EEO) is a broad concept holding that individuals should receive equal treatment in all employment-related actions. Individuals covered under equal employment laws are protected from illegal discrimination in which: (1) different standards are used to judge different individuals, or (2) the same standard is used, but it is not related to the individuals' jobs.

Various laws have been passed to protect individuals who share certain characteristics, such as race, age, or gender. Those having the designated characteristics are referred to as a **protected class**, which is composed of individuals who fall within a group identified for protection under equal employment laws and regulations. The following bases for protection have been identified by various federal, state, or local laws:

- Race, ethnic origin, color (African Americans, Hispanic Americans, Native Americans, Asian Americans)
- Sex/Gender (women, including those who are pregnant)
- Age (individuals over 40)
- Individuals with disabilities (physical or mental)
- Military experience (Vietnam-era veterans)
- Religion (special beliefs and practices)
- Marital status (some states)
- Sexual orientation (some states and cities)

EEO Concepts. A number of basic concepts relate to equal employment. The concepts depicted in Figure 3.2 are the bases for court decisions, regulations, and laws. As has been emphasized by both regulations and a variety of court decisions, employers are expected to use job-related employment practices. A **business necessity** is a practice necessary for safe and efficient organizational operations. Business necessity has been the subject of numerous court decisions. Educational

FIGURE 3.2   Equal Employment Opportunity Concepts

```
   ┌──────────────────┐              ┌──────────────────┐
   │ Business Necessity│              │   No Disparate   │
   │       and         │              │    Treatment     │
   │  Job Relatedness  │              │                  │
   └──────────────────┘              └──────────────────┘

┌──────────────────┐        ╭────────────╮        ┌──────────────────┐
│ Bona Fide Occupation│      │   EQUAL    │       │   No Disparate   │
│   Qualification    │       │ EMPLOYMENT │       │     Impact       │
│                    │       │OPPORTUNITY │       │                  │
└──────────────────┘        ╰────────────╯        └──────────────────┘

      ┌──────────────┐              ┌──────────────────┐
      │  Burden of   │              │ Non-Retaliatory  │
      │    Proof     │              │    Treatment     │
      └──────────────┘              └──────────────────┘
```

requirements often are based on business necessity. However, an employer who requires a minimum level of education, such as a high school diploma, must be able to defend the requirement as essential to the performance of the job. For instance, equating a degree or diploma with the possession of math or reading abilities is considered questionable.

Title VII of the 1964 Civil Rights Act specifically states that employers may discriminate on the basis of sex, religion, or national origin if the characteristic can be justified as a "bona fide occupational qualification." Thus, a **bona fide occupational qualification (BFOQ)** is a legitimate reason why an employer can exclude persons on otherwise illegal bases of consideration. What constitutes a BFOQ has been subject to different interpretations in various courts across the country.

Disparate treatment occurs when protected-class members are treated differently from others. For example, if female applicants must take a special skills test not given to male applicants, then disparate treatment may be occurring. If disparate treatment has occurred, the courts generally have ruled that intentional discrimination exists.

Disparate impact occurs when substantial underrepresentation of protected-class members results from employment decisions that work to their disadvantage. The landmark case that established the importance of disparate impact as a legal foundation of EEO law is *Griggs v. Duke Power* (1971).[1]

Another legal issue that arises when discrimination is alleged is the determination of which party has the *burden of proof*. Based on the evolution of court decisions, current laws and regulations state that the plaintiff charging discrimination: (1) must be a *protected-class member*, and (2) must prove that *disparate impact* or *disparate treatment* existed. Once a court rules that a *prima facie* (preliminary) case has been made, the burden of proof shifts to the employer. The employer then must show that the bases for making employment-related decisions were specifically job-related and consistent with considerations of business necessity.

Employers are prohibited by EEO laws from retaliating against individuals who file discrimination charges. **Retaliation** occurs when employers take punitive actions against individuals who exercise their legal rights.

Affirmative Action

Affirmative action occurs when employers identify problem areas, set goals, and take positive steps to enhance opportunities for protected-class members. Affirmative action focuses on hiring, training, and promoting of protected-class members where they are *underrepresented* in an organization in relation to their availability in the labor markets from which recruiting occurs.

Court Decisions and Legislation on Affirmative Action. Increasingly, court decisions and legislative efforts have focused on restricting the use of affirmative action. Federal court decisions have addressed admission standards at various universities, including the University of Texas and the University of Michigan.

Affirmative Action and Reverse Discrimination. Two U.S. Supreme Court decisions regarding admission practices at the University of Michigan provided some legal guidance. The Supreme Court ruled that race can be a consideration, but race cannot be the only factor utilized. When employment regulations are discussed, probably the most volatile issue concerns the view that affirmative action leads to *quotas* or *preferential selection*. At the heart of the conflict is the employers' role in selecting, training, and promoting protected-class members when they are underrepresented in various jobs in an organization. Those who are not members of any protected class have claimed **reverse discrimination**, which may exist when a person is denied an opportunity because of preferences given to a member of a protected class who may be less qualified.

Regardless of the viewpoints held about affirmative action, diversity is a reality that is a strategic HR concern to be addressed in all organizations. Also, despite the differing philosophical views of affirmative action, a large number of EEO regulations and laws still exist. HR professionals must ensure that their organizations comply with EEO requirements for different protected groups. The following sections examine the nature, issues, and HR practices to be addressed in managing diversity and equal employment on the bases of race/national origin, sex/gender, disabilities, age, and other factors.

EEO LEGAL REQUIREMENTS AND COMPLIANCE

Most organizations must follow federal, state, and local EEO laws and some affirmative action regulations to avoid costly penalties. Numerous federal, state, and local laws address equal employment opportunity concerns, as shown in Appendix B. Some laws have a general civil rights emphasis, while others address specific EEO issues and concerns. An overview of the major laws, regulations, and concepts follows next.

Civil Rights Act of 1964, Title VII

The passage of the Civil Rights Act of 1964 is the keystone of antidiscrimination employment legislation. As part of this act, the Equal Employment Opportunity Commission (EEOC) was established to enforce the provisions of Title VII, the portion of the act that deals with employment.

Title VII covers most employers in the United States. Any organization meeting one of the criteria in the following list is subject to rules and regulations that specific government agencies have established to administer the act:

- ▶ All private employers of 15 or more persons who are employed 20 or more weeks per year
- ▶ All educational institutions, public and private
- ▶ State and local governments
- ▶ Public and private employment agencies
- ▶ Labor unions with 15 or more members
- ▶ Joint labor/management committees for apprenticeships and training

Civil Rights Act of 1991

The Civil Rights Act of 1991 requires employers to show that an employment practice is *job-related for the position* and is consistent with *business necessity.* The act clarifies that the plaintiffs bringing the discrimination charges must identify the particular employer practice being challenged and must show only that protected-class status played *some factor. Also,* the 1991 act allows victims of discrimination on the basis of sex, religion, or disability to receive both compensatory and punitive damages in cases of intentional discrimination.

Affirmative Action Regulations

The changing laws over the last 30 years have forced employers to address additional areas of potential discrimination. Several acts and regulations apply specifically to government contractors. These acts and regulations specify a minimum number of employees and size of government contracts. The requirements primarily come from federal Executive Orders 11246, 11375, and 11478.

Affirmative Action Plans (AAPs). Federal, state, and local regulations require many government contractors to compile affirmative action plans to report on the composition of their workforces. An **affirmative action plan (AAP)** is a formal document that an employer compiles annually for submission to enforcement agencies. Generally, contractors with at least 50 employees and

$50,000 in government contracts annually must submit these plans. The contents of an AAP and the policies flowing from it must be available for review by managers and supervisors within the organization. Plans vary in length; some are long and require extensive staff time to prepare.

A crucial part of preparing an AAP requires two different types of analyses and comparisons. The **availability analysis** identifies the number of protected-class members available to work in the appropriate labor markets in given jobs. This analysis can be developed with data from a state labor department, the U.S. Census Bureau, and other sources. Another major section of an AAP is the **utilization analysis**, which identifies the number of protected-class members employed and the types of jobs they hold in an organization.[2]

EEO Enforcement Agencies

Government agencies at several levels can investigate illegal discriminatory practices. At the federal level, the two most prominent agencies are the *Equal Employment Opportunity Commission (EEOC)* and the *Office of Federal Contract Compliance Programs (OFCCP)*. The EEOC has enforcement authority for charges brought under a number of federal laws. While the EEOC is an independent agency, the OFCCP is part of the Department of Labor and ensures that federal contractors and subcontractors follow nondiscriminatory practices. A major thrust of OFCCP efforts is to require that covered employers take affirmative action to counter prior discriminatory practices.

In addition to federal laws and orders, many states and municipalities have passed their own laws prohibiting discrimination on a variety of bases, and have established state and *local enforcement agencies*. However, state and local laws sometimes provide greater remedies, require different actions, or prohibit discrimination in areas beyond those addressed by federal law.

Uniform Guidelines on Employee Selection Procedures

The Uniform Guidelines on Employee Selection Procedures apply to the federal EEOC, the U.S. Department of Labor's OFCCP, the U.S. Department of Justice, and the federal Office of Personnel Management. These guidelines affect virtually all phases of HR management, not just the initial hiring process. Two major compliance approaches are identified by the guidelines: (1) no disparate impact, and (2) job-related validation.

"No Disparate Impact" Approach. Generally, the most important issue regarding discrimination in organizations is the *effect* of employment policies and procedures, regardless of employer *intent*. **Disparate impact** occurs when a substantial underrepresentation of protected-class members is evident in employment decisions.

Under the guidelines, disparate impact is determined with the **4/5ths rule**. If the selection rate for a protected group is less than 80% (4/5ths) of the selection rate for the majority group or less than 80% of the group's representation in the relevant labor market, discrimination exists. Thus, the guidelines have attempted to define discrimination in statistical terms. Disparate impact can be checked both internally and externally.

Job-Related Validation Approach. Under the job-related validation approach virtually every factor used to make employment-related decisions—recruiting, selection, promotion, termination, discipline, and performance appraisal—must be shown to be specifically job related. Hence, the concept of validity affects many of the common tools used to make HR decisions.

Validity is simply the extent to which a test actually measures what it says it measures. The concept relates to inferences made from tests. For instance, it may be valid to assume that performance on a mechanical knowledge test may predict performance of a machinist in a manufacturing plant. However, it is probably invalid to assume these same test scores measure general intelligence or promotability for a manufacturing sales representative.

An **employment "test"** is any employment procedure used as the basis for making an employment-related decision. For instance, for a general intelligence test to be valid, it must actually measure intelligence, not just a person's vocabulary. An employment test that is valid must measure the person's ability to perform the job for which he or she is being hired. The ideal condition for employment-related tests is to be both valid and reliable. **Reliability** refers to the consistency with which a test measures an item. For a test to be reliable, an individual's score should be about the same every time the individual takes that test (allowing for the effects of practice).

The 1978 Uniform Selection Guidelines recognize validation strategies measuring three types of validity:

1.   Content validity
2.   Criterion-related validity (concurrent and predictive)
3.   Construct validity

Content validity is a logical, nonstatistical method used to identify the KSAs and other characteristics necessary to perform a job. A test has content validity if it reflects an actual sample of the work done on the job in question. Content validity is especially useful if the workforce is not large enough to allow other, more statistical approaches.

Employment tests of any kind attempt to predict how well an individual will perform on the job. In measuring **criterion-related validity**, a test is the *predictor* and the desired knowledge, skills, and abilities (KSAs) and measures for job performance are the *criterion variables*. The two different approaches to criterion-related validity are *concurrent validity*, which is an "at-the-same-time" approach, and *predictive validity*, a "before-the-fact" approach.

When an employer measures **concurrent validity**, a test is given to current employees and the scores are correlated with their performance ratings. These ratings are determined by such measures as accident rates, absenteeism records, and supervisory performance appraisals. To measure **predictive validity**, test results of applicants are compared with their subsequent job performance. Success on the job is measured by such factors as absenteeism, accidents, errors, and performance appraisals. If those employees who had one year of experience at the time of hire demonstrate better performance than those without such experience, as calculated by statistical comparisons, then the experience requirement is considered a valid predictor of performance and may be used in hiring future employees.

Construct validity shows a relationship between an abstract characteristic inferred from research and job performance. Common constructs for which tests have been devised include creativity, leadership potential, and interpersonal sensitivity. Construct validity is used less frequently in employment situations than the other types of validity.

Elements of EEO Compliance

Employers must comply with a variety of EEO regulations and guidelines. To do so, management should have an *EEO policy statement* and maintain all required *EEO-related records.* All employers with 15 or more employees are required to keep certain records that can be requested by enforcement agencies. The length of time documents must be kept varies, but generally three years is recommended as a minimum. Complete records are necessary to enable an employer to respond should a charge of discrimination be made. Also, a basic report that must be filed with the EEOC is the annual report form EEO-1.

Under EEO laws and regulations, employers may be required to show that they do not discriminate in the recruiting and selection of members of protected classes. Because collection of racial data on application blanks and other pre-employment records is not permitted, the EEOC allows employers to use a "visual" survey or a separate *applicant flow form* that is not used in the selection process. This form is filled out voluntarily by the applicant, and the data must be maintained separately from other selection-related materials.

Pre-employment vs. After-Hire Inquiries. Appendix C lists pre-employment inquiries and identifies whether they may or may not be discriminatory. The pre-employment inquiries labeled as "may be discriminatory" have been so designated because of findings in a variety of court cases. Those labeled "may not be discriminatory" are practices that are legal, but only if they reflect a business necessity or are job-related.

Once an employer tells an applicant he or she is hired (the "point of hire"), inquiries that were prohibited earlier may be made. After hiring, medical examination forms, group insurance cards, and other enrollment cards containing inquiries related directly or indirectly to sex, age, or other bases may be requested.

EEO and International Employees. The extent to which U.S. Equal Employment regulations apply to U.S. employees working for U.S. firms internationally was finally decided when the Civil Rights Act of 1991 extended coverage of EEO laws and regulations to U.S. citizens working internationally for U.S.-controlled companies. However, the act states that if laws in a foreign country require actions in conflict with U.S. EEO laws, the foreign laws will apply.

Most EEO regulations and laws do not apply to foreign-owned firms operating in the United States. For example, some women have brought sexual harassment charges against foreign managers, and other protected-class individuals have brought EEO charges against foreign-owned firms with U.S. operations for refusal to hire or promote them. In those cases, courts have treated the foreign-owned firms just as they would U.S.-owned employers, and in well-known cases involving Mitsubishi and other foreign firms, courts have found them guilty of violating U.S. EEO laws.

GENDER DISCRIMINATION AND SEXUAL HARASSMENT

A number of laws and regulations address discrimination on the bases of sex/gender. Historically, women experienced employment discrimination in a variety of ways. The inclusion of sex as a basis for protected-class status in Title VII of the 1964 Civil Rights Act has led to various areas of protection for women.

Sexual Harassment

The Equal Employment Opportunity Commission (EEOC) has issued guidelines designed to curtail this behavior. **Sexual harassment**, which refers to actions that are sexually directed, are unwanted, and subject the worker to adverse employment conditions or create a hostile work environment. As shown in Figure 3.3, individuals in different roles can be sexual harassers. Most

---

FIGURE 3.3 Potential Sexual Harassers

frequently, sexual harassment occurs by a male in a supervisory or managerial position who harasses women within his "power structure." However, women managers have been found guilty of sexually harassing male employees. Also, same sex harassment has occurred.

Types of Sexual Harassment. EEOC regulations and a large number of court cases define two basic types of sexual harassment:

1. *Quid pro quo* is harassment in which employment outcomes are linked to the individual granting sexual favors.
2. *Hostile environment* harassment exists when an individual's work performance or psychological well-being is unreasonably affected by intimidating or offensive working conditions.

In the *quid pro quo* type, an employee may be told he or she may get promoted, receive a special raise, or be given a desirable work assignment, but only if the employee submits to granting some sexual favors to the supervisor. Unfortunately, *hostile environment* harassment is much more prevalent, partially because the standards and consequences are more varied.

In cases of sexual harassment, only if the employer can produce evidence of an *affirmative defense* in which the employer took reasonable care to prohibit sexual harassment does the employer have the possibility of avoiding liability. Components of ensuring reasonable care include the following:

▶ Establishing a sexual harassment policy
▶ Communicating the policy regularly
▶ Training employees and managers on avoiding sexual harassment
▶ Investigating and taking action when complaints are voiced

Pregnancy Discrimination

The Pregnancy Discrimination Act (PDA) of 1978 requires that any employer with 15 or more employees treat maternity leave the same as other personal or medical leaves. Closely related to the PDA is the Family and Medical Leave Act (FMLA) of 1993, which requires that individuals be given up to 12 weeks of family leave without pay and also requires that those taking family leave be allowed to return to jobs. The FMLA applies to both men and women.

Equal Pay and Pay Equity

The Equal Pay Act of 1963 requires employers to pay similar wage rates for similar work without regard to gender. A *common core of tasks* must be similar, but tasks performed only intermittently or infrequently do not make jobs different enough to justify significantly different wages. Differences in pay may be allowed because of: (1) differences in seniority, (2) differences in performance, (3) differences in quality or quantity of production, and (4) factors other than sex, such as skill, effort, and working conditions.

A related idea is **pay equity**, which is the notion that the pay for jobs requiring comparable levels of knowledge, skill, and ability should be similar, even if actual duties differ significantly. This theory has also been called *comparable worth* in earlier cases. But except where state laws have mandated pay equity for public-sector employees, U.S. federal courts generally have ruled that the existence of pay differences between jobs held by women and jobs held by men is not sufficient to prove that illegal discrimination has occurred.

Glass Ceiling

For years, women's groups have alleged that women in workplaces encounter a **glass ceiling**, which refers to discriminatory practices that have prevented women and other protected-class members from advancing to executive-level jobs. A related problem is that women have tended to advance to senior management in a limited number of support areas, such as HR and corporate communications. Because jobs in these "supporting" areas tend to pay less than jobs in sales, marketing, operations, or finance, the overall impact is to reduce women's career progression and income. Limits that keep women from progressing only in certain fields have been referred to as "glass walls" or "glass elevators."

AMERICANS WITH DISABILITIES ACT (ADA)

The passage of the Americans with Disabilities Act (ADA) in 1990 expanded the scope and impact of laws and regulations on discrimination against individuals with disabilities. All employers with 15 or more employees are covered by the provisions of the ADA, which are enforced by the EEOC, and it applies to private employers, employment agencies, and labor unions.

Who Is Disabled?

As defined by the ADA, a **disabled person** is someone who has a physical or mental impairment that substantially limits that person in some major life activities, who has a record of such an impairment, or who is regarded as having such an impairment. In spite of the EEOC guidelines, some confusion still remains as to who is disabled. A growing area of concern under the ADA is individuals with mental disabilities. A mental illness is often more difficult to diagnose than a physical disability. Employers must be careful when considering "emotional" or "mental health" factors when making employment-related decisions. However, employers must not stereotype individuals with mental disabilities, but base their evaluation on sound medical information.[3]

ADA and Job Requirements

The ADA contains a number of specific requirements that deal with employment of individuals with disabilities. The major ones are discussed next.

Discrimination is prohibited against individuals with disabilities who can perform **essential job functions**—the fundamental job duties of the employment position that an individual with a disability holds or desires. These functions do not include marginal functions of the position. For persons with disabilities, employers must make a **reasonable accommodation**, which is a modification or adjustment to a job or work environment that enables a qualified individual with a disability to have equal employment opportunity.

Reasonable accommodation is restricted to actions that do not place an "undue hardship" on an employer. An **undue hardship** is a significant difficulty or expense imposed on an employer in making an accommodation for individuals with disabilities. The ADA offers only general guidelines in determining when an accommodation becomes unreasonable and places undue hardship on an employer. However, most accommodation expenditures by employers have been relatively inexpensive.

AGE, RACE, AND OTHER TYPES OF DISCRIMINATION

Several other types of discrimination have been identified as illegal. A growing number of issues in the various areas of discrimination require attention by employers.

Age Discrimination

The Age Discrimination in Employment Act of 1967, amended in 1978 and 1986, prohibits discrimination in compensation terms, conditions, or privileges of employment against all individuals age 40 or older working for employers having 20 or more workers. However, the U.S. Supreme Court has ruled that state employees may not sue state government employers in federal courts because the ADEA is a federal law.[4]

Age Discrimination and Workforce Reductions. In the past decade, early retirement programs and organizational downsizing have been used by many employers to reduce their employment costs. Illegal age discrimination sometimes occurs when an individual over the age of 40 is forced into retirement or is denied employment or promotion on the basis of age. If disparate impact or treatment for those over 40 exists, age discrimination occurs.

Older Workers Benefit Protection Act (OWBPA). The Older Workers Benefit Protection Act (OWBPA) of 1990 was passed to amend the ADEA to ensure that equal treatment for older workers occurs in early retirement or severance situations. Additionally, guidelines issued by the EEOC are designed to ensure that older workers are protected when early retirement and downsizing programs include severance agreements and employee waivers.[5]

EEO Issues and Race, National Origin, and Citizenship

The original purpose of the Civil Rights Act of 1964 was to address race and national origin discrimination. This concern continues to be important today, and employers must be aware of practices that may be discriminatory on the basis of race, national origin, and citizenship.

Immigration Reform and Control Acts (IRCA). Race is often a factor in discrimination on the basis of national origin. The Immigration Reform and Control Acts (IRCA) and later revisions made it illegal for an employer to discriminate in recruiting, hiring, disciplining, or terminating employees based on an individual's national origin or citizenship. In addition, the IRCA requires that employers who knowingly hire illegal aliens be penalized. Employers must ask for proof of identity, such as a driver's license with a picture, Social Security card, birth certificate, immigration permit, or other documents. The required I-9 form must be completed by all new employees within 72 hours.

Bilingual Employees and English-Only Requirements. As the diversity of the workforce has increased, more employees have language skills beyond English. Interestingly, some employers attempt to restrict the use of foreign languages, while other employers recognize that bilingual employees have valuable skills. The EEOC has issued guidelines clearly stating that employers may require workers to speak only English at certain times or in certain situations, but the business necessity of the requirements must be justified.[6]

Racial/Ethnic Harassment. The area of harassment is such a concern that the EEOC has issued guidelines on racial/ethnic harassment. It is recommended that employers adopt policies against harassment of any type, including ethnic jokes, vulgar epithets, racial slurs, or physical actions.

Other Types of Discrimination

Several other types of discrimination have been identified as illegal. A growing number of issues in the area of religious discrimination require attention by employers.

Religious Discrimination. Title VII of the Civil Rights Act identifies discrimination on the basis of religion as illegal. However, religious schools and institutions can use religion as a bona fide occupational qualification (BFOQ) for employment practices on a limited scale. Also, the employers must make *reasonable accommodation* efforts regarding an employee's religious beliefs.

Appearance and Weight Discrimination. Several EEO cases have been filed concerning the physical appearance of employees. Court decisions consistently have allowed employers to have dress codes as long as they are applied uniformly. For example, requiring a dress code for women but not for men has been ruled to be discriminatory. Also, employers should be cautious when enforcing dress standards for women employees who are members of certain religions that prescribe appropriate and inappropriate dress and appearance standards.

Sexual Orientation. Some states and cities have passed laws prohibiting discrimination based on sexual orientation or lifestyle. Even the issue of benefits coverage for "domestic partners," whether heterosexual or homosexual, has been the subject of state and city legislation. At the federal level no laws of a similar nature have been passed. Whether gay men and lesbians have rights under the equal protection amendment to the U.S. Constitution has not been decided by the U.S. Supreme Court.

NOTES

1. *Griggs v. Duke Power Co.*, 401 U.S. 424 (1971).
2. Reginald E. Jones and Dara L. Dehaven, "OFCCP's Revised 60-2 Regulations," *Legal Report,* January/February 2001, 1–4.
3. Jonathan A. Segal, "I'm Depressed—Accommodate Me," *HR Magazine,* February 2001, 139–148.
4. *Kimel v. Florida, Board of Regents*, U.S. S.Ct., 98-791, 2000.
5. Darryl Van Duch, "New EEOC Rules Target 'Won't Sue' Severance Pledges," *The National Law Journal,* March 5, 2001, 1.
6. T. Shawn Taylor, "A New Language Barrier," *Chicago Tribune,* June 10, 2001, G-1.

INTERNET RESEARCH

U.S. Equal Employment Opportunity Commission The commission's Web site provides information about its purpose, facts about employment discrimination, enforcement statistics, and details on technical assistance programs. **http://www.eeoc.gov**

Diversity Inc. Provides news, resources, and other commentary on the role of diversity in corporations. **http://www.diversityinc.com**

SUGGESTED READINGS

Ed Fortson and Mari Florence, *Sex at Work,* Silver Lake Publishing, 2000.

Equal Employment Opportunity, Compliance Guide, Aspen Publishing, 2000.

How to Write an Affirmative Action Plan, Business & Legal Reports, 2001.

Lee Garderswartz and Anita Rowe, *Diverse Teams at Work,* Society for Human Resource Management, 2003.

Chapter 4

Jobs

The work that needs to be done in an organization, and how it gets done matters to both employers and employees. Important elements for *employers* are: (1) having work done properly that will lead to organization goals, (2) making sure that work is logically organized into jobs that can be compensated fairly, and (3) having work that people are willing (even eager) to do. Important factors for *employees* are: (1) having a clear understanding of what is expected in the job, (2) doing tasks they personally enjoy, (3) being rewarded appropriately for their work, and (4) having a sense that what they do is important and respected.

HR MANAGEMENT AND JOBS

Several areas associated with jobs involve human resources professionals. Figure 4.1 shows how organizational values, strategies, and customer needs influence the work the organization has to do. **Work** is effort directed toward producing or accomplishing results. A **job** is a grouping of tasks, duties, and responsibilities that constitutes the total work assignment for employees. These tasks, duties, and responsibilities may change over time and therefore the job may change. Ideally, when all the jobs are added together they should equal the amount of work that the organization needs to have done—no more, no less.

Workflow Analysis

Workflow analysis studies the way work moves through the organization and usually begins with an examination of the desired and actual *outputs* (goods and services) in terms of both quantity and quality. Then the *activities* (tasks and jobs) that lead to the outputs are evaluated to see whether they can achieve the desired outputs. Finally the *inputs* (people, material, information, data,

FIGURE 4.1 Influences Affecting Jobs, People, and Related HR Policies

equipment, etc.) must be assessed to determine whether these inputs make the outputs and activities more efficient and better.

Re-Engineering Business Processes

After workflow analysis provides an understanding of how work is being done, re-engineering generates the needed changes in the business processes. The purpose of business process re-engineering is to improve such activities as product development, customer service, and service delivery. Re-engineering consists of three different phases:

1. *Rethink.* Examine how the current organization of work and jobs affects customer satisfaction and service.
2. *Redesign.* Analyze how jobs are put together, the workflow, and results achieved; then redesign as necessary.
3. *Retool.* Look at new technologies (equipment, computers, software, etc.) as opportunities to improve product and service quality and customer satisfaction.

Job Design

Individual responses to jobs vary because a job may be motivating to one person but not to someone else. Also, depending on how jobs are designed, they may provide more or less opportunity for employees to satisfy their job-related needs.

Designing or redesigning jobs encompasses many factors. **Job design** refers to organizing tasks, duties, and responsibilities into a productive unit of work. It addresses the content of jobs and the effect of jobs on employees. Identifying the components of a given job is an integral part of job design. Currently, job design is receiving greater attention for three major reasons:

▶ Job design can influence *performance* in certain jobs, especially those where employee motivation can make a substantial difference. Lower costs through reduced turnover and absenteeism also are related to good job design.

▶ Job design can affect *job satisfaction.* Because people are more satisfied with certain job configurations than with others, identifying what makes a "good" job becomes critical.

▶ Job design can affect both *physical and mental health.* Problems such as hearing loss, backache, and leg pain sometimes can be traced directly to job design, as can stress, high blood pressure, and heart disease.

The *person/job fit* is a simple but important concept that involves matching characteristics of people with characteristics of jobs. Obviously, if a person does not fit a job, either the person can be changed or replaced, or the job can be altered. In the past, it was much more common to try to make the "round" person fit the "square" job. However, successfully reshaping people is not easy to do. By redesigning jobs, the person/job fit may be improved more easily.

Job Enlargement and Job Enrichment. Attempts to alleviate some of the problems encountered in excessive job simplification fall under the general headings of job enlargement and job enrichment. **Job enlargement** involves broadening the scope of a job by expanding the number of different tasks to be performed. **Job enrichment** is increasing the depth of a job by adding responsibility for planning, organizing, controlling, or evaluating the job. A manager might enrich a job by promoting variety, requiring more skill and responsibility, providing more autonomy, and adding opportunities for personal growth. Giving an employee more planning and controlling responsibilities over the tasks to be done also enriches.

Job Rotation. One technique that can break the monotony of an otherwise simple, routine job is **job rotation**, which is the process of shifting an employee from job to job. The advantage is that job rotation develops an employee's capabilities for doing several different jobs. Because of the effects of job design on performance, employee satisfaction, health, and other factors, organizations are changing or have already changed the design of some jobs.[1]

Using Teams in Jobs. Typically, a job is thought of as something done by one person. However, jobs may be designed for teams, where it is appropriate. In an attempt to make jobs more meaningful and take advantage of the increased productivity and commitment that can follow, more organizations are using teams of employees instead of individuals for jobs. Some firms have gone as far as dropping such terms as *workers* and *employees,* replacing them with *teammates, crew members, associates,* and other titles that emphasize teamwork.

Doing work with teams has been a popular form of job redesign for the last decade. Improved productivity, increased employee involvement, more widespread employee learning, and greater employee ownership of problems are among the potential benefits. Even *virtual teams* linked primarily through advanced technology can contribute despite geographical dispersion of essential employees.

Not every use of teams as a part of job design has been successful, however. In some cases employers find that teams work better with employees who are "group oriented," than with more individually focused workers. Further, much work does not really need a team, but many companies use teamwork without much thought. Too often, *teamwork* can be a buzzword or "feel-good" device that may actually get in the way of good decisions. Another problem is how to measure the performance of teams.[2] Finally, compensating individual team members so that they see themselves as a team rather than just a group of individuals is another issue not adequately addressed in many team-oriented situations.

Work Schedules and Locations

Jobs include the tasks an employee does, the relationships required on the job, the tools one works with, and many other elements as well. Two of these important elements are when and how the work is scheduled, and where an employee is located when working.

The traditional work schedule, in which employees work full time, eight hours a day, five days a week at the employer's place of operations, is in transition. Organizations have been experimenting with many different possibilities for change: the 4-day, 40-hour week; the 4-day, 32-hour week; the 3-day week; and flexible scheduling. One type of schedule redesign is **flextime**, in which employees work a set number of hours per day but vary starting and ending times. The traditional starting and ending times of the eight-hour work shift can vary up to one or more hours at the beginning and end of the normal workday.

Another way to change work patterns is with the **compressed workweek**, in which a full week's work is accomplished in fewer than five days. Compression simply alters the number of hours per day per employee, usually resulting in longer working times each day and a decreased number of days worked per week.

Shift Work. Using an 8-hour standard, the 24-hour day can be divided into three "shifts." Many organizations need 24-hour coverage and therefore schedule three shifts each day. Many employers provide some form of additional pay for working evening or night shifts. The average shift differential is about

50¢ per hour.[3] Also, shift work has long been known to cause difficulties for many people with families. Twelve-hour shifts, which some employees choose, involve significant life changes for many too.

Telecommuting. A growing number of employers are allowing workers to use widely different working locations. Some employees work partly at home and partly at an office, while others share office space with other "office nomads." **Telecommuting** is the process of going to work via electronic computing and telecommunications equipment. Many U.S. employers have telecommuting employees or are experimenting with them.[4]

THE NATURE OF JOB ANALYSIS

The most basic building block of HR management, **job analysis**, is a systematic way to gather and analyze information about the content, context, and human requirement of jobs.

Approaches to Job Analysis

There are two different approaches to job analysis. One approach looks at the tasks performed in jobs, while the other approach focuses on the competencies needed to perform jobs satisfactorily.

Job analysis involves a system for formally collecting information on the characteristics of a job that differentiates it from other jobs. That information will be used to differentiate among jobs for compensation and other purposes.

Much of the current interest in analyzing jobs stems from the importance assigned to the activity by federal and state courts. The legal defensibility of an employer's recruiting and selection procedures, performance appraisal system, employee disciplinary actions, and pay practices rests in part on the foundation of job analysis.

It is useful to clarify the differences between job design and job analysis. Job design attempts to develop jobs that fit effectively into the flow of the organizational work that needs to be done. The more narrow focus of job analysis centers on gathering data in a formal and systematic way about what people do in their jobs.

Task-Based Job Analysis. Task-based job analysis is the most common form and focuses on the tasks, duties, and responsibilities performed in a job. A **task** is a distinct, identifiable work activity composed of motions, whereas a **duty** is a larger work segment composed of several tasks that are performed by an individual. Because both tasks and duties describe activities, it is not always easy or necessary to distinguish between the two. For example, if one of the employment supervisor's duties is to interview applicants, one task associated with that duty would be asking questions. **Responsibilities** are obligations to perform certain tasks and duties.

The Competency Approach to Job Analysis. Focusing on the competencies that individuals need to perform jobs, rather than on the tasks, duties, and responsibilities composing a job, emphasizes how significantly people's capabilities influence organizational performance. Instead of thinking of individuals having jobs that are relatively stable and can be written up into typical job descriptions, it may be more relevant to focus on the competencies used.

Competencies are basic characteristics that can be linked to enhanced performance by individuals or teams. A growing number of organizations use some facets of competency analysis. The three primary reasons organizations use a competency approach are: (1) to communicate valued behaviors throughout the organization, (2) to raise the competency levels of the organization, and (3) to emphasize the capabilities of people to enhance organizational competitive advantage.

Unlike the traditional approach to analyzing jobs, which identifies the tasks, duties, knowledge, and skills associated with a job, the competency approach considers how the knowledge and skills are used.[5] The competency approach also attempts to identify the hidden factors that are often critical to superior performance. For instance, many supervisors talk about employees' attitudes, but they have difficulty identifying what they mean by *attitude*. The competency approach uses some methodologies to help supervisors articulate examples of what they mean by attitude and how those factors affect performance.

Job Analysis Methods

There are several facets of job analysis, as Figure 4-2 depicts. The first one to examine is job analysis networks. Job analysis information about what people are doing in their jobs can be gathered in a variety of ways. Common methods are observations, interviews, questionnaires, and specialized methods of analysis. The use of a combination of these approaches depends on the situation and the organization. Each of these methods is discussed next.

Observation. With the observation method, a manager, job analyst, or industrial engineer observes the individual performing the job and takes notes to describe the tasks and duties performed. Observation may be continuous or based on intermittent sampling. Use of the observation method is limited because many jobs do not have complete and easily observed job duties or complete job cycles. Thus, observation may be more useful for repetitive jobs and in conjunction with other methods.

Interviewing. The interview method of gathering information requires that a manager or HR specialist visit each job site and talk with the employees performing each job. A standardized interview form is used most often to record the information. Frequently, both the employee and the employee's supervisor must be interviewed to obtain a complete understanding of the job. The interview method can be quite time consuming, especially if the interviewer talks with two or three employees doing each job. Professional and managerial jobs often

FIGURE 4.2   Job Analysis in Perspective

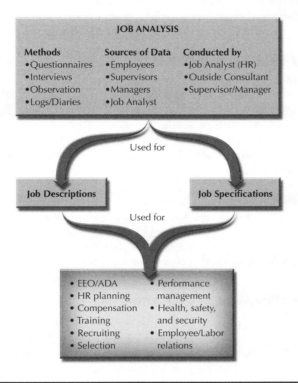

are more complicated to analyze and usually require longer interviews. For these reasons, combining the interview with one of the other methods is suggested.

Questionnaires. The questionnaire is a widely used method of gathering data on jobs. A survey instrument is developed and given to employees and managers to complete. The questionnaire method offers a major advantage in that information on a large number of jobs can be collected inexpensively in a relatively short period of time. However the questionnaire method assumes that employees can accurately analyze and communicate information about their jobs. Employees may vary in their perceptions of the jobs, and even in their literacy. For these reasons, the questionnaire method used in combination with interviews and observations allows analysts to clarify and verify the questionnaire information.

Computerized Job Analysis. With the expansion of information technology, researchers have developed computerized job analysis systems. An important feature of computerized job analysis is the specificity of data that can be gathered. All of these specific data are compiled into a job analysis database. As a result, a computerized job analysis system often can reduce the time and effort involved in writing job descriptions. These systems store banks of job duty statements that relate to each of the task and scope statements of the questionnaires.

Job Analysis and O*Net Online. A variety of resources related to job analysis are available from the U.S. Department of Labor (DOL). The DOL has made a major commitment to provide usable information on skills, abilities, knowledge, work activities, and interests associated with a wide range of jobs and occupations. This information is available online and can be used to develop job descriptions, job specifications, and career opportunity information. O*Net transforms mountains of data into precise, focused information that anyone can understand and use.

Combination Methods. There are a number of different ways to obtain and analyze information about a job. Therefore, in dealing with issues that may end up in court, HR specialists and others doing job analysis must carefully document all of the steps taken. Each of the methods has strengths and weaknesses, and a combination of methods generally is preferred over one method alone.

Behavioral Aspects of Job Analysis

A detailed examination of jobs, although necessary, can be a demanding and threatening experience for both managers and employees, in part because job analysis can identify the difference between what currently is being performed in a job and what *should* be done. Employees and managers have some tendency to inflate the importance and significance of their jobs. Because job analysis information is used for compensation purposes, both managers and employees hope that "puffing up" their jobs will result in higher pay levels. Titles of jobs often get inflated too, and some HR specialists believe the problem continues to grow.

Through the information developed in a job analysis, the job description is supposed to capture the nature of a job. However, if it fails—if some portions of the job are mistakenly left out of the description—some employees may use any omission to limit managerial flexibility. The resulting attitude, "It's not in my job description," puts a straitjacket on a manager. Because of such difficulties, the final statement in many job descriptions is a *miscellaneous clause,* which consists of a phrase similar to "Performs other duties as needed upon request by immediate supervisor."

Also, some employees may fear that an analysis of their jobs will put a "straitjacket" on them, limiting their creativity and flexibility by formalizing their duties. However, analyzing a job does not necessarily limit job scope or depth. In fact, having a well-written, well-communicated job description can assist employees by clarifying their roles and the expectations within those roles. One effective way to handle anxieties is to involve the employees in the revision process.

Legal Aspects of Job Analysis

The 1978 Uniform Selection Guidelines make it clear that HR requirements must be tied to specific job-related factors if employers are to defend their actions as a business necessity. Also, the Americans with Disabilities Act (ADA) increased emphasis by employers on conducting job analysis, as well as developing and maintaining current and accurate job descriptions and job specifications.

The ADA requires that organizations identify the **essential job functions**, which are the fundamental duties of a job. The term *essential functions* does not include the marginal functions of the positions. **Marginal functions** are those duties that are part of a job but are incidental or ancillary to the purpose and nature of a job. Job analysts, HR staff members, and operating managers must evaluate and make decisions when the information on the three considerations is not clear.

THE JOB ANALYSIS PROCESS

The process of job analysis must be conducted in a logical manner, following appropriate management and professional psychometric practices. Therefore, analysts usually follow a multistage process, regardless of the specific job analysis methods used. The stages for a typical job analysis, as outlined next and shown in Figure 4.3, may vary somewhat with the number of jobs included.

Planning the Job Analysis

A crucial aspect of the job analysis process is the planning done before gathering data from managers and employees. It is vital to obtain top management support. The backing of senior managers is essential as issues arise regarding changes in jobs or the organizational structure. Support from the highest levels of management also helps when managerial and employee anxieties and resistance arise.

Preparing and Introducing the Job Analysis

Preparation for job analysis begins by identifying the jobs under review. For example, are the jobs to be analyzed hourly jobs, clerical jobs, all jobs in one division, or all jobs in the entire organization? This phase identifies those who will be involved in conducting the job analysis and the methods to be used. It also specifies how current incumbents and managers will participate in the process and how many employees' jobs will be considered.

A crucial step is to communicate and explain the process to managers, affected employees, and other concerned people, such as union stewards. Explanations should address the natural concerns and anxieties people have when someone closely scrutinizes their jobs. Items to be covered often include the

FIGURE 4.3 Stages in the Job Analysis Process

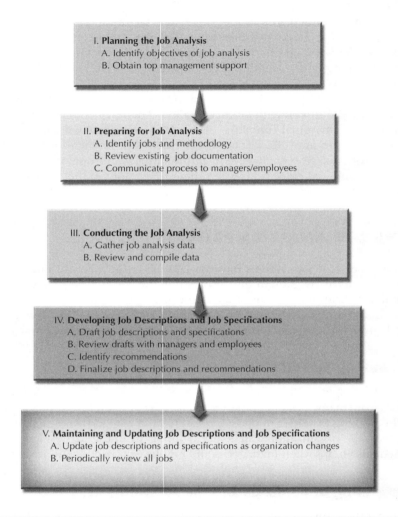

I. **Planning the Job Analysis**
   A. Identify objectives of job analysis
   B. Obtain top management support

II. **Preparing for Job Analysis**
   A. Identify jobs and methodology
   B. Review existing job documentation
   C. Communicate process to managers/employees

III. **Conducting the Job Analysis**
   A. Gather job analysis data
   B. Review and compile data

IV. **Developing Job Descriptions and Job Specifications**
   A. Draft job descriptions and specifications
   B. Review drafts with managers and employees
   C. Identify recommendations
   D. Finalize job descriptions and recommendations

V. **Maintaining and Updating Job Descriptions and Job Specifications**
   A. Update job descriptions and specifications as organization changes
   B. Periodically review all jobs

purpose of the job analysis, the steps involved, the time schedule, how managers and employees will participate, who is doing the analysis, and whom to contact as questions arise.

Conducting the Job Analysis

With the preparation completed, the job analysis can be conducted. The methods selected will determine the timeline for the project. Sufficient time should be allotted for obtaining the information from employees and managers. If questionnaires are used, it is often helpful to have employees return them to supervisors or managers for review before giving them back to those conducting the job analysis. The questionnaire should be accompanied by a letter explaining the process and instructions for completing and returning the job analysis questionnaires.

Typically, job analysis also identifies the percentage of time spent on each duty in a job. This information helps determine whether someone should be classified as *exempt* or *non-exempt* under the wage/hour laws. Other legal-compliance efforts, such as those involving workplace safety and health, can also be aided through the data provided by job analysis. In summary, it is extremely difficult for an employer to have a legal staffing system without performing job analysis. Truly, job analysis is the most basic HR activity.

Developing Job Descriptions and Job Specifications

The output from analysis of a job is used to develop a job description and its job specifications. Together, they summarize job analysis information in a readable format and provide the basis for defensible job-related actions. They also identify individual jobs for employees by providing documentation from management.

In most cases, the job description and job specifications are combined into one document that contains several different sections. A **job description** identifies the tasks, duties, and responsibilities of a job. It describes what is done, why it is done, where it is done, and briefly, how it is done. Then, **performance standards** can flow directly from a job description and indicate what the job accomplishes and how performance is measured in key areas of the job description.

While the job description describes activities to be done, the **job specifications** list the knowledge, skills, and abilities (KSAs) include education, experience, work skill requirements, personal abilities, and mental and physical requirements.

Generally, organizations find that having managers and employees write job descriptions is not recommended for several reasons. First, it reduces the consistency in format and details, both of which are important given the legal consequences of job descriptions. Second, managers and employees vary in their writing skills. Also, they may write the job descriptions and job specifications to reflect what they do and what their personal qualifications are, not what the job requires. A typical job description contains several major parts. Overviews of the most common components are presented next.

Identification. The first part of the job description is the identification section, in which the job title, reporting relationships, department, location, and date of analysis may be given. Usually, it is advisable to note other information that is useful in tracking jobs and employees through human resource information systems (HRIS).

General Summary. The second part, the general summary, is a concise statement of the general responsibilities and components that make the job different from others. One HR specialist has characterized the general summary statement as follows: "In thirty words or less, describe the essence of the job."

Essential Functions and Duties. The third part of the typical job description lists the essential functions and duties. It contains clear, precise statements on the major tasks, duties, and responsibilities performed. Writing this section is the most time-consuming aspect of preparing job descriptions.

Job Specifications. The next portion of the job description gives the qualifications needed to perform the job satisfactorily. The job specifications typically are stated as: (1) knowledge, skills, and abilities (KSAs), (2) education and experience, and (3) physical requirements and/or working conditions. The components of the job specifications provide information necessary to determine what accommodations might and might not be possible under Americans with Disabilities Act (ADA) regulations.

Disclaimer and Approvals. The final section on many job descriptions contains approval signatures by appropriate managers and a legal disclaimer. This disclaimer allows employers to change employees' job duties or request employees to perform duties not listed, so that the job description is not viewed as a "contract" between the employer and the employee. Appendix D shows a sample job description that contains job specifications also.

Maintaining and Updating Job Descriptions and Job Specifications

Once job descriptions and specifications have been completed and reviewed by all appropriate individuals, a system must be developed for keeping them current. One effective way to ensure that appropriate reviews occur is to use job descriptions and job specifications in other HR activities. For example, each time a vacancy occurs, the job description and specifications should be reviewed and revised as appropriate *before* recruiting and selection efforts begin. Similarly, in some organizations, managers review the job description during each performance appraisal interview. For many organizations, a complete review is done once every three years, or as technology shifts occur, and more frequently when organization changes are made.

NOTES

1. Eric Raimy, "Back to the Table," *Human Resource Executive,* March 2001, 1.
2. Bradley L. Kirkman, Paul E. Tesluk, and Benson Rosen, "Assessing the Incremental Validity of Team Consensus Ratings," *Personnel Psychology* 54 (2001), 645–667.
3. "Survey Spotlights Shiftwork Practices," *Occupational Hazards,* October 2000, 56.
4. Susan J. Wells, "Making Telecommuting Work," *HR Magazine,* October 2001, 34–45.
5. Carla Joinson, "Refocusing Job Descriptions," *HR Magazine,* January 2001, 67–72.

INTERNET RESEARCH

Job-Analysis.NETwork This Web site has resources for conducting a job analysis, including different types of methods, legal issues, questionnaires, and job descriptions.
http://www.job-analysis.net

O*Net O*Net is a database compiled by the U.S. Department of Labor to provide basic occupational data.
http://online.onetcenter.org

SUGGESTED READINGS

Michael T. Brannick and Edward L. Levine, *Job Analysis*, Corwin Press, 2002.

Jackson Lewis, *Recruiting, Retaining, & Terminating Employees*, American Chamber of Commerce, 2002.

John C. Maxwell, *The Laws of Teamwork*, Thomas Nelson, 2001.

Standard Occupational Classification Manuel. JIST Works, 2002.

Chapter 5

Staffing

Effective staffing helps minimize problems in an organization through recruiting and selecting qualified people using established criteria and predictors. Having the right people in the right jobs makes it more likely that the organization will have better performance.

The staffing process matches people with jobs through recruiting and selection. **Recruiting** is the process of generating a pool of qualified applicants for organizational jobs. **Selection** is the process of choosing people to fill those jobs. If the number of available candidates only equals the number of people to be hired, no real selection is required—the choice has already been made. The organization must either leave some openings unfilled or take all the candidates.

LABOR MARKETS AND RECRUITING ISSUES

The supply of and demand for workers in various labor markets substantially affect the staffing strategies of organizations. An organization can use a number of different ways to identify labor markets, including by geographic area, industry and occupation, and education/technical qualifications.

Geographic Labor Markets

One common way to classify labor markets is based on geographic location. Some markets are local, some area or regional, and others national. International labor markets also can be tapped. Local and area labor markets vary significantly in terms of workforce availability and quality.

Attempting to recruit locally or in a limited geographic area for a job market that is really national likely will result in disappointing applicant rates. For example, trying to recruit a senior merchandising manager for a catalog retailer only in the small town where the firm is located is not likely to be successful. Conversely, it may not be necessary to recruit nationally for workers to fill administrative support jobs.

Industry and Occupational Labor Markets

Labor markets also can be classified by industry and occupation. For example, the demand for truck drivers, healthcare workers, teachers, and others has been strong, creating tight labor markets in those industries. Occupational labor markets are based on the KSAs required for the jobs. Examples include physical therapists, HR managers, engineers, accountants, welders, and bank tellers. One occupational area of extreme volatility in the past several years is composed of information technology jobs.

STRATEGIC RECRUITING DECISIONS

Based on the recruiting needs identified as part of HR planning, a number of recruiting decisions must be made. The most important ones are discussed next.

Organizational-Based vs. Outsourcing

An initial and basic decision is whether recruiting will be done by HR staff and/or other organizational employees. Otherwise, outsourcing of some or most recruiting can be done. It need not be an "either-or" decision where all recruiting is done by organizational staff or external resources are used exclusively.

A common means of outsourcing is use of search firms and employment agencies who are retained to recruit candidates. Also, employers who list or advertise openings externally frequently are contacted by search firms who have possible candidates for referral.

Professional Employer Organizations and Employee Leasing. A specific type of outsourcing uses professional employer organizations (PEOs) and employee leasing. This approach has grown rapidly in recent years. Some sources estimate that more than 2 million individuals are employed by PEOs doing employee leasing.[1]

The employee leasing process is simple: An employer signs an agreement with the PEO, after which the existing staff is hired by the leasing firm and leased back to the company. For a fee, a small business owner or operator turns the staff over to the leasing company, which then writes the paychecks, pays the taxes, prepares and implements HR policies, and keeps all the required records. One advantage for employees of leasing companies is that they may receive better benefits than they otherwise would get in many small businesses.

All this service comes at a cost. Leasing companies often charge employers between 4% and 6% of employees' monthly salaries. Thus, while leasing may save employers money on benefits and HR administration, it may also increase total costs of payroll.

Regular vs. Flexible Staffing

Another decision affects how much recruiting will be done to fill staffing needs with regular full-time and part-time employees. Decisions as to who should be recruited hinge on whether to seek traditional employees or use more flexible approaches, which might include temporaries or independent contractors.

Flexible staffing makes use of recruiting sources and workers who are not traditional employees. Using flexible staffing arrangements allows an employer to avoid some of the cost of full-time benefits such as vacation pay and pension plans, as well as to recruit in a somewhat different market. These arrangements use temporary workers, independent contractors, and employee leasing.

Some employers hire temporary workers as a way for individuals to move into full-time, regular employment. After 90 days or some other period as a "temp," better-performing workers may move to regular positions when they become available. This "try before you buy" approach is potentially beneficial both to employers and employees. However, most temporary service firms bill client companies a placement charge if a temporary worker is hired full-time within a certain time period—usually 90 days.

Some firms employ **independent contractors**, or workers who perform specific services on a contract basis. However, those contractors must be independent as determined by a 20-item test used by the U.S. Internal Revenue Service and the U.S. Department of Labor. Independent contractors are used in a number of areas, including building maintenance, security, and advertising/public relations. Some estimates indicate that employers get significant savings by using independent contractors because benefits do not have to be provided.

Recruiting and EEO/Diversity Considerations

A number of factors go into ensuring that recruiting decisions meet diversity considerations. Recruiting as a key employment-related activity is subject to various legal considerations, especially equal employment laws and regulations. As part of legal compliance in the recruiting process, organizations must work to reduce external disparate impact, or underrepresentation of protected-class members compared to the labor markets utilized by the employer. If disparate impact exists, then the employer may need to make special efforts to persuade protected-class individuals to apply for jobs.

Recruiting Source Choices: Internal vs. External

Recruiting strategy and policy decisions entail identifying where to recruit, whom to recruit, and how recruiting will be done. One of the first decisions determines the extent to which internal or external sources and methods will be used. Both promoting from within the organization (internal recruitment) or hiring from outside the organization (external recruitment) to fill openings come with associated advantages and disadvantages. Figure 5.1 shows some of the major advantages and disadvantages of internal versus external recruiting.

FIGURE 5.1   Advantages and Disadvantages of Internal and External Recruiting Sources

Recruiting Source	Advantages	Disadvantages
Internal	• *Morale of promotee* • *Better assessment of abilities* • *Lower cost for some jobs* • *Motivator for good performance* • *Causes a succession of promotions* • *Have to hire only at entry level*	• *Inbreeding* • *Possible morale problems of those not promoted* • *"Political" infighting for promotions* • *Need for management development program*
External	• *New "blood" brings new perspectives* • *Cheaper and faster than training professionals* • *No group of political supporters in organization already* • *May bring new industry insights*	• *May not select someone who will "fit" the job or organization* • *May cause morale problems for internal candidates not selected* • *Longer "adjustment" or orientation time*

Internal Recruiting Processes

Databases, job postings, promotions, and transfers within the organization are ways to allow current employees to move to other jobs. The design of these processes outlines ways for employees to "surface" and be considered for openings as they occur. Filling openings internally may add motivation for employees to stay and grow in the organization rather than pursuing career opportunities elsewhere.

The major means for recruiting employees for other jobs within the organization is job posting, a system in which the employer provides notices of job openings and employees respond by applying for specific openings. Without some sort of job posting system, it is difficult for many employees to find out what jobs are open elsewhere in the organization. The organization can notify employees of job vacancies in a number of ways, including posting notices on bulletin boards, using employee newsletters, and sending out e-mails to managers and employees.

Employee-Focused Recruiting

One reliable source of potential recruits is suggestions from current or former employees. Because current and former employees are familiar with the employer, their references often are high-potential candidates, because most employees usually do not refer individuals who are likely to be unqualified or make the employees look bad.

Former employees and former applicants represent another source for recruitment. Both cases offer a time-saving advantage, because something is already known about the potential employees.[2] Known as *re-recruiting* because the individuals previously were successfully recruited, former employees are considered an internal source in the sense that they have ties to the employer and may be called "boomerangers" because they left and came back.

INTERNET RECRUITING

Organizations first started using computers as a recruiting tool by advertising jobs on a bulletin board service from which prospective applicants would contact employers. Then some companies began to take e-mail applications. Today the Internet has become a primary means for employers to search for job candidates and for applicants to look for jobs. The explosive growth in Internet use is a key reason, with more than 160 million Internet users in the United States and 1.2 billion worldwide. In the United States it is estimated that 74% of those with Internet access, aged 18 years or older, annually use the Internet as part of job searching.[3] Internet users tap the Internet to search for jobs almost as frequently as reading newspaper classified ads. Also many of these Internet users post or submit resumes on the Internet.

HR professionals and recruiters are using the Internet regularly also. When HR recruiters were asked what sources generate more new hires, 77% of those responding indicated Internet job postings, compared with 17.5% citing newspaper ads.[4] Various surveys have found that 80% to 90% of employers use the Internet for recruiting. As many as 100,000 recruiting Web sites are available to employers and job candidates on which to post jobs and review resumes of various types. But the explosive growth of Internet recruiting also means that HR professionals can be overwhelmed by the breadth and scope of Internet recruiting.

E-Recruiting Methods

Several different methods are used for Internet recruiting. The most commons ones are job boards, professional/career Web sites, and employer Web sites.

Job Boards. Numerous job boards, such as *http://www.monster.com* and *http://www.hotjobs.com*, provide places for employers to post jobs or search for candidates. Another prevalent one is America's Job Bank, operated in conjunction with the U.S. Department of Labor and state job services.

Even though job boards provide access to numerous candidates, many individuals accessing the sites are "job lookers" who are not serious about changing jobs, but checking out compensation levels and what job availability exists in their areas of interest. One estimate is that about one-third of all visitors to the job boards are just browsing, not seriously considering changing employment.[5] Despite these concerns, HR recruiters find the general job boards useful for generating applicant responses.

Professional/Career Web Sites. Many professional associations have employment sections at their Web sites. As illustration, for HR jobs see *http://www. shrm.org* or *http://www.astd.org.* A number of private corporations maintain specialized career or industry Web sites in order to focus on IT, telecommunications, engineering, physicians, or other areas. Using these more targeted Web sites limits somewhat the recruiters' search time and efforts. Also, posting jobs on such Web sites is likely to target applicants specifically interested in the job field and may reduce the number of less-qualified applicants who actually apply.

Employer Web Sites. Aside from the popularity of job boards and other job sites, many employers have found their Web sites to be more effective and efficient when recruiting candidates. Numerous employers have included employment and career information as part of their organizational Web sites. On many of these sites, job seekers are encouraged to e-mail resumes or complete on-line applications.

Advantages and Disadvantages of Internet Recruiting

Employers have found a number of advantages in using Internet recruiting. A primary one is that many employers have realized cost savings using Internet recruiting compared to other sources such as newspaper advertising, employment agencies and search firms, and other external sources. Some employers experience savings from several hundred dollars per hire to as high as $4,000 to $6,000 for senior professional and management jobs.[6]

Internet recruiting also can save considerable *time.* Applicants can respond quickly to job postings by sending e-mails, rather than using "snail mail." Recruiters can respond to qualified candidates more quickly and establish times for interviews or request additional candidate information.

The positives associated with Internet recruiting come with a number of disadvantages. By getting broader exposure, employers also may get more unqualified applicants. A survey of HR recruiters found that one-third of them felt Internet recruiting created additional work for HR staff members.[7] More resumes must be reviewed, more e-mails dealt with, and specialized applicant tracking software may be needed to handle the increase in applicants caused in many Internet recruiting efforts.

EXTERNAL RECRUITING

Many different external sources are available for recruiting. In some tight labor markets multiple sources and methods may be used to attract candidates for the variety of jobs available in organizations. Some of the more prominent methods are highlighted next.

College and University Recruiting

At the college or university level, the recruitment of students is a significant source for entry-level professional and technical employees. Most colleges and universities maintain career placement offices in which employers and applicants can meet. The major determinants affecting an employer's selection of colleges and universities at which to conduct interviews are:

▸ Current and anticipated job openings
▸ College reputation
▸ Experiences with placement offices and previous graduates
▸ Organizational budget constraints
▸ Cost of available talent and typical salaries
▸ Market competition

School Recruiting

High schools or vocational/technical schools may be a good source of new employees for some organizations. Many schools have a centralized guidance or placement office. Promotional brochures that acquaint students with starting jobs and career opportunities can be distributed to counselors, librarians, or others. Participating in career days and giving tours of the company to school groups are other ways of maintaining good contact with school sources. Cooperative programs in which students work part-time and receive some school credits also may be useful in generating qualified future applicants for full-time positions.

Labor Unions. Labor unions are a source of certain types of workers. In some industries, such as construction, unions have traditionally supplied workers to employers. A labor pool is generally available through a union, and workers can be dispatched to particular jobs to meet the needs of the employers.

In some instances, the union can control or influence recruiting and staffing needs. An organization with a strong union may have less flexibility than a non-union company in deciding who will be hired and where that person will be placed. Unions also can work to an employer's advantage through apprenticeship and cooperative staffing programs, as they do in the building and printing industries.

Employment Agencies and Search Firms

Every state in the United States maintains its own state-sponsored employment agency. These agencies operate branch offices in many cities throughout the states and do not charge fees to applicants or employers.

Private employment agencies also operate in most cities. For a fee collected from either the employee or the employer, these agencies do some preliminary screening and put the organization in touch with applicants. Private employment agencies differ considerably in the level of service, costs, policies, and types of applicants they provide. Employers can reduce the range of possible problems from these sources by giving complete job descriptions and specifications on jobs to be filled.

Competitive Sources

Other sources for recruiting include professional and trade associations, trade publications, and competitors. Many professional societies and trade associations publish newsletters or magazines and have Web sites containing job ads. Such sources may be useful for recruiting specialized professionals needed in an industry.

Media Sources

Media sources such as newspapers, magazines, television, radio, and billboards are widely used. Some firms use direct mail by purchasing lists of individuals in certain fields or industries. Whatever medium is used, it should be tied to the relevant labor market and provide sufficient information on the company and the job.

Job Fairs and Special Events

Employers in tight labor markets or needing to fill a large number of jobs quickly have used job fairs and special recruiting events. Job fairs also have been held by economic development entities, employer associations, HR associations, and other community groups in order to assist bringing employers and potential job candidates together.

Creative Recruiting Methods

In tight labor markets and industries with significant shortages of qualified applicants, employers turn to more creative recruiting methods. Regardless of the methods used, the goal is to generate a pool of qualified applicants so that the jobs in organizations are filled in a timely manner. Some methods may be more effective at recruiting for certain jobs than others. To illustrate, some examples include the following:

- Using a plane towing an advertising banner over beach areas
- Advertising jobs on local movie theater screens as part of the pre-show entertainment
- Holding raffles for employees who refer candidates, with cars and trips being prizes
- Offering free rock concert tickets to the first 20 applicants hired
- Setting up recruiting tables at bowling alleys, minor league baseball games, or stock car races

In order to determine how effective various recruiting sources and methods have been, it is important to evaluate recruiting efforts. The primary way to find out whether recruiting efforts are cost effective is to conduct formal analyses as part of recruiting evaluation.

SELECTION AND PLACEMENT

Selection is the process of choosing individuals who have needed qualifications to fill jobs in an organization. Organizations on average reject a high percentage of applicants. In some situations about five out of six applicants for jobs are rejected. Perhaps the best perspective on selection and placement comes from two HR truisms that clearly identify the importance of effective employment selection.

▸ *"Good training will not make up for bad selection."* When the right people with the appropriate capabilities are not selected for jobs, employers have difficulty later trying to train those individuals.
▸ *"Hire hard, manage easy."* The amount of time and effort spent in selecting the right people for jobs may make managing them as employees much less difficult because more problems will be eliminated.

Placement

The ultimate purpose of selection is **placement,** or fitting a person to the right job. More than anything else, placement of human resources should be seen as a matching process. How well an employee is matched to a job affects the amount and quality of the employee's work.

Person-Job Fit. Selection and placement entail much more than just choosing the best available person. Selecting the appropriate capabilities and talents—which come packaged in a human being—attempts to "fit" what the applicant can and wants to do with what the organization needs. Much of selection is concerned with gathering needed information from applicants through application forms, resumes, interviews, tests, and other means.

Person-Organization Fit. In addition to matching individuals to jobs, employers also increasingly try to determine the congruence between individuals and organizational factors to achieve **person-organization fit**. The person-organization fit is important when general factors of job success are as important as specific knowledge, skills, and abilities (KSAs). For example, if an employer hires at the entry level and promotes from within for most jobs, specific KSAs might be less important than general cognitive and problem-solving abilities and work ethic.

Criteria, Predictors, and Job Performance

Whether an employer uses specific KSAs or the more general approach, effective selection of employees involves using criteria and predictors of job performance. At the heart of an effective selection system is knowledge of what constitutes appropriate job performance and what employee characteristics are associated with that performance. First, an employer defines employee success (performance) and then, using that definition as a basis, determines the employee specifications required to achieve success. A **selection criterion** is a characteristic that a person must have to do the job successfully. A pre-existing ability is often a selection criterion. Figure 5.2 shows that ability, motivation, intelligence, conscientiousness, appropriate risk, and permanence might be good selection criteria for many jobs.

To predict whether a selection criterion (such as "motivation" or "ability") is present, employers try to identify predictors as measurable indicators of selection criteria. For example, in Figure 5.2 three good predictors for some criteria might be individual interests, salary requirements, and tenure on previous jobs.

THE SELECTION PROCESS

Organizations take common steps to process applicants for jobs. Variations on the process depend on organizational size, nature of jobs to be filled, number of people to be selected, the use of electronic technology, and other factors. This process can take place in a day or over a much longer period of time. If the applicant is processed in one day, the employer usually checks references after selection. One or more phases of the process may be omitted or the order changed, depending on the employer.

FIGURE 5.2   Job Performance, Selection Criteria, and Predictors

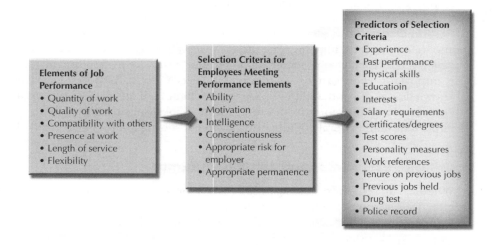

Legal Concerns in the Selection Process

Selection is subject to a number of legal concerns, especially all the equal employment opportunity (EEO) regulations and laws. Throughout the selection process, application forms, interviews, tests, background investigations, and any other selection activities must be conducted in a nondiscriminatory manner. Also, applicants not hired should be rejected only for job-related reasons, not based on protected-class or personal factors, which are illegal.

Defining Who Is an Applicant. It is increasingly important for employers to carefully define exactly who is an applicant because many employers are required to do applicant tracking and reporting as part of equal employment and affirmative action plans. Also, it is important because of "scams" involving individuals who try to apply for jobs, but their primary purpose is to then file lawsuits. Without clear definition of who is an applicant, all individuals who submit unsolicited resumes, respond electronically to Web site employment postings, and persons who walk in to apply for jobs might have to be counted as "applicants."

Applicant Flow Documentation. One interesting point to remember is that many employers must collect data on the race, sex, and other demographics on applicants to fulfill EEO reporting requirements. Many employers use an applicant flow form for applicants to provide EEOC reporting data separately. It is important that this form be filed separately and not be used in any other HR selection activities, or the employers may be accused of using applicant information inappropriately.

Pre-Employment Screening

Many employers conduct pre-employment screening in order to determine whether applicants meet the minimum qualifications for open jobs. Areas typically covered by employers include types of available jobs, applicants' pay expectations, job location, and travel requirements.

Pre-employment screening done electronically has increased dramatically in the past few years. One type of screening uses computer software to scan resumes or applications submitted electronically for key words.[8] Hundreds of large companies use types of "text searching" or artificial intelligence (AI) software to scan, score, and track resumes of applicants.

Application Forms

Application forms are widely used and can take many different formats. Many employers use only one application form, but others need several. For example, a hospital might need one form for nurses and medical technicians, another form for clerical and office employees, another for managers and supervisors, and another for support persons in housekeeping and food-service areas.

Immigration Forms. The Immigration Reform and Control Act (IRCA) of 1986, as revised in 1990, requires that within 72 hours of hiring, an employer must determine whether a job applicant is a U.S. citizen, registered alien, or illegal alien. Those applicants not eligible to work in this country must not be hired. Employers use the I-9 form to identify the status of potential employees. Employers have a responsibility that documents submitted by new employees, such as U.S. passports, birth certificates, original Social Security cards, and driver's licenses, appear to be genuine. Also, employers who hire employees on special visas must maintain appropriate documentation and records.

Selection Testing

A number of different types of tests are used as part of the selection process. A look at the most common types of tests follows.

Ability Tests. Tests that assess an individual's ability to perform in a specific manner are grouped as ability tests. **Cognitive ability tests** measure an individual's thinking, memory, reasoning, and verbal and mathematical abilities. Tests such as these can be used to test applicants' basic knowledge of terminology and concepts, word fluency, spatial orientation, comprehension and retention span, and general and conceptual reasoning.

Physical ability tests measure individual abilities such as strength, endurance, and muscular movement. At an electric utility, line workers regularly must lift and carry equipment, climb ladders, and perform other physical tasks. Testing applicants' mobility, strength, and other physical attributes is job-related.

Different skill-based tests can be used, including **psychomotor tests** that measure a person's dexterity, hand-eye coordination, arm-hand steadiness, and other factors. Additionally, many organizations use situational or **work sample tests**, which require an applicant to perform a simulated job task that is part of the target job. Having an applicant for a financial analyst's job prepare a computer spreadsheet is one such test.

Personality Tests. Personality is a unique blend of individual characteristics that affect interaction with the environment and help define a person. Of the many different types of personality tests, one of the most widely known and used is the Minnesota Multiphasic Personality Inventory (MMPI). It was originally developed to diagnose major psychological disorders and has become widely used as a selection test. From this and many other personality tests, an extensive number of personality characteristics can be identified and used. The Myers-Briggs test is another widely used test of this type.

Honesty/Integrity Testing. Different types of tests are being used by employers to assess the honesty and integrity of applicants and employees. They include standardized honesty/integrity tests and polygraphs. Honesty/integrity tests may be valid as broad screening devices for organizations if used properly. However, it is important that the tests be chosen, used, and evaluated to ensure that they are and remain valid and reliable.

Employers use these tests for several reasons. Firms such as retailers use honesty tests to screen out potentially dishonest individuals and decrease the incidence of employee theft. These firms believe that giving honesty tests not only helps them to screen out potentially dishonest individuals, but also sends a message to applicants and employees alike that dishonesty will not be tolerated.

The polygraph, more generally and incorrectly referred to as the "lie detector," is a mechanical device that measures a person's galvanic skin response, heart rate, and breathing rate. The theory behind the polygraph is that if a person answers incorrectly, the body's physiological responses will "reveal" the falsification through the polygraph's recording mechanisms. As a result of concerns, Congress passed the Employee Polygraph Protection Act, which prohibits polygraph use for pre-employment screening purposes by most employers.

SELECTION INTERVIEWING AND BACKGROUND INVESTIGATORS

Selection interviewing of job applicants is done to both obtain additional information and to clarify information gathered throughout the selection process. Typically, interviews are conducted at two levels: first in the HR department as an initial interview, and then second as an in-depth interview often involving HR staff members and operating supervisors and managers in the departments where the individuals will work. Figure 5.3 shows the different types of selection interviews.

FIGURE 5.3   Types of Selection Interviews

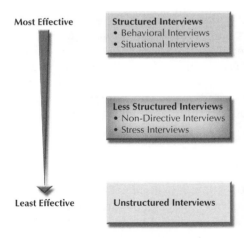

Structured Interviews

A **structured interview** uses a set of standardized questions asked of all applicants. The interviewer asks every applicant the same basic questions, so that comparisons among applicants can more easily be made. This type of interview allows an interviewer to prepare job-related questions in advance and then complete a standardized interviewee evaluation form that provides documentation indicating why one applicant was selected over another. Sample questions that might be asked of all applicants for a retail sales clerk opening are as follows:

▸ I noticed on your application that you were previously employed with _____. How did you get a job there?
▸ Tell me about your responsibilities and duties with _____.
▸ Describe a time you were frustrated as a customer because of the way a store clerk treated you. What do you think should have been done?
▸ How many hours can you work a week without your school work or personal life being negatively affected?

Behavioral Interview. More and more interviewers are using an experienced-based type of structured interview. In the **behavioral interview** applicants are asked to give specific examples of how they have performed a certain task or handled a problem in the past. For example, applicants might be asked the following questions:

▸ How did you handle a situation that had no rules or guidelines for employee discipline?
▸ Why did you choose that approach?
▸ How did your supervisor react?
▸ How was the situation finally resolved?

Situational Interview. The **situational interview** is a type of structured interview that is composed of questions about how applicants might handle specific job situations. Interview questions are based on job analysis and checked by experts in the job so they will be content valid. For some situational interviews, job experts also rate responses to the questions to facilitate ranking candidates. The interviewer can code the suitability of the answer, assign point values, and add up the total number of points an interviewee received.

Who Does Interviews?

Interviews can be done individually, by several individuals in sequence, or by panels or teams of interviewers. For some jobs, such as entry-level, lesser skilled jobs, applicants are interviewed by an HR representative alone. Other jobs are filled using multiple interviews, beginning with an HR interviewer, followed by interviews conducted by appropriate supervisors and managers.

In a **panel interview**, several interviewers interview the candidate at the same time. All the interviewers hear the same responses. On the negative side, without planning by the panel of interviewers, an unstructured interview can result. Also, applicants are frequently uncomfortable with the group interview format. The prevalence of work teams, has increased the use of **team interviews**, in which applicants are interviewed by the "team members" with whom they will work. To be successful, team members may be involved in selecting their co-workers.

Video Interviewing. A number of employers use video interviewing to augment or replace in-depth telephone interviews. Applicants are asked to go to video conferencing facilities scheduled by the employer. At the designated time, the applicant and those conducting the interview are video linked. The greatest use of video interviewing is done by large corporations, executive recruiting firms, and colleges and university placement offices, who offer such facilities to aid both students and employers.[9]

Background Investigation

Background investigation may take place either before or after the in-depth interview. It costs the organization some time and money, but it generally proves beneficial when making selection decisions. Background references can be obtained from several sources. Some information tends to be useful and relevant, depending on the jobs for which applicants are being considered. The most commonly used background investigation methods are:

▶ Employment verification
▶ Criminal records check
▶ Drug screen
▶ Education verification
▶ Previous employer reference check
▶ Professional licenses/Certifications
▶ Motor vehicles records
▶ Credit history
▶ Integrity tests

Personal references, such as those from relatives, clergy, or friends, often are of little value, and should not even be used. No applicant asks somebody who would give a negative response to write a recommendation. Instead, greater reliance should be placed on work-related references from previous employers and supervisors.

Giving References on Former Employees. In a number of court cases, individuals sued their former employers for slander, libel, or defamation of character as a result of what the employers said to other potential employers that prevented the individuals from obtaining jobs. Because of such problems, lawyers advise organizations who are asked about former employees to give out only name, employment date, and title; many organizations have adopted policies restricting the release of reference information. To address these concerns, 35 states have laws that protect employers from civil liability when giving reference information in good faith that is objective and factual in nature.[10]

Risks of Negligent Hiring. The costs of failing to check references may be high. Some organizations have become targets of lawsuits that charge them with negligence in hiring workers who have committed violent acts on the job. Lawyers say that an employer's liability hinges on how well it investigates an applicant's background. Prior convictions and frequent moves or gaps in employment should be cues for further inquiry. Details provided on the application form by the applicant should be investigated to the greatest extent possible, so the employer can show that due diligence was exercised.

Medical Examinations and Inquiries

Medical information on applicants may be used to determine the individual's physical and mental capability for performing jobs. Physical standards for jobs should be realistic, justifiable, and geared to the job requirements. Workers with disabilities can perform satisfactorily in many jobs. The Americans with Disabilities Act (ADA) prohibits the use of pre-employment medical exams, except for drug tests, until a job has been conditionally offered. Also, the ADA prohibits a company from rejecting an individual because of a disability and from asking job applicants any question relative to current or past medical history until a conditional job offer is made. Assuming a conditional offer of employment is made, then some organizations ask applicants to complete a pre-employment health checklist or are given a physical examination paid for by the employer.

Drug testing may be a part of a medical exam, or it may be done separately. Using drug testing as a part of the selection process has increased in the past few years, although some employers facing tight labor markets have discontinued drug testing. If used, employers should remember that the accuracy of drug tests varies according to the type of test used, the item tested, and the quality of the laboratory where the test samples are sent.

Making the Job Offer

The final step of the selection process is making a job offer. Often extended over the phone, many job offers are formalized in letters and sent to applicants. It is important that the offer document be reviewed by legal counsel and that the terms and conditions of employment be clearly identified. Care should be taken to avoid vague, general statements and promises about bonuses, work schedules, or other matters that might change later. These documents also should provide for the individuals to sign an acceptance of the offer and return it to the employer, who should place it in the individual's personnel files.

STAFFING GLOBAL ASSIGNMENTS

The staffing of global openings involves selecting, placing, and locating employees in other countries. The need for individuals who can provide leadership in global organizations emphasizes the importance of global staffing. When staffing global assignments, cost is a major factor to be considered. The cost of establishing a manager or professional in another country can run as high as $1 million for a three-year job assignment. The actual costs for placing a key manager outside the United States often are twice the manager's annual salary. For instance, if the manager is going to Japan, the costs may be even higher when housing costs, schooling subsidies, and tax equalization payment are calculated. Further, if a manager, professional, or executive quits an international assignment prematurely or insists on a transfer home, associated costs can equal or exceed the annual salary. "Failure" rates for managers sent to other countries may run as high as 40% to 50% in some firms or countries.

Types of Global Employees

Global organizations can be staffed in a number of different ways. Each staffing option presents some unique HR management challenges. For instance, when staffing with citizens of different countries, different tax laws and other factors apply. HR professionals need to be knowledgeable about the laws and customs of each country. They must establish appropriate payroll and record-keeping procedures, among other activities, to ensure compliance with varying regulations and requirements. International employees typically are placed in three different classifications, as discussed next.

Expatriates. An **expatriate** is an employee, working in an operation, who is not a citizen of the country in which the operation is located, but is a citizen of the country of the headquarters organization. Also referred to as *parent-country nationals (PCN)*, expatriates are used to ensure that foreign operations are linked effectively with the parent corporations. Generally, expatriates also are used to develop global capabilities within an organization.

Host-Country Nationals. A **host-country national** is an employee working for a firm in an operation who is a citizen of the country where the operation is located, but where the headquarters for the firm are in another country. Using host-country nationals is important for several reasons. One reason is that the organization wants to establish clearly that it is making a commitment to the host country and not just setting up a foreign operation. Host-country nationals often know the culture, politics, laws, and business customs better than an outsider would.

Third-Country Nationals. A **third-country national** is a citizen of one country, working in a second country, and employed by an organization headquartered in a third country. For example, a U.S. citizen working for a British oil company as a manager in Norway is a third-country national. Staffing with use of third-country nationals shows a truly global approach.

Recruiting for Global Assignments

Recruiting employees for global assignments requires approaches and understanding different from the typical recruiting efforts in a home-country setting. The recruiting processes must consider cultural differences, laws, and language considerations. For instance, in Eastern Europe potential recruits like to work for European and U.S. firms, so recruiters emphasize the "western" image. In Hong Kong recruiting ads often stress success factors by showing "typical employees" of a firm wearing expensive watches and stylish clothes.

The growth of the Internet has made global recruiting much more accessible, particularly for individuals in search of professional management jobs. Those individuals and more technologically knowledgeable candidates can be reached using Internet advertising. Global search firms also can be used to locate specialized global managerial talent.

Selection for Global Assignments

The selection process for an international assignment should provide a realistic picture of the life, work, and culture to which the employee may be sent. HR managers start by preparing a comprehensive description of the job to be done. This description notes responsibilities that would be unusual in the home nation, including negotiating with public officials; interpreting local work codes; and responding to ethical, moral, and personal issues such as religious prohibitions and personal freedoms.

NOTES

1. "Outsourcing HR," *Industry Week,* May 15, 2000, 71.
2. Carolyn Hirschman, "Reserve Space for Rehires," *HR Magazine,* January 2000, 58–64.
3. John R. Hall, "Recruiting Via the Internet," *Air Conditioning, Heating, & Refrigeration News,* April 9, 2001, 26.
4. *Internet Recruiting Newsletter,* available at *http://www.recruitersnetwork.com,* March 9, 2001.
5. Kate Dale, "Making the Net Work," *HR World,* May–June 2000, 32–36.
6. Skip Corsini, "Wired to Hire," *Training,* June 2001, 50–54.
7. "Online Recruiting: What Works, What Doesn't," *HR Focus,* March 2000, 1+.
8. Jim Meade, "Where Did They Go?" *HR Magazine,* September 2000, 81–84.
9. Mike Frost, "Video Interviewing," *HR Magazine,* August 2001, 93–98.
10. Carolyn Hirschman, "Laws Protect Reference Checks," *HR Magazine,* June 2000, 91.

INTERNET RESEARCH

Job Web This Web site offers a job outlook section containing a special report about labor markets and jobs. Also, it contains information on career fairs, starting salaries, and researching potential employers.
http://www.jobweb.com

HR-Guide.com This Web site is a guide to the selection process and includes information on methods, laws, best practices, tests, and software programs that can be used for selection.
http://www.hr-guide.com/selection.htm

SUGGESTED READINGS

Edward Hoffman, *Psychological Testing at Work*, McGraw-Hill, 2001.

Sherrie G. Taguchi, *Hiring the Best and Brightest*, AMACOM, 2001.

Robert Wendover, *Smart Hiring*, Sourcebooks. 2002.

Aggie White, *Interview Styles and Strategies*, South-Western Educational Publishers, 2003.

Chapter 6

Training, Careers, and HR Development

The competitive pressures facing organizations today require employees whose knowledge and ideas are current, and whose skills and abilities can deliver results. As organizations compete and change, training becomes even more critical than before. Employees who must adapt to the myriad of changes facing organizations need to be trained continually in order to maintain and update their capabilities. Also, managers must have training and development to enhance their leadership skills and abilities. In a number of situations, employers have documented that effective training and HR development can produce productivity gains.

THE NATURE OF TRAINING

Training is a process whereby people acquire capabilities to aid in the achievement of organizational goals. Because this process is tied to a variety of organizational purposes, training can be viewed either narrowly or broadly. In the narrow sense, training provides employees with specific, identifiable knowledge and skills for use in their present jobs. Sometimes a distinction is drawn between *training* and *development,* with development being broader in scope and focusing on individuals gaining new capabilities useful for both present and future jobs.

The Context of Training

More employers are recognizing that properly training their human resources is vital. Currently, U.S. employers spend at least $60 billion annually on training. For many employers, training expenditures average at least 1½ to 2% of payroll expenses, and run $677 per eligible employee according to a study by the American Society of Training & Development (ASTD). However, organizations that see training as especially crucial to their business competitiveness average $1,665 in training expenditures per eligible employee.[1]

Job performance, training, and employee learning must be integrated to be effective. First, as training progressively moves "closer to the job" in order to achieve "real-time" learning, the linkage between training and job performance becomes more important.

Second, organizations are seeking more authentic (and hence more effective) training experiences for their trainees using real business problems to advance employee learning. Rather than separating the training experience from actual job performance context, trainers who incorporate everyday business issues as learning examples increase the realism of training exercises and scenarios. It is yet another way that the lines between training, learning, and job performance merge.

STRATEGIC TRAINING

Training adds value to an organization by linking training and HR development to organizational objectives, goals, and business strategies. *Strategic training* focuses on efforts that develop competencies, value, and competitive advantages for the organization, which basically means that training and learning interventions must be based on organizational strategic plans and HR planning efforts.

Linking Training to Business Strategies

Organizational business strategies emphasize the need for training programs and activities to support those strategies. For instance, if a company is trying to distinguish itself from its competition based on customer service quality, then significant customer service training is needed to support the firm's strategic thrust. However, if another firm differentiates itself from competitors with products or services that customers perceive as distinctive and unique, then training resources should be shifted to keeping employees abreast of the latest advertising and marketing ideas.

The Training Process

Effective implementation of strategic training requires use of a systematic process. Figure 6.1 depicts the four phases of the training process: assessment, design, delivery, and evaluation. Using such a process reduces the likelihood that unplanned, uncoordinated, and haphazard training efforts will occur. A discussion of each phase of the training process follows next.

TRAINING NEEDS ASSESSMENT

Training needs can be diagnosed through analyzing what the organization or certain departments might need. One important source for organizational analyses comes from various operational measures of organizational performance. On a continuing basis, analyses of HR data might reveal training

FIGURE 6.1   Training Process

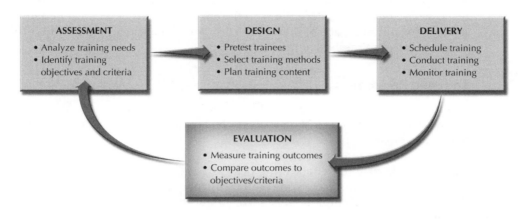

weaknesses. Departments or areas with high turnover, high absenteeism, low performance, or other deficiencies can be pinpointed. Following an analysis of such problems, training objectives can be developed.

The second way to diagnose training needs is through analyses of jobs and the tasks performed in those jobs. By comparing the requirements of jobs with the knowledge, skills, and abilities of employees, training needs can be identified. As an example, at a manufacturing firm job analyses identified tasks to be performed by engineers who served as technical instructors for other employees. By listing the tasks required of a technical instructor, management established a program to teach specific instruction skills; thus the engineers were able to become more successful instructors.

The third means of diagnosing training needs focuses on individuals and how they perform their jobs. The use of performance appraisal data in making these individual analyses is the most common approach. In some instances, a good HR information system can be used to identify individuals who require training in specific areas. To assess training needs through the performance appraisal process, an employee's performance inadequacies first must be determined in a formal review. Then some type of training can be designed to help the employee overcome the weaknesses.

TRAINING DESIGN

Once training objectives have been determined, designing the training can be done. Whether job-specific or broader in nature, training is designed to address the assessed needs. Effective training design considers learning concepts, legal issues, and different approaches to training.

Learning: The Focus of Training

Three primary considerations are central to designing training: (1) determining learner readiness, (2) understanding different learning styles, and (3) designing training for transfer. Each of these elements must be considered in order for the training design to mesh together.[2]

Learner Readiness

For training to be successful, learners must be ready to learn. This readiness means they must have the basic skills necessary for learning, the motivation to learn, and possess self-efficacy.

Ability to Learn. Learners must possess basic skills, such as fundamental reading and math proficiency, and sufficient cognitive abilities. Companies may discover that some employees lack the requisite skills to comprehend their training effectively.

Motivation to Learn. A person's desire to learn training content is referred to as motivation to learn and is influenced by multiple factors. For example, the extent to which a student taking a college course is motivated to learn the course content is influenced by several variables. That student might desire to learn the content because of personal career interests and values, degree plan requirements and area of study, the positive value the student has on getting an A in the course, or simply due to personal expectations of doing well in school.

Self-Efficacy. Learners must also possess **self-efficacy**, which refers to a person's belief that he/she can successfully learn the training program content. For learners to be ready and receptive to the training content, they must feel like they can learn it.

Learning Styles

In designing training interventions, trainers also should consider individual learning styles. For example, *auditory* learners are ones who learn best by listening to someone else tell them about the training content. Others are *tactile* learners who must "get their hands on" and use the training resources. Still others are *visual* learners who think in pictures and figures and need to see the purpose and process of the training. Trainers who address all of these styles by using multiple training methods can design more effective training.

Adult Learning. The classic work of Malcolm Knowles on adult learning suggests five principles for designing training for adults. This and subsequent work by others suggest that adults:[3]

1. Have the need to know why they are learning something.
2. Have a need to be self-directed.

3. Bring more work-related experiences into the learning process.
4. Enter into a learning experience with a problem-centered approach to learning.
5. Are motivated to learn by both extrinsic and intrinsic factors.

Behavior Modeling. The most elementary way in which people learn—and one of the best—is **behavior modeling**, or copying someone else's behavior. The use of behavior modeling is particularly appropriate for skill training in which the trainees must use both knowledge and practice. For example, a new supervisor receives mentoring and training on how to handle disciplinary discussions with employees by observing as the HR director or department manager deals with such problems.

Reinforcement and Immediate Confirmation. The concept of **reinforcement** is based on the *law of effect*, which states that people tend to repeat responses that give them some type of positive reward and avoid actions associated with negative consequences. Closely related is another learning concept called **immediate confirmation**: people learn best if reinforcement and feedback are given as soon as possible after training. Immediate confirmation corrects errors that, if made throughout the training, might establish an undesirable pattern that would need to be unlearned. It also aids with the transfer of training to the actual work done.

Transfer of Training

Finally, trainers should design training interventions for the highest possible transfer of training. This transfer occurs when trainees actually use on the job what they learned in training.

Effective transfer of training meets two conditions. First, the trainees can take the material learned in training and apply it to the job context in which they work. Second, employees maintain their use of the learned material over time.

A number of methods can increase the transfer of training. Offering trainees an overview of the training content and process prior to the actual training seems to help with both short-term and longer-term training transfer. One specific way to aid transfer of training to job situations is to ensure that the training mirrors the job context as much as possible. For example, training managers to be better interviewers should include role playing with "applicants" who respond in the same way that real applicants would.

Orientation: Training for New Employees. The most important and widely conducted type of regular training is done for new employees. **Orientation** is the planned introduction of new employees to their jobs, co-workers, and the organization, and is offered by most employers. It requires cooperation between individuals in the HR unit and other managers and supervisors. In a small organization without an HR department, the new employee's supervisor or manager usually assumes most of the responsibility for orientation. In large organizations, managers and supervisors, as well as the HR department, generally work as a team to orient new employees. Effective orientation achieves several key purposes for the organization:

▸ Establishes a favorable employee impression of the organization and the job
▸ Provides organization and job information
▸ Enhances interpersonal acceptance by co-workers
▸ Accelerates socialization and integration of the new employee into the organization
▸ Ensures employee performance and productivity begin more quickly

One way to expand the efficiency of orientation is through use of electronic orientation. A number of employers place general employee orientation information on company intranets or corporate Web sites. New employees can log on and go through much of the general material on organizational history, structure, products and services, mission statements, and other background information instead of sitting in a classroom where the information is delivered in person or by videotape.

Training for Global Assignments. A unique type of training is for individuals and their families with global assignments. Unfortunately, many global employers do not provide formal training programs for such assignments. When offered, most individuals participate in this training, which generally produces a positive effect on cross-cultural adjustment.

The most common topics covered in pre-departure training include:

▸ Daily living conditions
▸ Cultural customs
▸ Business issues
▸ Country history
▸ Geographical climate
▸ Transportation and communication systems

Growing numbers of global employers are providing intercultural competence training for their global employees. Intercultural competence incorporates a wide range of human social skills and personality characteristics.

▸ *Cognitive:* What does the person know about other cultures?
▸ *Emotional:* How does the person view other cultures and how much sensitivity exists to cultural customs and issues?
▸ *Behavioral:* How does the person act in intercultural situations?

TRAINING DELIVERY

Once training has been designed, then the actual delivery of training can begin. It is generally recommended that the training be pilot-tested or conducted on a trial basis in order to ensure that the training meets the needs identified and that the design is appropriate. Regardless of the type of training done, a number of different training approaches and methods can be used. The growth of training technology continues to expand the available choices.

Internal Training

Generally, internal training is very specifically job-focused. It is also popular because it saves the cost of sending employees away for training and often avoids the cost of outside trainers. Often, skills-based, technical training is conducted inside organizations. Due to rapid changes in technology, the building and updating of technical skills have become crucial training needs.

One internal source of training that has grown is **informal training**, which occurs through interactions and feedback among employees. Much of what employees know about their jobs they learn informally from asking questions and getting advice from other employees and their supervisors, rather than from formal training programs. Such information may or may not be accurate.

On-the-Job Training (OJT). The most common type of training at all levels in an organization is **on-the-job training** (OJT). Different from informal training that often occurs spontaneously, OJT should be planned. The supervisor or manager conducting the training must be able to both teach and show the employees what to do. Based on a special guided form of training known as **job instruction training** (JIT), on-the-job training is most effective if a logical progression of stages is used, as shown in Figure 6.2.

External Training

Whatever the size of the organization, external training occurs for several reasons:

▶   It may be less expensive for an employer to have an outside trainer conduct training in areas where internal training resources are limited.

FIGURE 6.2   Stages for On-the-Job Training

Prepare the Learners	Present the Information	Trainees Practice	Do Follow-Up
• Put them at ease • Find out what they know • Get them interested	• Tell, show, question • Present one point at a time • Make sure they know	• Trainees perform tasks • Ask questions • Observe and correct • Evaluate mastery	• Put them on their own • Check frequently • Reduce follow-up as performance improves

▶ The organization may have insufficient time to develop internal training materials.

▶ The HR staff may not have the necessary level of expertise for the subject matter in which training is needed.

▶ Advantages can be realized when employees interact with managers and peers in other companies in training programs held externally.

Outsourcing of Training. Many employers of all sizes outsource training to external training firms, consultants, and other entities. According to data from ASTD, approximately 20% of training expenditures go to outside training sources. Interestingly, over a recent three-year period, the outsourcing of training declined some, especially in firms with fewer than 500 employees.[4] The reasons for the decline may be cost concerns, greater emphasis on internal linking of training to organizational strategies, or others.

E-Learning: Training Online

E-learning is defined as the use of the Internet or an organizational intranet to conduct training online. Many people possess a familiarity with the Internet, which has so dramatically altered the way people do business, locate information, and communicate. An intranet is similar to the Internet, but it is a private organizational network behind "firewall" software that restricts access to authorized users, including those employees participating in e-learning.

Developing E-Learning. E-learning does not simply mean putting existing training courses and materials on a Web site. Rather than being adopted just for its "gee-whiz" effect, e-learning is meant to meet strategic training needs.

Modularizing of content permits trainees to complete segments of training materials, rather than sitting for several hours at a time to complete an entire course. Once modules are developed, then the e-learning must be made "learner centric," which means that users can customize their learning. For instance, rather than taking an entire module or course, an employee wanting to learn one segment could access that information specifically.

Finally, e-learning should be measured, usage tracked, and training evaluated to see whether it meets objectives. To establish and implement e-learning requires considerable investment in resources and time by HR and training staff, managers, and employees, and the return on that investment should be assessed. Often, employers turn to outside consultants and firms specializing in e-learning for assistance. Frequently, application service providers (ASPs) are used to facilitate and implement e-learning for individual employers.

Advantages and Disadvantages of E-Learning. The rapid growth of e-learning makes the Internet or an intranet a viable means for delivering training content. A study of 700 e-learners found that 62% had positive experiences with online learning, but only 38% indicated they preferred e-learning to classroom training.[5] These findings support the view that e-learning has both advantages and disadvantages that must be considered.

Training Methods

Whether delivered internally, externally, or through e-learning, appropriate training methods must be chosen. The following overview classifies common training methods into several major groups. Some methods are used more frequently for job-based training. Others are utilized more for human resource development.

Cooperative Training. Cooperative training methods mix classroom training and on-the-job experiences. This training takes several forms. One method, generally referred to as *school-to-work* transition, helps individuals move into jobs while still in school or upon completion of formal schooling.

A form of cooperative training called *internships* usually combines job training with classroom instruction at schools, colleges, and universities. Internships offer advantages to both employers and interns. Interns get "real-world" exposure, a line on their resumes, and a chance to examine a possible employer closely. Employers who hire interns get a cost-effective source that includes a chance to see an intern at work before making a final hiring decision.

Another form of cooperative training used by employers, trade unions, and government agencies is *apprentice training*. An apprenticeship program provides an employee with on-the-job experience under the guidance of a skilled and certified worker. Apprenticeships usually last two to five years, depending on the occupation. During this time the apprentice usually receives lower wages than the certified individual.

Instructor-Led Classroom and Conference Training. Instructor-led training is still the most prevalent method for training. Employer-conducted short courses, lectures, and meetings usually consist of classroom training, whereas numerous employee development courses offered by professional organizations, trade associations, and educational institutions are examples of conference training.

Distance Training/Learning. A growing number of college and university classes use some form of Internet-based course support. Blackboard and WebCT, two of the more popular support packages that thousands of college professors use to make their lecture content available to students, and enable virtual chat and electronic file exchange among course participants.

EVALUATION OF TRAINING

Evaluation of training compares the post-training results to the objectives expected by managers, trainers, and trainees. Too often, training is conducted with little thought of measuring and evaluating it later to see how well it worked. Because training is both time-consuming and costly, evaluation always should be done.

Levels of Evaluation

It is best to consider how training is to be evaluated before it begins. Donald L. Kirkpatrick identified four levels at which training can be evaluated.[6]

Reaction. Organizations evaluate the reaction level of trainees by conducting interviews or by administering questionnaires to the trainees. However, immediate reactions may measure only how much the people liked the training rather than how it benefited them or how they conduct interviews.

Learning. Learning levels can be evaluated by measuring how well trainees have learned facts, ideas, concepts, theories, and attitudes. Tests on the training material are commonly used for evaluating learning and can be given both before and after training to compare scores.

Behavior. Evaluating training at the behavioral level means: (1) measuring the effect of training on job performance through interviews of trainees and their co-workers, and (2) observing job performance. For instance, a behavioral evaluation of the managers who participated in the interviewing workshop might be done by observing them conduct actual interviews of applicants for jobs in their departments.

Results. Employers evaluate results by measuring the effect of training on the achievement of organizational objectives. Because results such as productivity, turnover, quality, time, sales, and costs are relatively concrete, this type of evaluation can be done by comparing records before and after training. For the interviewing training, records of the number of individuals hired to the offers of employment made prior to and after the training could be gathered.

Cost-Benefit Analyses

Training results can also be examined on the basis of costs and benefits associated with the training through a **cost-benefit analysis**. Even though some benefits (such as attitude changes) are hard to quantify, comparison of costs and benefits associated with training remains a way to determine whether training is cost effective.

Return on Investment (ROI)

In organizations training often is expected to produce a return on investment (ROI). Unfortunately, in too many circumstances, training is justified because someone liked it, rather than based on resource accountability.

Benchmarking Training

Rather than evaluating training internally, some organizations use benchmark measures of training that are compared from one organization to others. To do benchmarking, HR professionals in an organization gather data on training and compare them to data on training at other organizations in the industry and of their size. Comparison data are available through the American Society of Training and Development (ASTD) and its Benchmarking Service.

CAREERS

A **career** is the series of work-related positions a person occupies throughout life. People pursue careers to satisfy deeply individual needs. At one time, identifying with one employer seemed to fulfill many of those needs. Now, the distinction between the way individuals and organizations view careers is significantly different.

Organization-Centered Career Planning

Organization-centered career planning focuses on jobs and on identifying career paths that provide for the logical progression of people between jobs in an organization. Individuals follow these paths as they advance in certain organizational units. For example, a person might enter the sales department as a sales representative, then be promoted to account director, to sales manager, and finally to vice president of sales.

Top management is responsible for developing career planning programs. A good program identifies career paths and includes performance appraisal, development, opportunities for transfer and promotion, and some planning for succession.

Individual-Centered Career Planning

Individual-centered career planning focuses on an individual's career rather than organizational needs. It is done by employees themselves analyzing their individual goals and skills. Such efforts might consider situations both inside and outside the organization that could expand a person's career. Even though individuals are the only ones who know for certain what they consider a successful career, that definition is not always apparent even to the individuals involved.

General Career Progression

Many theorists in adult development describe the first half of life as the young adult's quest for competence and a way to make a mark in the world. According to this view, a person attains happiness during this time primarily through achievement and the acquisition of capabilities. The second half of life is different. Once the adult starts to measure time from the expected end of his or her life rather than from the beginning, the need for competence and acquisition changes to the need for integrity, values, and well-being. For many people internal values take precedence over external scorecards or accomplishments such as wealth and job title status. In addition, mature adults already possess certain skills, so their focus may shift to other interests. Career-ending concerns reflect additional shifts also.

Career Transitions and HR

Three career transitions are of special interests to HR: organizational entry and socialization, transfers and promotions, and job loss. Starting as a new employee can be overwhelming. "Entry shock" is especially difficult for younger new hires who find the work world very different from school.

Training and development of employees present obvious career implications for both the employee and the organization. Traditionally, career development efforts targeted managerial personnel to look beyond their current jobs and to prepare them for a variety of future jobs in the organization. But development for all employees, not just managers, is necessary for organizations to have the needed human resource capabilities for future growth and change.

Mergers, acquisitions, restructurings, and layoffs all have influenced the way people and organizations look at careers and development. In the "new career," the individual—not the organization—manages his or her own development. Such self-development consists of personal educational experiences, training, organizational experiences, projects, and even changes in occupational fields. Under this system, the individual defines career success, which may or may not coincide with the organizational view of success.

SPECIAL CAREER ISSUES FOR ORGANIZATIONS AND EMPLOYEES

Although the goals and perspectives in career planning may differ for organizations and employees, three issues can be problematic for both, perhaps for different reasons: (1) career plateaus (or the lack of opportunity to move up), (2) dealing with technical professionals who do not want to go into management, and (3) dual-career couples.

Career Plateaus

Those who do not change employers may face career plateaus. As the baby-boomer generation reaches midlife, and as large employers cut back on their workforces, increasing numbers of employees find themselves at a career plateau where they are "stuck" at a career level. This plateauing may seem a sign of failure to some people, and plateaued employees can cause problems for employers if their frustrations affect their job performance.

Technical and Professional Workers

Technical and professional workers, such as engineers, scientists, physical therapists, IT systems experts, and others, present a special challenge for organizations.[7] Many of these individuals want to stay in their technical areas rather than enter management; yet advancement in many organizations frequently requires a move into management. Most of these people like the idea of the responsibility and opportunity associated with advancement, but they do not want to leave the professional and technical puzzles and problems at which they excel.

The *dual-career ladder* is an attempt to solve this problem. A person can advance up either the management ladder or a corresponding ladder on the technical/professional side.

Dual-Career Couples

As the number of women in the workforce, particularly in professional careers, continues to increase, so does the number of dual-career couples. For dual-career couples with children, family issues may conflict with career progression. Thus, in job transfer situations, one partner's flexibility may depend on what is "best" for the family. Companies may consider part-time work, flextime, and work-at-home arrangements as possible options, especially for parents with younger children.

Recruitment Problems with Dual-Career Couples. Recruiting a member of a dual-career couple may mean having an equally attractive job available for the candidate's partner at the new location. Dual-career couples may lose some income when relocating; thus they often have higher expectations, request more help, and expect higher salaries in such situations.

Relocation of Dual-Career Couples. Traditionally, employees accepted transfers as part of upward mobility in organizations. However, for some dual-career couples the mobility required because of one partner's transfer often interferes with the other's career. In addition having two careers, dual-career couples often have established support networks of co-workers, friends, and business contacts to cope with both their careers and personal lives. Relocating one partner in a dual-career couple may mean upsetting this carefully constructed network for the other person or creating a "commuting" relationship.

DEVELOPING HUMAN RESOURCES

Development represents efforts to improve employees' ability to handle a variety of assignments and to cultivate capabilities beyond those required by the current job. Development benefits both organizations and individuals. Employees and managers with appropriate experiences and abilities may enhance organizational competitiveness and the ability to adapt to a changing environment. In the development process, individuals' careers also may evolve and gain new or different focus.

Development differs from training. It is possible to train most people to run a copy machine, answer customer service questions, drive a truck, operate a computer, or assemble a radio. However, developing abilities in areas such as judgment, responsibility, decision making, and communications presents a bigger challenge. These areas may or may not develop through life experiences by individuals. However, a planned system of development experiences for all employees, not just managers, can help expand the overall level of capabilities in an organization.

Make or Buy?

To some extent, employers face a "make-or-buy" choice: Develop competitive human resources, or "buy" them already developed from somewhere else. Current trends indicate that technical and professional people usually are hired based on the amount of skill development already achieved, rather than on their ability to learn or their behavioral traits. Many organizations show an apparent preference to buy rather than "make" scarce employees in today's labor market. However, buying rather than developing human resource capabilities may not contribute to a strategy of sustained competitive advantage through human resources. As in finance, the make-or-buy decision can be quantified and calculated.[8]

Developing Specific Capabilities

Exactly what kind of development a given individual might need to expand his or her capabilities depends on both the person and the capabilities needed. However, some important and common management capabilities often include action orientation, quality decision making, ethical values, and technical skills.

For high-demand tech specialties (tech support, database administrator, network designer, etc.) certain non-technical abilities must be developed as well:

▶ Ability to work under pressure
▶ Ability to work independently
▶ Ability to solve problems quickly
▶ Ability to use past knowledge in a new situation

Team building, developing subordinates, directing others, and dealing with uncertainty are equally important but much less commonly developed capabilities for successful managers.

Lifelong Learning

Learning and development are not one-time occurrences. For most people, lifelong learning and development are much more likely and desirable. For many professionals, lifelong learning may mean continuing education requirements to keep certified. For example, lawyers, CPAs, teachers, dentists, and others must complete continuing education requirements in most states to keep their licenses to practice. For semi-skilled employees, learning and development may involve training to expand existing skills and prepare for different jobs, promotions, or even for new jobs after retirement.

Re-development

Whether due to a desire for career change or because the employer needs different capabilities, people may shift jobs mid-life or mid-career. Re-developing or re-training people in the capabilities they need is logical and important. In the last decade the number of college enrollees over age 35 increased by more than 25%.[9] But going back to college is only one way to redevelop individuals. Some companies offer redevelopment programs in order to recruit experienced workers from other fields. For example, firms needing truck drivers, reporters, and IT workers sponsor second-career programs. Public-sector employers have been using redevelopment as a recruiting tool as well.

DEVELOPMENT NEEDS ANALYSES

Either the company or the individual can analyze what a given person needs by way of development. The goal, of course, is to identify strengths and weaknesses. Methods used by organizations to assess development needs include use of assessment centers, psychological testing, and performance appraisals.

Assessment Centers

Assessment centers are collections of instruments and exercises designed to diagnose an individual's development needs. Organizational leadership uses assessment centers for both developing and selecting managers. Many types of large organizations, such as police departments, use assessment centers.

In a typical assessment-center experience, an individual spends two or three days away from the job, performing many activities. These activities might include role playing, pencil-and-paper tests, cases, leaderless group discussions, computer-based simulations, management games, and peer evaluations. Frequently, in-basket exercises are used also, in which the individual handles typical problems coming across a manager's desk. For the most part, the exercises represent situations that require the use of managerial skills and behaviors.

Psychological Testing

Psychological pencil-and-paper tests have been used for several years to determine employees' development potential and needs. Intelligence tests, verbal and mathematical reasoning tests, and personality tests are often used. Even a test that supposedly assesses common sense is available. Such testing can furnish useful information on individuals about such factors as motivation, reasoning abilities, leadership style, interpersonal response traits, and job preferences.

Performance Appraisals

Well-done performance appraisals can be a source of development information. Performance data on productivity, employee relations, job knowledge, and other relevant dimensions can be gathered in this way. Appraisals designed for development purposes may be more useful in aiding individual employee development than appraisals designed strictly for administrative purposes.

CHOOSING A DEVELOPMENT APPROACH

To be effective, a development approach must mesh with HR strategies to meet organizational goals. Figure 6.3 summarizes the major advantages and disadvantages of various on-site and off-site approaches to development.

Management Development

Although development is important for all employees, it is essential for managers. Effective management development imparts the knowledge and judgment needed by managers. Without appropriate development, managers may lack the capabilities to best deploy and manage resources (including employees) throughout the organization.

Experience plays a central role in management development. Indeed, experience often contributes more to the development of senior managers than classroom training does, because much of their experience occurs in varying circumstances on the job over time. Yet, despite a need for effective managers, finding such managers for managerial jobs sometimes is difficult. At the first-line supervisor level, some individuals may refuse such jobs.

SUCCESSION PLANNING

Planning for the succession of key executives, managers, and other employees is an important part of HR development. **Succession planning** is a process of identifying a longer-term plan for the orderly replacement of key employees. The need to replace key employees results from promotions, transfers, retirements, deaths, disability, departures, or other reasons. Succession planning often focuses on top management, such as ensuring a CEO successor. However, limiting succession planning just to top executive jobs is one of the greatest mistakes made.[10]

Whether in small or large firms, succession planning is linked to strategic HR planning. Both the quantity and capabilities of potential successors must be linked to organizational strategies and HR plans. For example, a retailer whose

FIGURE 6.3   Advantages and Disadvantages of Major Development Approaches

Job-Site Methods	Advantage	Disadvantage
• Coaching	• Natural and job-related	• Difficulty in finding good coaches
• Committee Assignments/ Meetings	• Involve participants in critical processes	• Can be time waster
• Job Rotation	• Gives excellent overview of the organization	• Long start-up time
• Assistant-to Positions	• Provides exposure to an excellent manager	• Possible shortage of good assignments
• Online Development	• Flexible	• Niche not yet well defined
• Corporate Universities/ Development Centers	• Can combine academic and real world at work	• May be "university" in name only
• Learning Organization	• Perhaps the ideal mindset for development	• Essentially a theoretical, idealistic notion for most organizations

Off-Site Methods	Advantage	Disadvantage
• Classroom Courses and Degrees	• Familiar, accepted, status	• Does not always improve performance
• Human Relations Training	• Deals with important management skills	• Difficult to measure effectiveness
• Simulations	• Realism and integration	• Inappropriate "game playing"
• Sabbaticals	• Rejuvenating as well as developmental	• Expensive; employees may lose contact with job
• Outdoor Training	• Increases self-confidence and teamwork through physical challenges	• Not appropriate for all because of physical nature; dangerous

key merchandising managers are likely to retire soon must consider the implications for future merchandising and store expansion plans, particularly if the firm plans to enter or withdraw from offering certain lines of goods.

Managerial Modeling

A common adage in management development says that managers tend to manage as they were managed. In other words, managers learn by behavior modeling, or copying someone else's behavior. This tendency is not surprising, because a great deal of human behavior is learned by modeling. Children learn by modeling the behaviors of parents and older children. Management development efforts can take advantage of natural human behavior by matching young or developing managers with appropriate models and then reinforcing the desirable behaviors exhibited.

Management Coaching

Coaching combines observation with suggestions. Like modeling, it complements the natural way humans learn. A brief outline of good coaching pointers often includes the following:

- ▸ Explaining appropriate behavior
- ▸ Making clear why actions were taken
- ▸ Accurately stating observations
- ▸ Providing possible alternatives/suggestions
- ▸ Following up/reinforcing

Mentoring

Mentoring is a relationship in which experienced managers aid individuals in the earlier stages of their careers. Such a relationship provides an environment for conveying technical, interpersonal, and organizational skills from the more-experienced to the less-experienced person. Not only does the inexperienced employee benefit, but the mentor may enjoy the challenge of sharing his or her wisdom.

However, mentoring is not without its problems. Young minority managers frequently report difficulty finding mentors. Also, men generally show less willingness than women to be mentors. Further, mentors who are dissatisfied with their jobs and those who teach a narrow or distorted view of events may not help a young manager's development.

Women and Management Development

In virtually all countries in the world, the proportion of women holding management jobs is lower than the proportion of men holding such jobs. The term *glass ceiling* has been used to describe the situation in which women fail to progress into top management positions. Women are making slow but steady strides into management and the executive suite.

Executive Education

Executives in an organization often face difficult jobs due to changing and unknown circumstances. "Churning" at the top of organizations and the stresses of executive jobs contribute to increased turnover in these positions. In an effort to decrease turnover, some organizations are experimenting with a relatively recent phenomenon: special education for executives. This type of training supplements executive education traditionally offered by university business schools and includes strategy formulation, financial models, logistics, alliances, and global issues.

Problems with Management Development Efforts

Development efforts are subject to certain common mistakes and problems. Most of the management development problems in the United States have resulted from inadequate HR planning and a lack of coordination of HR development efforts. Common problems include the following:

- ▶ Inadequate needs analysis
- ▶ Relying on fad programs or training methods
- ▶ Abdicating responsibility for development to HR staff alone
- ▶ Trying to substitute training for selection
- ▶ Lack of training among those who lead the development activities
- ▶ Using only "courses" as the road to development

NOTES

1. *http://www.astd.org.*
2. Based on concepts and models suggested by Lisa A. Burke, PhD, SPHR.
3. Shawn B. Merriam and Rosemary Caffarella, *Learning in Adulthood: A Comprehensive Guide*, 2nd ed. (San Francisco: Jossey-Bass, 1999).
4. Mark E. Van Buren, *ASTD State of the Industry Report, 2003* (Alexandria VA: American Society of Training and Development, 2003).
5. Paula Santonocito, "Employees and E-Learning: Increasing Acceptance and Satisfaction," available from *http://www.hr-esource*, August 6, 2001.
6. Donald L. Kirkpatrick, *Evaluating Training Programs: The Four Levels* (New York: Barret-Kohler, 1998).
7. Carol Hymowitz, "What Happens When Your Valued Employee Makes Bad Manager," *The Wall Street Journal*, January 23, 2001, B1.
8. Wayne F. Cascio, *Costing Human Resources*, 4th Ed. (Cincinnati: South-Western College Publishing, 2000).
9. "The Boom," *Business Week*, February 14, 2000, 103.
10. Scott T. Fleischmann, "Succession Management for the Entire Organization," *Employee Relations Today*," Summer 2000, 53–62.

INTERNET RESEARCH

Learnativity.com This Web site on adult learning contains articles and other readings on adult learning, training, and evaluation, as well as frequently asked questions about training resources. **http://www.learnativity.com**

Career Planning.Org This Web site can assist individuals with career planning. **http://www.career-planning.org**

SUGGESTED READINGS

Karen Lawson, *New Employee Orientation Training*, ASTD, 2002.

John H. McConnell, *How to Identify Your Organization's Training Needs*, AMACOM, 2003.

Darlene Russ-Eft and Hallie Preskill, *Evaluation in Organizations*, Perseus Book Group, 2002.

Peter A. Topping, *Managerial Leadership*, McGraw-Hill, 2001.

Chapter 7

Performance Management and Appraisal

All employers want employees who perform their jobs well. However, an effective performance management system increases the likelihood that such performance will occur. A **performance management system** consists of the processes used to identify, encourage, measure, evaluate, improve, and reward employee performance. As shown in Figure 7.1, performance management links organizational strategy to results. The figure lists common performance management practices and outcomes in the strategy-results loop. As identified by HR professionals, a performance management system should do the following:[1]

- ▶ Provide accurate information to employees about their performance.
- ▶ Clarify what the organization expects.
- ▶ Identify development needs.
- ▶ Document performance for personnel records.

IDENTIFYING AND MEASURING EMPLOYEE PERFORMANCE

Performance is essentially what an employee does or does not do. Specific **job criteria** or dimensions of job performance identify the most important elements in a given job. They define what the organization pays an employee to do. Therefore, the performance of individuals on job criteria should be measured and compared against standards, and then the results communicated to the employee.

Most jobs have more than one job criterion or dimension. Often a given individual might demonstrate better performance on some job criteria than others. Also, some criteria might be more important than others to the organization. Weights can be used to show the relative importance of several job criteria in one job.

FIGURE 7.1   Linkage Between Strategy, Outcomes, and Organizational Results

Types of Performance Information

Managers receive three different types of information about how employees are performing their jobs. *Trait-based* information identifies a subjective character trait of the employee—such as attitude, initiative, or creativity—and may have little to do with a specific job. Traits tend to be ambiguous, and court decisions generally have held that performance appraisals based on traits such as "adaptability" and "general demeanor" are too vague to use when making performance-based HR decisions.

Behavior-based information focuses on specific behaviors that lead to job success. Although more difficult to identify, behavioral information clearly specifies the behaviors management wants to see. A potential problem arises when any of several behaviors can lead to successful performance in a given situation. For example, identifying successful "verbal persuasion" for a salesperson might be difficult because the approach used by one salesperson may not be successful when used by another.

Results-based information considers employee accomplishments. For jobs in which measurement is easy and obvious, a results-based approach works well and that which is measured tends to be emphasized. However, this emphasis may leave out equally important but unmeasurable parts of the job. Further, ethical or even legal issues may arise when only results are emphasized and not how the results were achieved.

Relevance of Performance Criteria

Measuring performance requires the use of relevant criteria that focus on the most important aspects of employees' jobs. For example, measuring customer service representatives in an insurance claims center on their "attitude" may be less relevant than measuring the number of calls handled properly. This example stresses that the most important job criteria should be identified and linked to the employees' job descriptions.

Performance measures that leave out some important job duties are considered *deficient*. For example, when measuring the performance of an employment interviewer, if only the number of applicants hired and not the quality of those hired is evaluated, performance measurement is likely to be deficient. On the other hand, including some irrelevant criteria *contaminates* the measure. An example of a contaminated criterion might be "appearance" for a telemarketing sales representative whom customers never see. Managers need to guard against using deficient or contaminated criteria in measuring performance.

Performance measures also can be thought of as objective or subjective. *Objective* measures can be directly measured or counted—for example, the number of cars sold or the number of invoices processed. *Subjective* measures require judgment on the part of the evaluator and are more difficult to measure. One example of a subjective measure is a supervisor's ratings of an employee's "motivation," which cannot be seen directly. Unlike subjective measures, objective measures tend to be more narrowly focused, which sometimes leads to them being inadequately defined. However, subjective measures may be prone to contamination or other random errors. Neither is a panacea, and both objective and subjective measures should be used carefully.[2]

Performance Standards

Performance standards define the expected levels of performance, and are "benchmarks," or "goals," or "targets"—depending on the approach taken. Realistic, measurable, clearly understood performance standards benefit both organizations and employees. In a sense, performance standards define what satisfactory job performance is, and they need to be established *before* the work is performed. Well-defined standards ensure that everyone involved knows the levels of accomplishment expected.

Both numerical and non-numerical standards can be established. Sales quotas and production output standards are familiar numerical performance standards. A standard of performance can also be based on non-numerical criteria. Consider the following performance standards as illustrating both types.

Job Criterion: Keep current on supplier technology.
Performance Standards: 1. Every four months, invite suppliers to make presentation of newest technology. 2. Visit supplier plants twice per year. 3. Attend trade shows quarterly.

Job Criterion: Do price or cost analysis as appropriate.
Performance Standard: Performance is acceptable when employee follows all requirements of the procedure "Price and Cost Analysis."

NATURE OF PERFORMANCE APPRAISALS

Performance appraisal is the process of evaluating how well employees perform their jobs when compared to a set of standards, and then communicating that information to those employees. Performance appraisal is widely used for administering wages and salaries, giving performance feedback, and identifying individual employee strengths and weaknesses. Most U.S. employers use performance appraisal systems for office, professional, technical, supervisory, middle management, and nonunion production workers. However, despite their widespread use, not everyone enthusiastically endorses performance appraisals. Criticisms revolve around the way they are done and the results. Those criticisms include:

▶ With today's emphasis on teamwork, appraisals focus too much on the individual and do too little to develop employees to perform better.[3]
▶ Most employees who receive reviews and supervisors who give them generally rate the process a resounding failure.
▶ Most appraisals are inconsistent, short-term oriented, subjective, and valuable only for identifying employees performing extremely well or poorly.

Organizations generally use performance appraisals in two potentially conflicting roles. One role is to measure performance for the purpose of making pay or other administrative decisions about employees. Promotions or terminations might hinge on these ratings, often creating stress for managers doing the appraisals. The other role focuses on the development of individuals. In that role, the manager acts more as counselor than as judge, which may change the atmosphere of the relationship. The developmental type of performance appraisal emphasizes identifying potential and planning employees' growth opportunities and direction. Figure 7.2 shows the two potentially conflicting roles for performance appraisal.

The use of teams provides a different set of circumstances for developmental appraisal. The manager may not see all of the employee's work, but team members do. Teams *can* provide developmental feedback. However, it is still an open question whether teams can handle administrative appraisals. When teams are allowed to

FIGURE 7.2   Conflicting Roles for Performance Appraisal

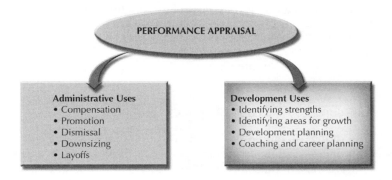

PERFORMANCE APPRAISAL

Administrative Uses
• Compensation
• Promotion
• Dismissal
• Downsizing
• Layoffs

Development Uses
• Identifying strengths
• Identifying areas for growth
• Development planning
• Coaching and career planning

design appraisal systems, they tend to "get rid of judgment," and avoid differential rewards. Perhaps, then, group appraisal is best suited to developmental purposes.

Informal vs. Systematic Appraisal

Performance appraisal can occur in two ways: informally or systematically. A supervisor conducts *informal appraisal* whenever necessary. The day-to-day working relationship between a manager and an employee offers an opportunity for the employee's performance to be evaluated. Informal appraisal is especially appropriate when time is an issue, because delays in giving feedback weaken its motivational effect. Frequent informal feedback to employees also can prevent surprises during a formal evaluation.

A *systematic appraisal* is used when the contact between manager and employee is formal, and a system is in place to report managerial impressions and observations on employee performance. One survey found that almost 90% of employers have a formal performance management system or process.[4]

Systematic appraisals feature a regular time interval, which distinguishes them from informal appraisals. Both employees and managers know that performance will be reviewed on a regular basis, and they can plan for performance discussions. Informal appraisals can be conducted whenever a manager feels they are desirable.

Appraisals and Pay Discussions. Many experts argue that performance appraisals and pay discussions should be separate. Two major reasons support this view. One is that employees often focus more on the pay amount received than on the appraisal feedback that identifies what they have done well or need to improve. Second, sometimes managers manipulate performance appraisal ratings to justify the desired pay treatment they wish to give specific individuals.

Who Conducts Appraisals?

Performance appraisal can be conducted by anyone familiar with the performance of individual employees. Possibilities include the following:

- ▸ Supervisors who rate their employees
- ▸ Employees who rate their superiors
- ▸ Team members who rate each other
- ▸ Outside sources
- ▸ Employees' self-appraisal
- ▸ Multisource (360° feedback) appraisal

The rating of employees by their supervisors or managers is the most common method. The immediate superior has the main responsibility for appraisals in most organizations, although often the supervisor's boss may review and approve the appraisals. The growing use of teams and a concern with customer input contribute to the two fast-growing sources of appraisal information: team members and sources outside the organization. Multisource appraisal (or 360° feedback) combines numerous methods and has grown in usage recently.

Supervisory Rating of Subordinates

Traditional rating of employees by supervisors is based on the assumption that the immediate supervisor is the person most qualified to evaluate the employee's performance realistically and fairly. Toward this end, some supervisors keep performance logs noting their employees' accomplishments. These logs provide specific examples to use when rating performance.

Employee Rating of Managers

A number of organizations today ask employees or group members to rate the performance of supervisors and managers. Having employees rate managers can be quite useful in identifying competent managers. The rating of leaders by combat soldiers is one example. Also, this type of rating program can help make the manager more responsive to employees, though this advantage can quickly become a disadvantage if the manager focuses on being "nice" rather than managing. This and other problems associated with having employees rate managers limit the usefulness of this appraisal approach to certain situations, except for managerial development uses. The traditional nature of most organizations restricts the applicability of employee rating to self-improvement purposes.

Team/Peer Ratings

The use of employee peers and team members as raters is another type of appraisal with potential both to help and to hurt. For example, when a group of salespeople meets as a committee to talk about one another's ratings, they may share ideas that could be used to improve the performance of lower-rated individuals. Alternatively, the criticisms could negatively affect future work relationships.

Team and peer ratings are especially useful when supervisors do not have the opportunity to observe each employee's performance, but other work group members do. However, some contend that any performance appraisal, including team/peer ratings, can affect teamwork and participative management efforts negatively.

Self-Ratings

Self-appraisal works in certain situations. As a self-development tool, it forces employees to think about their strengths and weaknesses and set goals for improvement. However, employees may not rate themselves as supervisors would rate them; they may use quite different standards. The research is mixed as to whether people tend to be more lenient or more demanding when rating themselves. Still, employee self-ratings can be a valuable and credible source of performance information.[5]

Outside Raters

Rating also may be done by outsiders who may be called in to conduct performance reviews. The customers or clients of an organization are obvious sources for outside appraisals. For salespeople and other service jobs, customers may provide useful input on the performance behaviors of salespeople. One firm measures customer service satisfaction to determine bonuses for top marketing executives.

Multisource Rating/360° Feedback

Multisource rating, or 360° feedback, has grown in popularity. Multisource feedback recognizes that the manager is no longer the sole source of performance appraisal information. Although participants generally view multisource feedback as useful, they identify follow-up on the development activities based on the feedback as the most critical factor in the future development of a person.

When using 360° feedback for administrative purposes, managers must anticipate potential problems. Differences among raters can present a challenge, especially in the use of 360° ratings for discipline or pay decisions. Also, some wonder whether multisource appraisals really create better decisions that offset the additional time and investment required.[6] These issues appear to be less threatening when the 360° feedback is used *only for development*. But those concerns may effectively eliminate multisource appraisals as an administrative tool in many situations.

METHODS FOR APPRAISING PERFORMANCE

Performance can be appraised by a number of methods. The various methods can be categorized into four groups, as discussed next.

Category Rating Methods

The simplest methods for appraising performance are category rating methods, which require a manager to mark an employee's level of performance on a specific form divided into categories of performance. The graphic rating scale and checklist are common category rating methods. The **graphic rating scale** allows the rater to mark an employee's performance on a continuum. Figure 7.3 presents a graphic rating scale form used by managers to rate employees. The rater checks the appropriate rating on the scale for each duty listed. More detail can be added in the space for comments following each element.

Comparative Methods

Comparative methods require that managers directly compare the performance of their employees against one another. The **ranking** method lists all employees from highest to lowest in performance. The primary drawback of the ranking method is that the size of the differences among individuals is not well defined. Further, the ranking task becomes unwieldy if the group to be ranked is large.

With the **forced distribution** method, the ratings of employees' performance are distributed along a bell-shaped curve. Using the forced distribution method, for example, a head nurse would rank nursing personnel along a scale, placing a certain percentage of employees at each performance level.

However, the forced distribution method suffers from several drawbacks. One problem is that a supervisor may resist placing any individual in the lowest (or the highest) group. Difficulties also arise when the rater must explain to the employee why he or she was placed in one grouping and others were placed in higher groupings. Finally, in some cases the manager may make distinctions among employees that may not exist in reality.

Narrative Methods

Managers and HR specialists frequently are required to provide written appraisal information. In the *critical incident method,* the manager keeps a written record of both highly favorable and unfavorable actions in an employee's performance during the entire rating period. When a "critical incident" involving an employee occurs, the manager writes it down.

Behavioral/Objectives Methods

In an attempt to overcome some of the difficulties of the methods just described, **behavioral rating approaches** attempt to assess an employee's *behaviors* instead of other characteristics. Some of the different behavioral approaches are *behaviorally anchored rating scales* (BARS), *behavioral observation scales* (BOS), and *behavioral expectation scales* (BES).

Behavioral rating approaches describe specific examples of employee job behaviors. In BARS, these examples are "anchored" or measured against a scale

FIGURE 7.3   Sample Performance Appraisal Form

Date Sent   **4/19/04**   Return by   **5/01/04**
Name   **Jane Doe**   Job Title   **Receiving Clerk**
Department   **Receiving**   Supervisor   **Fred Smith**
Full-time   **x**   Part-time _____   Date of Hire   **5/12/00**
Rating Period: From **5/12/03**   To: **5/12/04**
Reason for appraisal (check one):

        Regular Interval **x**   Introductory ___   Counseling only ___   Discharge ___

Utilizing the following definitions, rate the performance as I, M, or E.

I—Performance is below job requirements and **improvement is needed.**

M—Performance **meets** job requirements and standards.

E—Performance **exceeds** job requirements and standards a **majority** of the time.

SPECIFIC JOB RESPONSIBILITIES: List the principal activities from the job summary, rate the performance on each job duty by placing an "X" on the rating scale at the appropriate location, and make appropriate comments to explain the rating.

I ——————————— M ——————————— E

Job Duty #1:   **Inventory receiving and checking**
Explanation: _____
_____

I ——————————— M ——————————— E

Job Duty #2:   **Accuracy of records kept**
Explanation: _____
_____

I ——————————— M ——————————— E

Attendance (including absences and tardies): Number of absences ___   Number of tardies ___
Explanation: _____
_____

Overall Rating: Based on the total performance, place the letter **I, M, or E** in the box provided that best describes the employee's overall performance.

Explanation: _____
_____

of performance levels. Spelling out the behaviors associated with each level of performance helps minimize some of the problems noted earlier for other approaches.

Several problems associated with the behavioral approaches must be considered. First, developing and maintaining behavioral rating scales require extensive time and effort. In addition, different appraisal forms may be needed to accommodate different types of jobs in an organization.

Management by Objectives

Management by objectives (MBO) specifies the performance goals that an individual and a manager agree to try to attain within an appropriate length of time. Each manager sets objectives derived from the overall goals and objectives of the organization; however, MBO should not be a disguised means for a superior to dictate the objectives of individual managers or employees. Although not limited to the appraisal of managers, MBO is most often used for this purpose.

No single appraisal method is best for all situations. Therefore, a performance measurement system that uses a combination of the preceding methods may be sensible in certain circumstances. Using combinations may offset some of the advantages and disadvantages of individual methods.

When managers can articulate what they want a performance appraisal system to accomplish, they can choose and/or mix the methods just mentioned to realize the advantages they want. For example, one combination might include a graphic rating scale of performance on major job criteria, a narrative of developmental needs, and an overall ranking of employees in a department. Different categories of employees (e.g., salaried exempt, nonexempt salaried, maintenance) might require different combinations.

RATER ERRORS

There are many possible sources of errors in the performance appraisal process. One of the major sources is mistakes made by the rater. Although completely eliminating these errors is impossible, making raters aware of them through training is helpful.

Varying Standards

When appraising employees, a manager should avoid applying different standards and expectations for employees performing similar jobs. Inequities in assessments, whether real or perceived, generally anger employees. Such problems often result from the use of ambiguous criteria and subjective weightings by supervisors.[7]

Recency/Primacy Effect

The **recency effect** occurs when a rater gives greater weight to recent events when appraising an individual's performance. Giving a student a course grade based only on his performance in the last week of class, or giving a drill press operator a high rating even though she made the quota only in the last two weeks of the rating period are examples.

Central Tendency, Leniency, and Strictness Errors

Ask students, and they will tell you which professors tend to grade easier or harder. A manager also may develop a similar *rating pattern*. Appraisers who rate all employees within a narrow range (i.e., everyone is average) commit a **central tendency error**, where even the poor performers receive an average rating.

Rating patterns also may exhibit leniency or strictness. The *leniency error* occurs when ratings of all employees fall at the high end of the scale. The *strictness error* occurs when a manager uses only the lower part of the scale to rate employees. To avoid conflict, managers often rate employees higher than they should be rated. This "ratings boost" is especially likely when no manager or HR representative reviews the completed appraisals.

Rater Bias

Rater bias occurs when a rater's values or prejudices distort the rating. Such bias may be unconscious or quite intentional. For example, a manager's dislike of certain ethnic groups may cause distortion in appraisal information for some people. Judgments about age, religion, seniority, sex, appearance, or other arbitrary classifications also may skew appraisal ratings if the appraisal process is not properly designed. A review of appraisal ratings by higher-level managers may help correct this problem.

Halo Effect

The **halo effect** occurs when a manager rates an employee high on all job criteria because of performance in one area. For example, if a worker has few absences, her supervisor might give her a high rating in all other areas of work, including quantity and quality of output, because of her dependability. The manager may not really think about the employee's other characteristics separately, resulting in the halo effect. The "horns" effect is the opposite, where one characteristic may lead to an overall lower rating.

APPRAISAL FEEDBACK

After completing appraisals, managers need to communicate the results to give employees a clear understanding of how they stand in the eyes of their immediate superiors and the organization. Organizations commonly require managers to discuss appraisals with employees. The appraisal feedback interview provides an opportunity to clear up any misunderstandings on both sides. In this interview, the manager should focus on counseling and development, and not just tell the employee, "Here is how you rate and why." Emphasizing development gives both parties an opportunity to consider the employee's performance as part of appraisal feedback. Figure 7.4 summarizes hints for an effective appraisal interview for supervisors and managers.

Reactions of Managers and Employees

Managers and supervisors who must complete appraisals of their employees often resist the appraisal process. Many managers feel that their role calls on them to assist, encourage, coach, and counsel employees to improve their performance. However, being a judge on the one hand and a coach and counselor on the other may cause internal conflict and confusion for many managers.

Employees may well see the appraisal process as a threat and feel that the only way to get a higher rating is for someone else to receive a low rating. This win/lose perception is encouraged by comparative methods of rating. However, both parties can win and no one must lose. Emphasis on the self-improvement and developmental aspects of appraisal appears to be the most effective means to reduce zero-sum reactions from those participating in the appraisal process.

LEGAL AND EFFECTIVE PERFORMANCE APPRAISALS

A number of court decisions have focused attention on performance appraisals, particularly on equal employment opportunity (EEO) concerns. The Uniform Guidelines issued by the Equal Employment Opportunity Commission (EEOC) and other federal enforcement agencies make it clear that performance appraisals must be job-related and non-discriminatory.

FIGURE 7.4 Appraisal Interview Hints

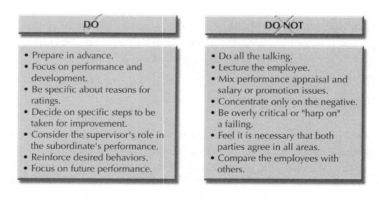

DO	DO NOT
• Prepare in advance.	• Do all the talking.
• Focus on performance and development.	• Lecture the employee.
• Be specific about reasons for ratings.	• Mix performance appraisal and salary or promotion issues.
• Decide on specific steps to be taken for improvement.	• Concentrate only on the negative.
• Consider the supervisor's role in the subordinate's performance.	• Be overly critical or "harp on" a failing.
• Reinforce desired behaviors.	• Feel it is necessary that both parties agree in all areas.
• Focus on future performance.	• Compare the employees with others.

Performance Appraisals and the Law

The elements of a performance appraisal system that can survive court tests can be determined from existing case law. Various cases have identified the elements of a legally defensible performance appraisal to include the following:

▶ Performance appraisal criteria based on job analysis
▶ Absence of disparate impact and evidence of validity
▶ Formal evaluation criteria that limit managerial discretion
▶ Formal rating instrument linked to job duties and responsibilities
▶ Personal knowledge of and contact with appraised individual
▶ Training of supervisors in conducting appraisals
▶ Review process that prevents one manager, acting alone, from controlling an employee's career
▶ Counseling to help poor performers improve

Clearly, employers should have fair and nondiscriminatory performance appraisals. To do so, employers must decide how to design their appraisal systems to satisfy the courts, enforcement agencies, and their employees.[8]

Effective Performance Management

Regardless of the approach used, managers must understand the intended outcome of performance management. When performance management is used to develop employees as resources, it usually works. When management uses one key part of performance management, the performance appraisal, to punish employees, or when raters fail to understand its limitations, performance management is less effective. Done well, performance management can lead to higher employee motivation and satisfaction. But in an era of continuous improvement, an ineffective performance management system poses a huge liability.

NOTES

1. "SHRM Performance Management Survey," *Society for Human Resource Management Research,* 2000, 7.
2. Mark A. Siders et al., "The Relationships of Internal and External Commitment Foci to Objective Job Performance Measures," *Academy of Management Journal,* 44 (2001), 570.
3. Dayton Fandray, "The New Thinking in Performance Appraisals," *Workforce,* May 2001, 36–40.
4. "Performance Management Practices," *http://www.ddi.com.*
5. José Goris et al., "Effects of Communica-tion Direction on Job Performance and Satisfaction," *The Journal of Business Communication,* October 2000, 348.
6. Joan F. Brett and Leanne E. Atwater, "360 Degree Feedback: Accuracy, Reactions, and Perceptions of Usefulness," *Journal of Applied Psychology* 86 (2001), 930–942.
7. Yitzhak Fried et al., "Rater Positive and Negative Mood Predisposition," *Journal of Occupational and Organizational Psychology,* September 2000, 373.
8. Timothy S. Bland, "Anatomy of an Employment Lawsuit," *HR Magazine,* March 2001, 145.

INTERNET RESEARCH

AHI's Employment Law Resource Center This Web site offers valuable legal management information on performance appraisals and other HR topics under the problem solver heading. **http://www.ahipubs.com/**

Zigon Performance Group This Web site contains many resources for measuring, managing, and improving employee performance. **http://www.zigonperf.com**

SUGGESTED READINGS

Tom Coens and Mary Jenkins, *Abolishing Performance Appraisals*, Barrett-Koehler, 2000.

Dick Grote, *The Performance Appraisal Question and Answer Book*, AMACOM, 20002.

Mark R. Edwards and Ann J. Ewen, *Providing 360-Degree Feedback*, WorldatWork, 2001.

Ferdinand F. Fournies, *Coaching for Improved Work Performance*, McGraw-Hill, 2000.

Chapter 8

Compensation Strategies and Practices

Compensation systems in organizations must be linked to organizational objectives and strategies. Employers must balance compensation costs at a level that both ensures organizational competitiveness and provides sufficient rewards to employees. In order to attract, retain, and reward employees, employers provide several types of compensation.

NATURE OF COMPENSATION

Compensation is an important factor affecting how and why people choose to work at one organization over others. Employers must be reasonably competitive with several types of compensation to attract and retain competent employees. The tangible components of a compensation program are of two general types (see Figure 8.1), direct and indirect.

Base Pay

The basic compensation that an employee receives, usually as a wage or salary, is called **base pay**. Many organizations use two base pay categories, *hourly* and *salaried*. Hourly pay is the most common means of payment based on time, and employees paid hourly receive **wages**, which are payments directly calculated on the amount of time worked. In contrast, people paid **salaries** receive consistent payments each period regardless of the number of hours worked.

Variable Pay

Another type of direct pay is **variable pay**, which is compensation linked directly to individual, team, or organizational performance. The most common types of variable pay for most employees take the form of bonuses and incentives. Executives often receive longer-term rewards such as stock options.

FIGURE 8.1 Components of a Compensation Program

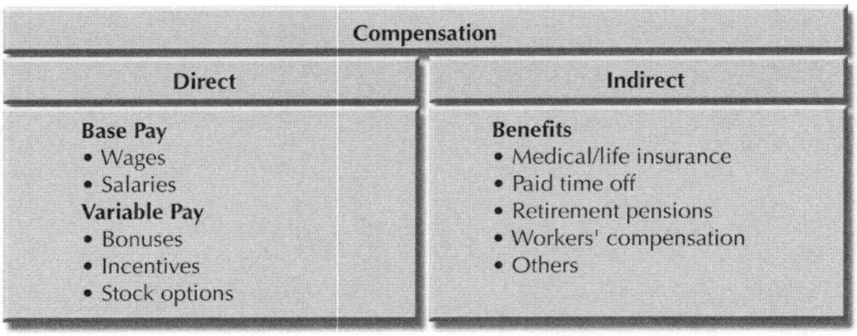

Compensation	
Direct	**Indirect**
Base Pay • Wages • Salaries **Variable Pay** • Bonuses • Incentives • Stock options	**Benefits** • Medical/life insurance • Paid time off • Retirement pensions • Workers' compensation • Others

Benefits

Many organizations provide numerous rewards in an indirect manner. With indirect compensation, employees receive the tangible value of the rewards without receiving the actual cash. A **benefit** is indirect compensation—health insurance, vacation pay, or retirement pensions—given to an employee or group of employees as a part of organizational membership, regardless of performance.

STRATEGIC COMPENSATION DESIGN

Compensation decisions must be viewed strategically. Because so many organizational funds are spent on compensation-related activities, it is critical for top management and HR executives to match compensation practices with what the organization is trying to accomplish. Organizations must make a number of important decisions about the nature of a compensation system, some of which are highlighted next.

Compensation Philosophies

The two basic compensation philosophies lie on opposite ends of a continuum.

Entitlement-oriented organizations give automatic increases to their employees every year. Further, most of those employees receive the same or nearly the same percentage increase each year. Employees and managers who subscribe to the entitlement philosophy believe that individuals who have worked another year are *entitled* to a raise in base pay. They also believe compensation and benefit programs should continue and be increased, regardless of changing industry or economic conditions. Commonly, in organizations following an entitlement philosophy, pay increases are referred to as *cost-of-living* raises, even if they are not tied specifically to economic indicators.

Where a *performance-oriented philosophy* is followed, organizations do not guarantee additional or increased compensation simply for completing another year of organizational service. Instead, pay and incentives reflect performance differences among employees. Employees who perform well receive larger compensation increases; those who do not perform satisfactorily see little or no increase in compensation. Thus, employees who perform satisfactorily or better maintain or advance in relation to market compensation levels, whereas poor or marginal performers may fall behind. Also, bonuses are determined on the basis of individual, group, and/or organizational performance.

Compensation Approaches

Figure 8.2 presents some of the choices organizations must make regarding compensation approaches. For some organizations a traditional compensation approach makes sense and offers certain advantages in specific competitive situations. It may be more legally defensible, less complex, and viewed as more "fair" by average and below-average employees. However, the total rewards approach helps retain top performers, can be more flexible when the economy goes up or down, and is favored by top-performing companies.

The total rewards approach tries to place a value on individuals rather than just the jobs. Managers factor in elements such as how much an employee knows or employee competence when determining compensation. The need for such an approach becomes more evident in trying to pay people with exceptional computer skills who, on the other hand, may lack traditional experience or educational degrees.

Competency-Based Pay. Some organizations are paying employees for the competencies they demonstrate rather than just for the specific tasks performed. Paying for competencies rewards employees who exhibit more versatility and continue to develop their competencies. In knowledge-based pay (KBP) or skill-based

FIGURE 8.2 Compensation Approaches

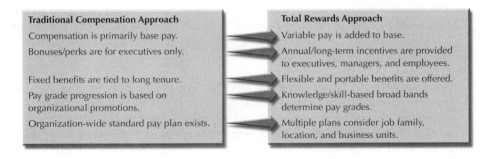

Traditional Compensation Approach	Total Rewards Approach
Compensation is primarily base pay.	Variable pay is added to base.
Bonuses/perks are for executives only.	Annual/long-term incentives are provided to executives, managers, and employees.
Fixed benefits are tied to long tenure.	Flexible and portable benefits are offered.
Pay grade progression is based on organizational promotions.	Knowledge/skill-based broad bands determine pay grades.
Organization-wide standard pay plan exists.	Multiple plans consider job family, location, and business units.

pay (SBP) systems, employees start at a base level of pay and receive increases as they learn to do other jobs or gain other skills and therefore become more valuable to the employer. The success of competency plans requires managerial commitment to a philosophy different from the traditional one in organizations.[1] This approach places far more emphasis on training employees and supervisors. Also, workflow must be adapted to allow workers to move from job to job as needed.

Individual vs. Team Rewards. As organizations have shifted to using work teams, they face the logical concern of how to develop compensation programs that build on the team concept. At issue is how to compensate the individual whose performance may also be evaluated on the basis of team achievement.

Many organizations provide team rewards as variable pay above base pay. For base pay, individual compensation is based on competency- or skill-based approaches. Variable pay rewards for teams are most frequently distributed annually as a specified dollar amount, not as a percentage of base pay.

Perceptions of Pay Fairness. The concept of **equity** is the perceived fairness of what a person does (inputs) and what the person receives (outcomes). Individuals judge equity in compensation by comparing the effort and performance they give to the effort and performance of others and the subsequent rewards received. Internally, equity means that employees receive compensation in relation to the knowledge, skills, and abilities (KSAs) they use in their jobs as well as their responsibilities and accomplishments. **Procedural justice** is the perceived fairness of the process and procedures used to make decisions about employees, including their pay. As it applies to compensation, the process of determining base pay for jobs, allocating pay increases, and measuring performance all must be perceived as fair.

Another related issue that must be considered is **distributive justice**, which refers to the perceived fairness in the distribution of outcomes. This facet of equity examines how pay relates to performance. As one example, if a hard-working employee whose performance is outstanding receives the same across-the-board raise as an employee with attendance problems and mediocre performance, then inequity may be perceived.

Another equity issue concerns the degree of *openness* or *secrecy* that organizations allow regarding their pay systems. Pay information kept secret in "closed" systems includes how much others make, what raises others have received, and even what pay grades and ranges exist in the organization. A crucial element in an open pay system is that managers be able to explain satisfactorily the pay differences that exist.

Decisions About Compensation Levels. Some organizations establish specific policies based on where they wish to be positioned in labor markets. Most employers choose to position themselves in the *second quartile* (median), in the middle of the market, based on pay survey data of other employers' compensation plans. Choosing this level attempts to balance employer cost pressures and the need to attract and retain employees by providing mid-level compensation levels.

International Compensation

Organizations with employees in many different countries face some special compensation pressures. Variations in laws, living costs, tax policies, and other factors all must be considered in establishing the compensation for expatriate managers and professionals. Even fluctuations in the value of the home-country currency must be tracked and adjustments made as the currency rises or falls in relation to currency rates in other countries. Add to all of these concerns the need to compensate employees for the costs of housing, schooling of children, and yearly transportation home for themselves and their family members. With all of these different issues involved, international compensation becomes extremely complex.

LEGAL CONSTRAINTS ON PAY SYSTEMS

Compensation systems must comply with a myriad of government constraints. Important areas addressed by the laws include minimum wage standards and hours of work.

Fair Labor Standards Act (FLSA)

The major federal law affecting compensation is the Fair Labor Standards Act (FLSA). Compliance with FLSA provisions is enforced by the Wage and Hour Division of the U.S. Department of Labor. The act focuses on the following major objectives:

▶ Establish a minimum wage floor.
▶ Discourage oppressive use of child labor.
▶ Encourage limits on the number of weekly hours employees work through overtime provisions (exempt and non-exempt status).

Minimum Wage. The FLSA sets a minimum wage to be paid to the broad spectrum of covered employees. The actual minimum wage can be changed only by congressional action. A lower minimum-wage level is set for "tipped" employees, such as restaurant workers, but their compensation must equal or exceed the minimum wage when average tips are included.

Child-Labor Provisions. The child-labor provisions of the FLSA set the minimum age for employment with unlimited hours at 16 years. For hazardous occupations, the minimum is 18 years of age. Individuals 14 to 15 years old may work outside school hours with certain limitations.

Exempt and Non-Exempt Status. Under the FLSA, employees are classified as exempt or non-exempt. **Exempt employees** hold positions classified as *executive, administrative, professional,* or *outside sales,* to whom employers are not required to pay overtime. **Non-exempt employees** must be paid overtime under the Fair Labor Standards Act.

Three major factors determine whether an individual holds an exempt position:

1. Discretionary authority for independent action
2. Percentage of time spent performing routine, manual, or clerical work
3. Earnings level

Overtime Provisions. The FLSA establishes overtime pay requirements. Its provisions set overtime pay at one and one-half times the regular pay rate for all hours in excess of 40 per week, except for employees who are not covered by the FLSA. Overtime provisions do not apply to farm workers, who also have a lower minimum-wage schedule. Also, if they wish to do so, hospitals and nursing homes are allowed to use a 14-day period instead of a 7-day week as long as over-time is paid for hours worked beyond 8 in a day or 80 in a 14-day period.

Compensatory Time Off. Often called *comptime,* **compensatory time off** is given in lieu of payment for extra time worked. However, unless it is given to non-exempt employees at the rate of one and one-half time for the hours worked over a 40-hour week, comp-time is illegal in the private sector. Also, comp-time cannot be carried over from one pay period to another. The only major excep-tion to those provisions is for public-sector employees, such as fire and police employees, and a limited number of other workers.

Independent Contractor Regulations

The growing use of contingent workers by many organizations has focused atten-tion on another group of legal regulations—those identifying the criteria that independent contractors must meet. Most federal and state entities rely on the criteria for independent contractor status identified by the Internal Revenue Service (IRS). The IRS considers 20 factors in making such a determination.

Equal Pay and Pay Equity

Various legislative efforts address the issue of wage discrimination on the basis of gender. The Equal Pay Act of 1963 applies to both men and women and pro-hibits using different wage scales for men and women performing substantially the same jobs. **Pay equity** is the concept that the pay for all jobs requiring com-parable knowledge, skills, and abilities should pay the same even if job duties and market rates differ significantly. However, simply showing the existence of pay differences for jobs that are different has *not been sufficient* to prove discrimi-nation in court in most cases.[2]

Garnishment Laws

Garnishment of an employee's wage occurs when a creditor obtains a court order that directs an employer to set aside a portion of one employee's wages to pay a debt owed a creditor. Regulations passed as a part of the Consumer Credit Protection Act established limitations on the amount of wages that can be garnished and restricted the right of employers to discharge employees whose pay is subject to a single garnishment order. All 50 states have laws applying to wage garnishments.

DEVELOPMENT OF A BASE PAY SYSTEM

As Figure 8.3 shows, development of a base wage and salary system assumes that accurate job descriptions and job specifications are available. The job descriptions then are used in two activities: *job evaluation* and *pay surveys*. These activities are designed to ensure that the pay system is both internally equitable and externally competitive. The data compiled in these two activities are used to design *pay structures*, including *pay grades* and minimum-to-maximum *pay ranges*. After the development of pay structures, individual jobs must be placed in the appropriate pay grades and employees' pay adjusted based on length of service and performance. Finally, the pay system must be monitored and updated.

FIGURE 8.3 Compensation Administration Process

Job Evaluation

Job evaluation provides a systematic basis for determining the relative worth of jobs within an organization and is a key part of a base pay system. In job evaluation, every job in an organization is examined and ultimately priced according to the following features:

▸ Relative importance of the job
▸ Knowledge, skills, and abilities (KSAs) needed to perform the job
▸ Difficulty of the job

Job evaluation flows from the job analysis process and relies on job descriptions and job specifications. Several methods are used to determine internal job worth through job evaluation.

Ranking Method. The ranking method is one of the simplest methods of job evaluation. It places jobs in order, ranging from highest to lowest in value to the organization. The entire job is considered rather than the individual components.

Classification Method. In the classification method of job evaluation, descriptions of each class of jobs are written, and then each job in the organization is put into a grade according to the class description it best matches.

Point Method. The point method, the most widely used job evaluation method, is more sophisticated than the ranking and classification methods. It breaks down jobs into various compensable factors and places weights, or *points,* on them. A **compensable factor** identifies a job value commonly present throughout a group of jobs. The factors are derived from the job analysis. Consequently, the compensable factors used and the weights assigned must reflect the nature of the jobs under study.

The point method has been widely used because it is a relatively simple system to use. Also, it considers the components of a job rather than the total job and is much more comprehensive than either the ranking or classification method. Although not perfect, the point method of job evaluation generally is better than the classification and ranking methods because it quantifies job elements.[3]

Factor Comparison. The factor-comparison method is a quantitative and quite complex combination of the ranking and point methods. A major advantage of the factor comparison method is that it is tailored specifically to one organization. The major disadvantages of the factor comparison method are its difficulty and complexity.

Integrated and Computerized Job Evaluation. Increasingly, organizations are linking the components of wage and salary programs through computerized and statistical techniques. Using a bank of compensable factors, employers can select those factors most relevant for the different job families in the organization.

These systems really are less a separate method and more an application of information technology and advanced statistics to the process of developing a wage and salary program.

Pay Surveys

Another part of building a pay system is surveying the pay that other organizations provide for similar jobs. A **pay survey** is a collection of data on compensation rates for workers performing similar jobs in other organizations. An employer may use surveys conducted by other organizations, or it may decide to conduct its own survey. Many different surveys are available from a variety of sources. The Internet provides a large number of pay survey sources and data online. However, use of these sources requires caution because their accuracy and completeness may not be verifiable.[4]

Pay Structures

Once survey data are gathered, pay structures can be developed. Tying pay survey information to job evaluation data can be done by plotting a *wage curve*, and *scattergram*. This plotting involves first making a graph that charts job evaluation points and pay survey rates for all surveyed jobs. The graph shows the distribution of pay for surveyed jobs, allowing development of a linear trend line via the *least-squares regression method*. Also, a curvilinear line can be developed by use of multiple regression and other statistical techniques. The end result is the development of a **market line**. This line shows the relationship between job value, as determined by job evaluation points and pay survey rates. (Details on these methods can be found in any basic compensation text.)

Establishing Pay Grades. In the process of establishing a pay structure, organizations use **pay grades** to group individual jobs having approximately the same job worth. Although no set rules govern establishing pay grades, some overall suggestions can be useful. Generally, from 11 to 17 grades are used in small and medium-sized companies with fewer than 500 employees. However, a growing number of employers are reducing the number of grades by broadbanding.

Broadbanding is the practice of using fewer pay grades with much broader ranges than in traditional compensation systems. Combining many grades into these broadbands is designed to encourage horizontal movement and therefore more skill acquisition. The primary reasons for broadbanding are: (1) creating more flexible organizations, (2) encouraging competency development, and (3) emphasizing career development.

Pay Ranges. The pay range for each pay grade also must be established. Using the market line as a starting point, the employer can determine minimum and maximum pay levels for each pay grade by making the market line the midpoint line of the new pay structure (see Figure 8.4).

FIGURE 8.4 Example of Pay Grades and Pay Ranges

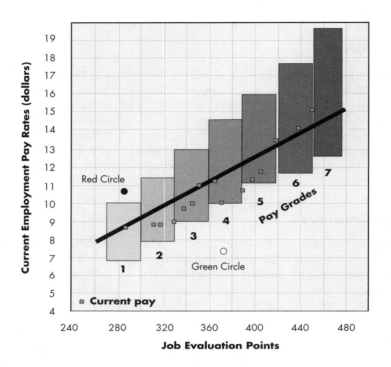

Individual Pay Issues

Once managers have determined pay ranges, they can set the pay for specific individuals. Setting a range for each pay grade gives flexibility by allowing individuals to progress within a grade instead of having to be moved to a new grade each time they receive a raise. A pay range also allows managers to reward the better-performing employees while maintaining the integrity of the pay system.

Regardless of how well constructed a pay structure is, usually a few individuals are paid lower than the minimum or higher than the maximum. A **red-circled employee** is an incumbent who is paid above the range set for the job. An individual whose pay is below the range is a **green-circled employee**.

Pay Compression. One major problem many employers face is **pay compression**, which occurs when the pay differences among individuals with different levels of experience and performance becomes small. Pay compression occurs for a number of reasons, but the major one involves situations in which labor market pay levels increase more rapidly than current employees' pay adjustments.

Pay Increases. Decisions about pay increases often are critical ones in the relationships among employees, their managers, and the organization. Individuals express expectations about their pay and about how much increase is "fair," especially in comparison with the increases received by other employees. Pay increases may be determined in several ways.

Seniority, or time spent in the organization or on a particular job, also can be used as the basis for pay increases. Pay adjustments based on seniority often are set as automatic steps once a person has been employed the required length of time, although performance must be at least satisfactory in many non-union systems.

Cost-of-Living Adjustments (COLA). A common pay-raise practice is the use of a *standard raise* or *cost-of-living adjustment* (COLA). Giving all employees a standard percentage increase enables them to maintain the same real wages in a period of economic inflation. Often, these adjustments are tied to changes in the Consumer Price Index (CPI) or some other general economic measure. However, numerous studies have revealed that the CPI overstates the actual cost of living.

Pay Adjustment Matrix. Many employers profess to have a pay system based on performance. However, relying on performance appraisal information for making pay adjustments assumes that performance appraisals are accurate and done well, which is not always the case. Consequently, some system for integrating appraisals and pay changes must be developed and applied equally. Often, this integration is done through the development of a *pay adjustment matrix,* or *salary guide chart.* Use of pay adjustment matrices bases adjustments in part on a person's **compa-ratio**, which is the pay level divided by the midpoint of the pay range.

Lump-Sum Increases (LSI). Most employees who receive pay increases, either for merit or seniority, first have their base pay adjusted and then receive an increase in the amount of their regular monthly or weekly paycheck. In contrast, a **lump-sum increase (LSI)** is a one-time payment of all or part of a yearly pay increase. The pure LSI approach does not increase the base pay. It also allows for the amount of the "lump" to be varied, without having to continually raise the base rate. Some organizations place a limit on how much of a merit increase can be taken as a lump-sum payment. Other organizations split the lump sum into two checks, each representing one-half of the year's pay raise.

EXECUTIVE COMPENSATION

A history of executive compensation shows that a combination of events created today's unsettled situation in the United States. Many organizations, especially large ones, administer executive compensation differently than compensation for lower-level employees.

The absolute amounts of the compensation packages and the questionable tie of pay to performance has made executive compensation a controversial item.

In some organizations, it appears that the total level of executive compensation may be unreasonable and not linked closely to organizational performance.

Elements of Executive Compensation

At the heart of most executive compensation plans is the idea that executives should be rewarded if the organization grows in profitability and value over a period of years. As Figure 8.5 shows, the common components of executive compensation are *salaries, annual bonuses, long-term incentives,* supplemental benefits, and perquisites.

Salaries of executives vary by type of job, size of organization, region of the country, and industry. On average, salaries make up about 40% to 60% of the typical top executive's annual compensation total.

Annual performance incentives or bonuses for executives can be determined in several ways. Whatever method is used, it is important to describe it so that executives trying to earn bonuses understand the plan; otherwise the incentive effect will be diminished.[5]

Performance-based incentives attempt to tie executive compensation to the long-term growth and success of the organization. A **stock option** gives an individual the right to buy stock in a company, usually at an advantageous price. The increase in stock options as a component of executive compensation during the past 10 years takes a variety of specialized and technical forms, which are beyond the scope of this discussion.

Executive benefits may take several forms, including traditional retirement, health insurance, vacations, and others. However, executive benefits may include

---

FIGURE 8.5   Executive Compensation Components

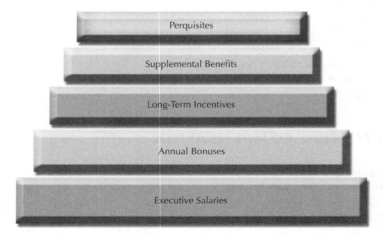

some items that other employees do not receive. For example, executive health plans with no co-payments and with no limitations on deductibles or physician choice are popular among small and medium-sized businesses.

In addition to the regular benefits received by all employees, executives often receive benefits called perquisites. **Perquisites (perks)** are special executive benefits—usually noncash items. Perks help tie executives to organizations and demonstrate their importance to their companies.

Executive Compensation and the Board of Directors

In most organizations, the board of directors is the major policy-setting entity. For publicly traded companies covered by federal regulatory agencies, such as the Securities and Exchange Commission (SEC), the board of directors must approve executive compensation packages. Even for many nonprofit organizations, Internal Revenue Service regulations require boards of directors review and approve the compensation for top-level executives.

The **compensation committee** usually is a subgroup of the board composed of directors who are not officers of the firm. Compensation committees generally make recommendations to the board of directors on overall pay policies, salaries for top officers, supplemental compensation such as stock options and bonuses, and additional perquisites ("perks") for executives. However, the independence of board compensation committees increasingly has been criticized. To counter criticism, some corporations have changed the composition of the compensation committee and given it more independence.

Debating the "Reasonableness" of Executive Compensation

The notion that monetary incentives tied to performance result in improved performance makes sense to most people. The debate about whether executive compensation in the United States goes too far occurs regularly. The question of whether or not executive compensation levels are linked to organizational performance has been the subject of numerous studies. In many settings, financial measures such as return on equity, return to shareholders, earnings per share, net income before taxes, and other criteria are used. Executives can even manipulate earnings per share by selling assets, liquidating inventories, or reducing research and development expenditures. All these actions may make organizational performance look better, but they may impair the long-term growth of the organization.[6]

Undoubtedly, the criticisms of executive compensation will continue as huge payouts occur, particularly if organizational performance has been weak. Hopefully, boards of directors of more corporations will address the need to better link organizational performance with variable pay rewards for executives and other employees.

NOTES

1. Jörgen Sandberg, "Understanding Competence at Work," *Harvard Business Review,* March 2001, 24.

2. Karen Caldwell, "Comparable Worth Comparisons Called Unfair," *HR News,* May 2001, 23.

3. Robert L. Heneman, "Work Evaluation," *WorldatWork Journal,* Third Quarter 2001, 65–70.

4. John A. Menefee, "The Value of Pay Data on the Web," *Workspan,* September 2000, 25–28.

5. M. C. Struman and J. C. Short, "Lump-Sum Bonus Satisfaction: Testing the Construct Validity of a New Pay Satisfaction Dimension," *Personnel Psychology,* 53 (2000), 673–700.

6. Jack Dolmat, "Executive Pay for Performance," *WorldatWork Journal,* First Quarter 2001, 19–27.

INTERNET RESEARCH

Economic Research Institute This institute provides national and geographic salaries for various positions. On this Web site, the database and samples of the product can be viewed. **http://www.erieri.com**

Wage and Hour Division This government Web site from the Wage and Hour Division of the U.S. Department of Labor provides an overview of the Fair Labor Standards Act and other laws. **http://www.dol.gov/esa/whd**

SUGGESTED READINGS

Lance A. Berger and Dorothy R. Berger, *The Compensation Handbook,* 4th ed. McGraw-Hill, 2000.

Bruce Ellig, *The Complete Guide to Executive Compensation,* McGraw-Hill, 2001.

Robert L. Heneman, *Strategic Reward Management,* Information Age Publishing, 2002.

Todd Manas and Michael Dennis Graham, *Creating a Total Rewards Strategy,* AMACOM, 2003.

Chapter 9

Variable Pay and Benefits

Employers increasingly are recognizing that the definition of compensation must be extended beyond base pay to include variable pay and employee benefits. While adding value to employees, variable pay and benefits can add significant costs to employers.

VARIABLE PAY: INCENTIVES FOR PERFORMANCE

Variable pay is compensation linked to individual, team, and organizational performance. Traditionally also known as *incentives,* variable pay plans attempt to provide tangible rewards to employees for performance beyond normal expectations. The assumptions are:

- ▸ Some jobs contribute more to organizational success than others.
- ▸ Some people perform better than others.
- ▸ Employees who perform better should receive more compensation.
- ▸ A portion of some employees' total compensation should be contingent on performance.

    Individual incentives are given to reward the effort and performance of individuals. Some of the most common means of providing individuals variable pay includes piece-rate systems, sales commissions, and bonuses. Others include special recognition rewards such as trips or merchandise. However, individual incentives can present drawbacks. One of the potential difficulties with individual incentives is that an employee may focus on what is best individually and may block or inhibit performance of other individuals with whom the employee is competing. Competition intensifies if only the top performer or winner receives incentives, which is why *team or group incentives* have been developed.

    When an organization rewards an entire work group or *team* for its performance, cooperation among the members usually increases. However, competition among different teams for rewards can lead to decline in overall performance under certain circumstances. The most common *team* or *group incentives* are gainsharing plans, where employee teams that meet certain goals share in the gains measured against performance targets. Often, gainsharing programs focus on quality improvement, cost reduction, and other measurable results.

Organizational incentives reward people based on the performance results of the entire organization. This approach assumes that all employees working together can generate greater organizational results that lead to better financial performance. These programs often share some of the financial gains to the firm with employees through payments calculated as a percentage of each employee's base pay. Figure 9.1 shows some of the programs under each type of incentive or variable pay plan.

Successes and Failures of Variable Pay Plans

Even though variable pay has grown in popularity, some attempts to implement it have succeeded and others have not. One study suggests that about 74% of companies have a variable pay plan of some sort. Of those, most feel these plans have been successful in aligning pay with performance for executives (79%), managers (73%), and exempt/professionals (60%). However, only 48% felt variable pay was effective for non-exempt/administrative personnel.[1]

Factors Affecting Successful Variable Pay Plans

Most employers adopt variable pay incentives in order to: (1) link individual performance to business goals, and (2) reward superior performance. A number of different elements can affect the success of a variable pay plan. In the case of

FIGURE 9.1 Types of Variable Pay Plans

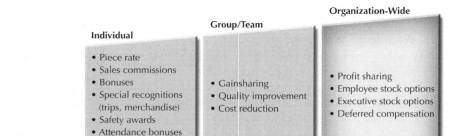

variable pay, one size does not fit all. A plan that has worked well for one company will not necessarily work well for another. Obviously the plan must be linked to the objectives of the organization.

Also, variable pay systems should be tied as much as possible to desired performance. Employees must see a direct relationship between their efforts and their financial rewards. Indeed, higher-performing companies give out far more incentive pay to their top performers than do lower-performing companies.[2]

A variable pay plan may be complex or simple, but it will not be successful if employees do not understand what they have to do to be rewarded. The more complicated a plan is, the more difficult it will be to communicate it meaningfully to employees. Experts generally recommend that a variable pay plan include several performance criteria. However, having two or three areas to focus on should not complicate the calculations necessary for employees to determine their own incentive amounts. Managers also need to be able to explain clearly what future performance targets need to be met.

Individual Incentives

As noted earlier, individual incentive systems try to relate individual effort to pay. The performance of each individual must be measured and identified because each employee has job responsibilities and tasks that can be separated from those of other employees. The most basic individual incentive system is the **piece-rate system**. Individual employees also may receive additional compensation payments in the form of a **bonus**, which is a one-time payment that does not become part of the employee's base pay. Generally, bonuses are less costly to the employer than other pay increases because they do not become part of employees' base wages, upon which future percentage increases are figured. Growing in popularity, individual bonuses often are used at the executive levels in organizations, but bonus usage also has spread to jobs at all levels in some firms.

Additionally, numerous special incentive programs that provide awards to individuals have been used, ranging from one-time contests for meeting performance targets to rewards for performance over time. Cash, merchandise, gift certificates, and travel are the most frequently used incentive rewards. Cash is highly valued by many employees because they have discretion on how to spend it. Also, studies have concluded that many employees like the continuing "trophy" value of merchandise.[3]

Another common type of reward given to individual employees is the *service award*. Although these awards often may be portrayed as rewarding performance over a number of years, in reality, they usually are determined by length of service, and performance plays little or no role.

Sales Compensation and Incentives

The compensation paid to employees involved with sales and marketing is partly or entirely tied to individual sales performance. Better-performing salespeople receive more total compensation than those selling less. Sales incentives are perhaps the most widely used individual incentive. Successfully using variable sales compensation requires establishing clear performance criteria and measures. Generally, no more than three sales performance measures should be used in a sales compensation plan.

Sales compensation plans are generally of several different types. The types are based on the degree to which total compensation includes some variable pay tied to sales performance. The *salary-only* approach is useful when an organization emphasizes serving and retaining existing accounts over generating new sales and accounts.

An individual incentive system widely used in sales jobs is the **commission**, which is compensation computed as a percentage of sales in units or dollars. Commissions are integrated into the pay given to sales workers in three common ways: *straight commission, salary plus commission,* and *bonuses.*

Some sales organizations combine both individual and group sales bonus programs. In these programs, a portion of the sales incentive is linked to the attainment of group sales goals. This approach encourages cooperation and teamwork for the salespeople to work together. Team incentives in situations other than sales jobs are discussed next.

Group/Team-Based Variable Pay

A group of employees is not necessarily a "team," but either one can be the basis for variable compensation. The use of work teams in organizations has implications for compensation of the teams and their members. Interestingly, although the use of teams has increased substantially in the past few years, the question of how to equitably compensate the individuals who compose the team remains a significant challenge.

The two primary approaches for distributing team rewards are as follows:

1. *Same size reward for each team member:* In this approach, all team members receive the same payout, regardless of job levels, current pay, or seniority.
2. *Different size rewards for each team member:* Using this approach, employers vary individual rewards based upon such factors as contribution to team results, current pay, years of experience, and skill levels of jobs performed.

Generally, more organizations use the first approach as an addition to different levels of individual pay. This method is used to reward team performance by making the team incentive equal, while still recognizing that individual pay differences exist and are important to many employees. The size of the team incentive can be determined either by using a percentage of base pay for the individuals or the team as a whole, or by offering a specific dollar amount.

How often team incentives are paid out is another important consideration. Some of the choices seen in firms with team-based incentives include payment monthly, quarterly, semiannually, or annually. The most common period used is annually. However, the shorter the time period, the more likely it is that employees will see a closer link to their efforts and the performance results that trigger the award payouts.

Successful Team Incentives

Generally, managers view the concept of people working in teams as beneficial. To a large extent many employees still expect to be paid based on individual performance. Until this individualism is recognized and compensation programs developed that are viewed as more equitable by more "team members," caution should be used in developing and implementing team-based incentives. Conditions for successful team incentives are shown in Figure 9.2. If these conditions cannot be met, then either individual or organizational incentives may be more appropriate.

Organizational Incentives

An organizational incentive system compensates all employees in the organization based on how well the organization as a whole performs during the year. The basic concept behind organizational incentive plans is that overall results depend on organizational or plant-wide cooperation. The purpose of these plans is to produce better results by rewarding cooperation throughout the organization. Common organizational incentive systems include profit sharing, stock options, and employee stock ownership plans (ESOPs).

FIGURE 9.2 Conditions for Successful Team Incentives

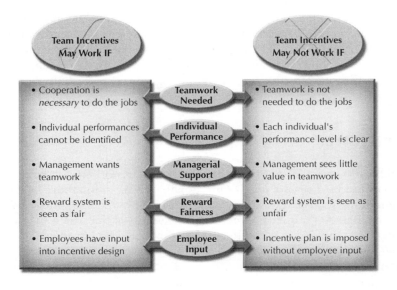

Profit Sharing. As the name implies, **profit sharing** distributes some portion of organizational profits to employees. Typically, the percentage of the profits distributed to employees is agreed on by the end of the year before distribution. In some profit-sharing plans, employees receive portions of the profits at the end of the year; in others, the profits are deferred, placed in a fund, and made available to employees on retirement or on their leaving the organization.

Employee Stock Options. Stock options, once the exclusive domain of executive compensation, have been used throughout some organizations. Employee stock options give employees the right to purchase a fixed number of shares of company stock at a specified price for a limited period of time. If the stock's market price exceeds the exercise price, employees can exercise the option and sell the stock at a profit. If the price falls below the exercise price, the option is worthless. Purchasing and holding company stock is thought to give employees a vested "ownership" in seeing the company do well. Obviously, stock prices do not always go up; and when stock values decline, employee anxiety increases. Nevertheless, using stock plans as a means of providing additional compensation to employees appears to help focus employee efforts on increasing organizational performance. Employees tend to like stock-related benefits but do not understand many of the complexities.[4]

Employee Stock Ownership Plans (ESOPs). An **employee stock ownership plan (ESOP)** is designed to give employees stock ownership in the organization for which they work. According to the National Center for Employee Ownership, an estimated 15,000 firms in the United States offer broad employee-ownership programs. Within these firms, approximately 10,000 have established ESOPs covering about 9 million workers.[5]

Establishing an ESOP creates several advantages. The major one is that the firm can receive favorable tax treatment of the earnings earmarked for use in the ESOP. Second, an ESOP gives employees a "piece of the action" so that they can share in the growth and profitability of their firm. As a result, employee ownership may be effective in motivating employees to be more productive and focused on organizational performance.

BENEFITS

Employers provide employee benefits to their workers for being part of the organization. *Employee benefits* are available in a smorgasbord of indirect compensation, such as pensions, health insurance, time off with pay, and other forms. Benefits influence employee's decisions about which employers to consider for employment, whether to stay or leave employment, and when they might retire. However, the unique demands of benefits make their administration by employers demanding. Benefits comprise a significant part of the total compensation package offered to employees. Total compensation includes money paid directly (such as wages and salaries) and money paid indirectly (such as benefits). Too often, both managers and employees think of only wages and salaries as compensation and fail to consider the additional costs associated with benefits expenditures.

Types of Benefits

A wide range of benefits are offered. Figure 9.3 shows the many different benefits classified by type. Employers in the United States must provide a number of **mandated benefits** to employees by law. Social Security and unemployment insurance are funded through a tax paid by the employer based on the employee's compensation. Workers' compensation laws exist in all states. In addition, under the Family and Medical Leave Act (FMLA), employers must offer unpaid leaves to employees with certain medical or family difficulties. Other mandated benefits are available through Medicare, which provides health care for those age 65 and over.

FIGURE 9.3   Types of Benefits

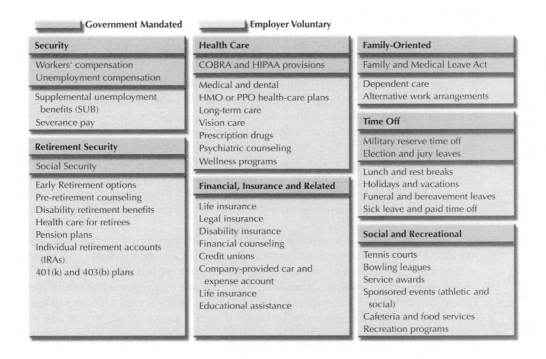

| Government Mandated | Employer Voluntary |

Security
Workers' compensation
Unemployment compensation

Supplemental unemployment benefits (SUB)
Severance pay

Retirement Security
Social Security

Early Retirement options
Pre-retirement counseling
Disability retirement benefits
Health care for retirees
Pension plans
Individual retirement accounts (IRAs)
401(k) and 403(b) plans

Health Care
COBRA and HIPAA provisions

Medical and dental
HMO or PPO health-care plans
Long-term care
Vision care
Prescription drugs
Psychiatric counseling
Wellness programs

Financial, Insurance and Related
Life insurance
Legal insurance
Disability insurance
Financial counseling
Credit unions
Company-provided car and expense account
Life insurance
Educational assistance

Family-Oriented
Family and Medical Leave Act

Dependent care
Alternative work arrangements

Time Off
Military reserve time off
Election and jury leaves

Lunch and rest breaks
Holidays and vacations
Funeral and bereavement leaves
Sick leave and paid time off

Social and Recreational
Tennis courts
Bowling leagues
Service awards
Sponsored events (athletic and social)
Cafeteria and food services
Recreation programs

Other benefits provide employee security. These benefits include some mandated by laws and others offered by employers voluntarily. The primary benefits found in most organizations include workers' compensation, unemployment compensation, and severance pay.

Workers' Compensation. Workers' compensation provides benefits to persons injured on the job. State laws require most employers to provide workers' compensation coverage by purchasing insurance from a private carrier or state insurance fund or by providing self-insurance.

Another benefit required by law is *unemployment compensation*, established as part of the Social Security Act of 1935. Because each U.S. state operates its own unemployment compensation system, provisions differ significantly from state to state.

Severance. Severance pay is a security benefit voluntarily offered by employers to employees who lose their jobs. Severed employees may receive lump-sum severance payments if their employment is terminated by the employer. The Worker Adjustment and Retraining Notification Act (WARN) requires that many employers give 60 days' notice if a mass layoff or facility closing is to occur. The act does not require employers to give severance pay. Regardless, a written severance policy is a good idea.[6]

Retirement Benefits

Few people set aside sufficient financial reserves to use when they retire, so employer retirement benefits attempt to provide income for retired employees. Most employers offer some kind of retirement plan.

As a result of a 1986 amendment to the Age Discrimination in Employment Act (ADEA), most employees cannot be forced to retire at a specific age. As a result, employers have had to develop different policies to comply with these regulations. In many employer pension plans, "normal retirement" is the age at which employees can retire and collect full pension benefits.

In many pension plans provisions for early retirement can be found in order to give workers opportunities to leave their jobs. After spending 25 to 30 years working for the same employer, individuals may wish to use their talents in other areas. Phased-in and part-time retirements offer alternatives to individuals and firms.

Some employers use early retirement buyout programs to cut back their workforces and reduce costs. Employers must take care to make these early retirement programs truly voluntary. Forcing workers to take advantage of an early retirement buyout program led to the passage of a federal law entitled the Older Workers Benefit Protection Act (OWBPA). This act requires equal treatment for older workers in early retirement or severance situations. It also sets forth some specific criteria that must be met when older workers sign waivers promising not to sue for age discrimination.

Social Security. The Social Security Act of 1935, with its later amendments, established a system providing *old age, survivor's, disability,* and *retirement benefits.* Administered by the federal government through the Social Security Administration, this program provides benefits to previously employed individuals. Employees and employers share in the cost of Social Security through a tax on employees' wages or salaries.

Pension Plans. **Pension plans** are retirement benefits established and funded by employers and employees. In **defined-benefit plans** the employees' contributions are based on actuarial calculations that focus on the *benefits* to be received by employees after retirement and the *methods* used to determine such benefits. A defined-benefit plan gives the employee greater assurance of benefits and greater predictability in the amount of benefits that will be available for retirement.

In a **defined-contribution plan**, the employer makes an annual payment to an employee's pension account. The key to this plan is the *contribution rate,* whereby employee retirement benefits depend on fixed contributions and employee earnings levels.

Employers are increasingly changing traditional pension plans to *cash balance plans,* a hybrid based on ideas from both defined benefit and defined contribution plans. Cash balance plans define retirement benefits for each employee not on years of service and salary, but by reference to a hypothetical account balance.

The Employee Retirement Income Security Act (ERISA) in 1974 essentially requires many companies to offer retirement plans to all employees if they are offered to any employees. The act also sets minimum funding requirements and plans not meeting these requirements are subject to IRS financial penalties.

Individual Retirement Benefit Options. The availability of several retirement benefit options makes the pension area more complex. The most prominent options are individual retirement accounts (IRAs), 401(k) and 403(b) plans, and Keogh plans. These plans may be available in addition to company-provided pension plans.

HEALTH-CARE BENEFITS

Employers provide a variety of health-care and medical benefits, usually through insurance coverage. The most common plans cover medical, dental, prescription drug, and vision care expenses for employees and their dependents. Basic health-care insurance to cover both normal and major medical expenses is also desired and expected by most employees. Dental insurance is also important to many employees.

The costs of health-care insurance have continued to escalate at a rate well in excess of inflation, as Figure 9.4 indicates. As a result of these large increases, many employers find that dealing with health-care benefits is time-consuming and expensive. Two approaches that focus specifically on what employers pay are

FIGURE 9.4   Increases in Health-Care Benefits Costs to Employers

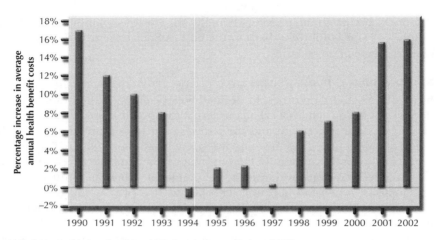

Source: U.S. Bureau of Labor Statistics, U.S. Department of Labor, 2003.

increasing co-payments and using *defined contribution* plans. As health insurance costs rise, employers have tried to shift some of those costs to employees. Using the **co-payment** strategy requires employees to pay some of the cost of both insurance premiums and medical care. Employers who have raised the deductible per person have realized significant savings in health-care expenses due to decreased employee usage of health-care services.

Rather than dropping health benefits or continuing to raise co-payments, a number of employers have implemented *defined contribution plans.* In this type of plan an employer makes a defined contribution of a set amount into each employee's "account." Then individual employees decide what type of health-care coverage they want to select and pay for from the alternatives identified by the employer. The advantage of such plans for employers is shifting more of the increases in health-care benefits to be paid by employees.[7] However, as would be expected, negative reactions from employees may result.

Managed Care

Several other types of programs attempt to reduce health-care costs paid by employers. **Managed care** consists of approaches that monitor and reduce medical costs through restrictions and market system alternatives. These managed care plans emphasize primary and preventative care, the use of specific providers who will charge lower prices, restrictions on certain kinds of treatment, and prices negotiated with hospitals and physicians. The most prevalent types of managed care are **Preferred Provider Organizations (PPOs)** and **Health Maintenance Organizations (HMOs)**.

Health-Care Legislation

The importance of health-care benefits to employers and employees has led to a variety of federal and state laws. Some laws have been enacted to provide protection for employees who leave their employers, either voluntarily or involuntarily. To date, the two most important ones are COBRA and HIPAA.

COBRA Provisions. Legal requirements in the Consolidated Omnibus Budget Reconciliation Act (COBRA) require that most employers (except churches and the federal government) with 20 or more employees offer extended health-care coverage to the following groups:

- Employees who voluntarily quit, except those terminated for "gross misconduct"
- Widowed or divorced spouses and dependent children of former or current employees
- Retirees and their spouses whose health-care coverage ends.

Employers must notify eligible employees and/or their spouses and qualified dependents within 60 days after the employees quit, die, get divorced, or otherwise change their status. The coverage must be offered for 18 to 36 months, depending on the qualifying circumstances.

HIPAA Provisions. The Health Insurance Portability and Accountability Act (HIPAA) allows employees to switch their health insurance plan from one company to another to get new health coverage, regardless of pre-existing health conditions. The legislation also prohibits group insurance plans from dropping coverage for a sick employee, and requires them to make individual coverage available to people who leave group plans.[8]

OTHER BENEFITS

Employers may offer workers a wide range of special benefits: financial benefits, insurance benefits (in addition to health-related insurance), educational benefits, social benefits, and recreational benefits. From the point of view of the employer, such benefits can be useful in attracting and retaining employees. Workers like receiving special benefits, which often are not taxed as income.

Insurance Benefits

In addition to health-related insurance, some employers provide other types of insurance. These benefits offer major advantages for employees because many employers pay some or all of the costs. Even when employers do not pay any of the costs, employees still benefit because of the lower rates available through group programs. The most common insurance benefits are *life insurance*, *disability insurance*, and *legal insurance*.

Educational Benefits

Another benefit used by employees comes in the form of *educational assistance* to pay for some or all costs associated with formal education courses and degree programs, including the costs of books and laboratory materials. Some employers pay for schooling on a proportional schedule, depending on the grades received; others simply require a passing grade of C or above.

Family-Oriented Benefits

The composition of families in the United States has changed significantly in the past few decades. To provide assistance, employers have established a variety of family-oriented benefits, and the federal government passed the Family and Medical Leave Act.

Family and Medical Leave Act (FMLA). Passed in 1993, the Family and Medical Leave Act (FMLA) covers all employers with 50 or more employees who live within 75 miles of the workplace and includes federal, state, and private employers. Only employees who have worked at least 12 months and 1,250 hours in the previous year are eligible for leaves under FMLA.

The law requires that employers allow eligible employees to take a total of 12 weeks' leave during any 12-month period for one or more of the following situations:

- ▶ Birth, adoption, or foster care placement of a child
- ▶ Caring for a spouse, child, or parent with a serious health condition
- ▶ Serious health condition of the employee

A **serious health condition** is one requiring inpatient, hospital, hospice, or residential medical care or continuing physician care. An employer may require an employee to provide a certificate from a doctor verifying such an illness. FMLA outlines the guidelines regarding employee leaves:

Family-Care Benefits. The growing emphasis on family issues is important in many organizations and for many workers. But those employees without families may feel some resentment against those who seem to get special privileges because they have families. Nevertheless, many employers provide maternity and paternity benefits to employees who give birth to children. In comparison to those giving birth, a relatively small number of employees adopt children, but in the interest of fairness, a growing number of organizations provide benefits for employees who adopt children.

Balancing work and family responsibilities is a major challenge for many workers. Some employers provide child care assistance by providing referral services to aid parents in locating child-care providers or by other means, including offering on-site child-care facilities.

Another family-related issue of growing importance is caring for elderly relatives. Various organizations have surveyed their employees and found that as many as 30% of them have had to miss work to care for an aging relative. Some responses by employers have included conducting needs surveys, providing resources, and giving referrals to elder-care providers.

Benefits for Domestic Partners and Spousal Equivalents. As lifestyles change in the United States, employers are being confronted with requests for benefits by employees who are not married but have close personal relationships with others. The terminology often used to refer to individuals with such living arrangements are *domestic partners* and *spousal equivalents.* The employees who are submitting these requests are unmarried employees who have living arrangements with individuals of the opposite sex, and gay and lesbian employees requesting benefits for their partners.

The argument made by these employees is that if an employer provides benefits for the spouses of married employees, then benefits should be provided for employees without spouses but with alternative lifestyles and relationships. Most employees using the domestic partner benefits are of the opposite sex and are involved in heterosexual relationships.

Time-Off Benefits

Employers give employees paid time off in a variety of circumstances. Paid lunch breaks and rest periods, holidays, and vacations are common. But leaves are given for a number of other purposes as well. Time-off benefits represent an estimated 5% to 13% of total compensation. Typical time-off benefits include holiday pay, vacation pay, and leaves of absence.

Employers grant *leaves of absence,* taken as time off with or without pay, for a variety of reasons. All of the different types of leaves add to employer costs even if unpaid, because the missing employee's work must be covered, either by other employees working additionally or by temporary employees working under contract. The most common types of leaves are *family leave, medical and sick leave, paid time off, election and jury leave*, and *funeral or bereavement leave.*

BENEFITS ADMINISTRATION

With the myriad of benefits and regulations, it is easy to see why many organizations must make coordinated efforts to properly administer benefits programs. The greatest role is played by HR specialists, but managers are responsible for some of the communication aspects of benefits administration.

Benefits Communication

Employees generally do not know much about the values and costs associated with the benefits they receive from employers. So benefits communication and benefits satisfaction are linked. Many employers have instituted special benefits communication systems to inform employees about the value of the benefits they provide. Some employers also give each employee an annual "personal statement of benefits" that translates benefits into dollar amounts.

Information technology allows employees to change their benefits choices, track their benefits balances, and submit questions to HR staff members and external benefits providers. HR professionals are utilizing information systems to communicate benefits information, conduct employee benefit surveys, and provide other benefits communications.

Flexible Benefits

A **flexible benefits plan**, sometimes called a *flex* or *cafeteria* plan, allows employees to select the benefits they prefer from groups of benefits established by the employer. By making a variety of "dishes" or benefits available, the organization allows each employee to select an individual combination of benefits within some overall limits. As a result of the changing composition of the workforce, flexible benefits plans have grown in popularity.

Flexible Spending Accounts.   Under current tax laws (Section 125 of the IRS Code), employees can divert some income before taxes into accounts to fund certain benefits. These **flexible spending accounts** allow employees to contribute pretax dollars to buy additional benefits. Under tax laws at the time of this writing, the funds in the account can be used only to purchase the following: (1) additional health care (including offsetting deductibles), (2) life insurance, (3) disability insurance, and (4) dependent-care benefits.

NOTES

1. "Study Questions If Incentive Pay Is Really Hitting Its Mark," *IOMA Report on Salary Surveys*, February 2000, 13.
2. "Towers Perrin Reveals How to Design the Most Effective Incentive Plans," *IOMA's Report on Salary Surveys*, March 2000, 14.
3. Marlen A. Prost, "New Worth," *Human Resource Executive*, February 2001, 78.
4. Barbara Estes et al., "Stock Options: Are They Still the Brass Ring?" *Workspan*, May 2001, 24.
5. Corey Rosen, NCEO, "A Brief Introduction to Employee Ownership," available at *http://www. nceo.org*.
6. Carolyn Hirschman, "The Kindest Cut," *HR Magazine*, April 2001, 48–53.
7. Robert J. Chitadore, "Defined Contribution," *WorldatWork Journal*, Third Quarter 2001, 11–17.
8. Alex M. (Kelly) Clarke, "The New HIPPA Regulations," *13th Annual Baird Holm Labor Law Forum 2001*, 57.

INTERNET RESEARCH

My Stock Options.com This Web site provides tools for communicating, educating, and training employees about stock options. http://www.mystockoptions.com

Benefit News.com This Web site consists of surveys, archived articles, and the latest trends and information regarding employee benefits. http://www.benefitnews.com

SUGGESTED READINGS

Paul Fronstin, *Consuer-Driven Health Benefits*, Employee Benefit Research Institute, 2002.

Managing Benefits Plans, IOMA, 2003.

Scott S. Roderick, *Stock Options: Beyond the Basics*, The National Center for Employee Ownership, 2003

Chapter 10

Health, Safety, and Employee Rights

Today employees expect their employers to provide work environments that are safe, secure, and healthy. The concept of using prevention and control to minimize or eliminate risks in workplaces is a key part of HR management.

NATURE OF HEALTH, SAFETY, AND SECURITY

The terms *health, safety,* and *security* are closely related. The broader and somewhat more nebulous term is **health**, which refers to a general state of physical, mental, and emotional well-being. A healthy person is free of illness, injury, or mental and emotional problems that impair normal human activity. Health management practices in organizations strive to maintain the overall well-being of individuals.

Typically, **safety** refers to protecting the physical well-being of people. The main purpose of effective safety programs in organizations is to prevent work-related injuries and accidents. The purpose of **security** is protecting employees and organizational facilities. With the growth of workplace violence, security at work has become an even greater concern for employers and employees alike.

The general goal of providing a safe, secure, and healthy workplace is reached by operating managers and HR staff members working together. As Figure 10.1 indicates, the primary health, safety, and security responsibilities in an organization usually fall on supervisors and managers.

Legal Requirements for Safety and Health

Employers must comply with a variety of federal and state laws as part of their efforts when developing and maintaining healthy, safe, and secure workforces and working environments. A look at some major legal areas follows next.

FIGURE 10.1   Typical Division of HR Responsibilities: Health, Safety, and Security

HR Unit	Managers
• *Coordinates health and safety programs* • *Develops safety reporting system* • *Provides accident investigation expertise* • *Provides technical expertise on accident prevention* • *Develops restricted-access procedures and employee identification systems* • *Trains managers to recognize and handle difficult employee situations*	• *Monitor health and safety of employees daily* • *Coach employees to be safety conscious* • *Investigate accidents* • *Observe health and safety behavior of employees* • *Monitor workplace for security problems* • *Communicate with employees to identify potentially difficult employees* • *Follow security procedures and recommend changes as needed*

Workers' Compensation. Under workers' compensation laws, employers contribute to an insurance fund to compensate employees for injuries received while on the job. Premiums paid reflect the accident rates at each employer, with those employers with higher incident rates being assessed higher comprehensive premiums. Also, these laws usually provide payments to injured workers for wage replacements, dependent on the amount of lost time and wage levels.[1] Workers' compensation payments also cover costs for medical bills, and for retraining if a worker cannot return to the job. Many of the safety and health management activities discussed later contribute to reducing workers' compensation costs.

Americans with Disabilities Act and Safety. The Americans with Disabilities Act (ADA) is another law affecting health and safety policies and practices of employers. Health and safety record-keeping practices have been affected by the following provision in the ADA:

> Information from all medical examinations and inquiries must be kept apart from general personnel files as a separate confidential medical record available only under limited conditions specified in the ADA.

As interpreted by attorneys and HR practitioners, this provision requires that all medical-related information be maintained separately from all other confidential files. Also, specific access restrictions and security procedures must be adopted for medical records of all types, including employee medical benefit claims and treatment records.

Child Labor Laws. Another area of safety concern is reflected in restrictions affecting younger workers, especially those under the age of 18. Child labor laws set the minimum age for most employment at 16 years. For "hazardous" occupations, 18 years is the minimum. In addition to complying with workers' compensation, ADA, and child labor laws, most employers must comply with the Occupational Health and Safety Act of 1970. This act has had a tremendous impact on the workplace, and is discussed next.

Occupational Safety and Health Act

The Occupational Safety and Health Act of 1970 was passed "to assure so far as possible every working man or woman in the Nation safe and healthful working conditions and to preserve our human resources." Every employer engaged in commerce who has one or more employees is covered by the act. Farmers having fewer than 10 employees are exempt. The 1970 act also established the Occupational Safety and Health Administration, known as OSHA, to administer its provisions. By making employers and employees more aware of safety and health considerations, OSHA has significantly affected organizations.[2]

OSHA Enforcement Standards. To implement OSHA, specific standards were established regulating equipment and working environments. National standards developed by engineering and quality control groups are often used. However, small-business owners and managers who do not have specialists on their staffs may find the standards difficult to read and understand.

A number of provisions have been recognized as key to OSHA compliance efforts by employers. Two of the most basic ones are as follows:

▶ *General duty:* The act requires that the employer has a "general duty" to provide safe and healthy working conditions, even in areas where OSHA standards have not been set. Employers who know or reasonably should know of unsafe or unhealthy conditions can be cited for violating the general duty clause.
▶ *Notification and posters:* Employers are required to inform their employees of safety and health standards established by OSHA. Also, OSHA posters must be displayed in prominent locations in workplaces.

Also, OSHA has enforcement responsibilities for the federal *Hazard Communication Standard*, which requires manufacturers, importers, distributors, and users of hazardous chemicals to evaluate, classify, and label these substances. Employers also must make available material safety data sheets (MSDSs), which must be kept readily accessible to those who work with chemicals and other substances. The MSDSs also indicate antidotes or actions to be taken should someone come in contact with the substances.

As part of hazard communications, OSHA has established **lock out/tag out regulations.** To comply, locks and tags are provided to mechanics and tradespersons for use when they make equipment inoperative for repair or adjustment to prevent accidental start-up of defective machinery.

OSHA issued an additional standard "to eliminate or minimize occupational exposure to hepatitis B virus (HBV), human immunodeficiency virus (HIV), and other *bloodborne pathogens.*" This regulation was developed to protect employees who regularly are exposed to blood and other such substances from AIDS.

One goal of OSHA has been to develop standards for *personal protective equipment.* These standards require that employers conduct analyses of job hazards, provide adequate PPE to employees in those jobs, and train employees in the use of PPE items.

Ergonomics and OSHA. **Ergonomics** is the study and design of the work environment to address physiological and physical demands on individuals. In a work setting, ergonomic studies look at such factors as fatigue, lighting, tools, equipment layout, and placement of controls.

For a number of years OSHA focused on the large number of work-related injuries due to repetitive stress, repetitive motion, cumulative trauma disorders, carpal tunnel syndrome, and other injuries in workplaces. **Cumulative trauma disorders (CTDs)** occur when workers repetitively use the same muscles to perform tasks, resulting in muscle and skeletal injuries. These problems occur in a variety of work settings. OSHA standards on ergonomics can be reviewed at the OSHA Web site, *http://www.osha.gov.*

OSHA Record-Keeping Requirements. OSHA has established a standard national system for recording occupational injuries, accidents, and fatalities. Many organizations must complete OSHA Form 300 to report workshop accidents and injuries. Four types of injuries or illnesses have been defined by the Occupational Safety and Health Act of 1970:

▸ *Injury- or illness-related deaths*
▸ *Lost-time or disability injuries:* Job-related injuries or disabling occurrences that cause an employee to miss his or her regularly scheduled work on the day following the accident
▸ *Medical care injuries:* Injuries that require treatment by a physician but do not cause an employee to miss a regularly scheduled work turn
▸ *Minor injuries:* Injuries that require first-aid treatment and do not cause an employee to miss the next regularly scheduled work turn

OSHA Inspections. The Occupational Safety and Health Act provides for on-the-spot inspections by OSHA representatives, called compliance officers or inspectors. Although OSHA inspectors can issue citations for violations of the provisions of the act, whether or not a citation is issued depends on the severity and extent of the problems, and on the employer's knowledge of them. In addition, depending on the nature and number of violations, penalties can be assessed against employers. Awareness of the types of violations and correction of them by employers are important as part of HR management.

The five types of violations ranging from the most severe to minimal, including a special category for repeated violations are:

- ▶ *Imminent danger*
- ▶ *Serious*
- ▶ *Other than serious*

- ▶ *De minimis*
- ▶ *Willful and repeated*

SAFETY MANAGEMENT

Effective safety management requires an organizational commitment to safe working conditions. But more importantly, well-designed and managed safety programs can pay dividends in reduced accidents and the associated costs, such as workers' compensation and possible fines. Also, accidents and other safety concerns usually decline as a result of management efforts emphasizing safety.

Components of Effective Safety Management

At the heart of safety management is an organizational commitment to a comprehensive safety effort. This effort should be coordinated from the top level of management to include all members of the organization. It also should be reflected in managerial actions. Employers can use a number of different approaches in managing safety. Figure 10.2 shows the organizational, engineering, and individual

FIGURE 10.2   Approaches to Effective Safety Management

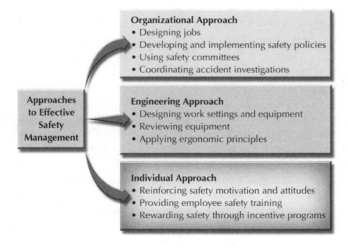

approaches and their components. Successful programs may use all three in dealing with safety issues.

Effective safety management programs usually contain the following elements:

▸ Organizational commitment and responsibility
▸ Safety policies and discipline
▸ Safety training and communications
▸ Safety committees
▸ Inspection, accident investigation, and research
▸ Evaluation of safety efforts

Designing safety policies and rules and disciplining violators are important components of safety efforts. Frequently reinforcing the need for safe behavior and supplying feedback on positive safety practices also are effective in improving worker safety. Such efforts must involve employees, supervisors, managers, safety specialists, and HR staff members, often using *safety committees* composed of workers from a variety of levels and departments. A safety committee generally meets at regularly scheduled times, has specific responsibilities for conducting safety reviews, and makes recommendations for changes necessary to avoid future accidents. Usually, at least one member of the committee comes from the HR department.

To reinforce *safety training*, continuous communication to develop safety consciousness is necessary. Merely sending safety memos is not enough. Producing newsletters, changing safety posters, continually updating bulletin boards, and posting safety information in visible areas also are recommended.

It is not necessary to wait for an OSHA inspector to inspect the work area for safety hazards. Inspections may be done by a safety committee or by a safety coordinator. They should be done on a regular basis, because OSHA may inspect organizations with above-average lost workday rates more frequently.

Organizations should monitor and evaluate their safety efforts.[3] Just as organizational accounting records are audited, a firm's safety efforts should be audited periodically as well. Accident and injury statistics should be compared with previous accident patterns to identify any significant changes. This analysis should be designed to measure progress in safety management.

HEALTH

Employee health problems are varied—and somewhat inevitable. They can range from minor illnesses such as colds to serious illnesses related to the jobs performed. Some employees have emotional health problems; others have alcohol or drug problems. Some problems are chronic; others are transitory. But all may affect organizational operations and individual employee productivity. Employers face a variety of workplace health issues. A number of concerns are associated with employee substance abuse, workplace air quality, and smoking.

Employers' concerns about substance abuse stem from the ways it alters work behaviors: tardiness, increased absenteeism, slower work pace, higher rate of mistakes, and less time spent at the workstation. Substance abuse also can cause altered behaviors at work such as increases in withdrawal symptoms and antagonistic behaviors that may lead to workplace violence. The Americans with Disabilities Act (ADA) affects how management can handle substance abuse cases. Current illegal drug users are specifically excluded from the definition of disabled under the act. However, those addicted to legal substances (alcohol, for example) and prescription drugs are considered disabled under the ADA. Also, recovering substance abusers are considered disabled under the ADA.

Many individuals today face work, family, and personal life pressures. Although most people manage these pressures successfully, some individuals have difficulties handling the demands. Stress, whereby individuals cannot successfully handle the multiple demands they face, is one concern. All people encounter stress, but when "stress overload" hits, work-related consequences can result. HR professionals, managers, and supervisors all must be prepared to handle employee stress.

Arguments and rebuttals characterize the smoking-at-work controversy, and statistics abound. A multitude of state and local laws deal with smoking in the workplace and public places. As a result of health studies, complaints by non-smokers, and state laws, many employers have no-smoking policies throughout their workplaces. Some employers also offer smoking cessation workshops as part of health promotion efforts.

Health Promotion

Employers concerned about maintaining a healthy workforce can move beyond simply providing healthy working conditions and begin promoting employee health and wellness in other ways. **Health promotion** is a supportive approach to facilitate and encourage employees to enhance healthy actions and lifestyles. Health promotion efforts can range from providing information and enhancing employee awareness of health issues to creating an organizational culture supportive of employee health enhancements, as Figure 10.3 indicates.

Employers' desires to improve productivity, decrease absenteeism, and control health-care costs have come together in **wellness programs** designed to maintain or improve employee health before problems arise and in **employee assistance programs** (EAPs) that provide counseling and other help to employees having emotional, physical, or other personal problems.

SECURITY

Traditionally, when employers addressed worker health, safety, and security, they were concerned about reducing workplace accidents, improving workers' safety practices, and reducing health hazards at work. However, over the past decade providing security for employees has grown in importance.

FIGURE 10.3 Health Promotion Levels

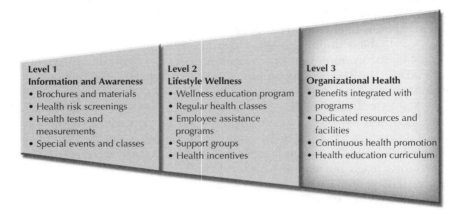

Level 1
Information and Awareness
- Brochures and materials
- Health risk screenings
- Health tests and measurements
- Special events and classes

Level 2
Lifestyle Wellness
- Wellness education program
- Regular health classes
- Employee assistance programs
- Support groups
- Health incentives

Level 3
Organizational Health
- Benefits integrated with programs
- Dedicated resources and facilities
- Continuous health promotion
- Health education curriculum

Source: Developed by Kay R. Ryan (Nebraska Methodist College) and Robert L. Mathis (University of Nebraska at Omaha). May not be reproduced without permission.

Workplace Violence

Estimates by the National Institute for Occupational Safety and Health (NIOSH) indicate that 10–15 workplace homicides occur every week. NIOSH estimates that an additional million people are attacked at work annually.[4] The increase in workplace violence has led many employers to develop workplace violence prevention and response policies and practices. As recommended by the American Society of Safety Engineers (ASSE), employers need to conduct a risk assessment of the organization and its employees, and then identify how workplace violence is to be dealt with in conjunction with disciplinary actions and referrals to employee assistance programs. Also, managers, HR staff members, supervisors, and employers should be trained on how to recognize the signs of a potentially violent employee and what to do when violence occurs.

Security Management

An overall approach to security management is needed to address a wide range of issues including workplace violence. Often HR managers have responsibility for security programs, or they work closely with security managers or consultants to address employee security issues. A key part of security involves controlling access to the physical facilities of the organization. Many organizations limit access to facilities, work areas, and computers by using electronic access or key-card systems. The growth of the Internet and e-mail systems has made computer security issues an even greater concern.

International Security and Terrorism. As more U.S. firms operate internationally, the threat of terrorist actions against those firms and the employees working for them increases. The extent to which employees are likely to experience security problems and violence depends upon the country. It is crucial that the HR staff regularly check the security conditions in countries where expatriates are traveling and working.

EMPLOYEE RIGHTS AND RESPONSIBILITIES ISSUES

Employees join organizations with certain rights established by the U.S. Constitution, including *freedom of speech, due process, protection against unreasonable search and seizure,* and others. Although the U.S. Constitution grants these and other rights to citizens, over the years laws and court decisions have identified limits on those rights in the workplaces.

Generally, **rights** do not exist in the abstract. Instead they exist only when someone is successful in demanding their application. Rights are offset by **responsibilities**, which are obligations to be accountable for actions. Employment is a reciprocal relationship where both sides have rights and obligations.

Employees' **statutory rights** are the result of specific laws or statutes passed by federal, state, or local governments. Various federal, state, and local laws have granted employees certain rights at work, such as equal employment opportunity, collective bargaining, and workplace safety. These laws and their interpretations also have been the subjects of a considerable number of court cases.

An employee's **contractual rights** are based on a specific contract agreement with an employer. For instance, a union and an employer may agree on a labor contract that specifies certain terms, conditions, and rights that employees have with the employer.

A formal **employment contract** outlines the details of an employment agreement. These written contracts often are very detailed. The idea that a contract (even an implied or unwritten one) exists between individuals and their employers affects the employment relationship. The rights and responsibilities of the employee may be spelled out in a job description, in an employment contract, in HR policies or a handbook, but often are not. The rights and responsibilities of the employee may also exist *only* as unwritten employer expectations about what is acceptable behavior or performance on the part of the employee. The discussion that follows focuses on major concepts in rights and responsibilities.

Employment-at-Will

Employment-at-will (EAW) is a common law doctrine stating that employers have the right to hire, fire, demote, or promote whomever they choose, unless there is a law or contract to the contrary. Conversely, employees can quit whenever they want and go to another job under the same constraints. Many court rulings have stressed that employees' job rights must be balanced against EAW.

Wrongful Discharge

Employers who run afoul of EAW restrictions may be found guilty of **wrongful discharge**, which occurs when an employer terminates an individual's employment for reasons that are illegal or improper. Additionally, courts generally have held that unionized workers cannot pursue EAW actions as at-will employees because they are covered by the grievance arbitration process.

Just Cause

What constitutes a "good reason" or **just cause** for disciplinary actions such as dismissal can usually be found in union contracts, but not in at-will situations. Even though definitions of *just cause* vary, the courts use well-defined criteria.

Just cause is about fairness. To be viewed by others as being *just,* any disciplinary action must be based on facts in each individual case. Generally *not* viewed as just cause is the act of **constructive discharge**, which occurs when an employer deliberately makes conditions intolerable in an attempt to get an employee to quit.

Due Process

Due process, like just cause, is also about fairness. **Due process** addresses the fairness of means used to determine employee wrongdoing and/or disciplinary measures, and includes the opportunity for individuals to explain and defend their actions. Figure 10.4 shows some factors to be considered when evaluating whether an individual received due process. How HR managers and their employers address these factors of just cause and due process figures prominently in whether the courts perceive employers' actions as fair.

FIGURE 10.4   Criteria for Just Cause and Due Process

Just Cause Determinants	Due Process Considerations
• Was the employee warned of the consequences of the conduct?	• How have precedents been handled?
• Was the employer's rule reasonable?	• Is a complaint process available?
• Did management investigate before disciplining?	• Was the complaint process used?
• Was the investigation fair and impartial?	• Was retaliation used against the employee?
• Was there evidence of guilt?	• Was a decision made based on facts?
• Were the rules and penalties applied in an evenhanded fashion?	• Were the actions and processes viewed as "fair" by outside entities?
• Was the penalty reasonable, given the offense?	

Alternative Dispute Resolutions (ADR) as Due Process

Disputes between management and employees over different work issues are normal and inevitable. How they resolve their disputes becomes important. Formal grievance procedures or lawsuits provide two methods to resolve disputes. However, more and more companies look to alternative means of ensuring that due process occurs in cases involving employee rights. Dissatisfaction with the expense and delays common in the court system when lawsuits are filed explains the growth in alternative dispute resolution (ADR) methods such as arbitration, peer review panels, and ombudsmen.

Rights Issues and Employee Records

As a result of concerns about protecting individual privacy rights, the Privacy Act of 1974 was passed. It includes provisions affecting HR record-keeping systems. This law applies *only* to federal agencies and organizations supplying services to the federal government; but similar state laws, somewhat broader in scope, also have been passed. The following legal issues concern employee rights to privacy and HR records:

- ▸ Access to personal information
- ▸ Response to unfavorable information
- ▸ Correction of erroneous information
- ▸ Knowledge of when information is given to a third party

It is important that specific access restrictions and security procedures for employee records be established. These restrictions and procedures are designed to protect both the privacy of employees and employers from potential liability for improper disclosure of personal information.

Employees' Free Speech Rights

The right of individuals to have freedom of speech is protected by the U.S. Constitution. However, that freedom is *not* an unrestricted one in the workplace. One area in which employees' freedom of speech has collided with employers' restrictions surrounds individuals who report real or perceived wrongs committed by their employers, called **whistle-blowers**. Employers need to address two key questions in regard to whistle-blowing: (1) When do employees have the right to speak out with protection from retribution? (2) When do employees violate the confidentiality of their jobs by speaking out? Even though the answers maybe difficult to determine, retaliation against whistle-blowers clearly is not allowed, based on a number of court decisions.

Monitoring of E-Mail, Voice Mail, and Internet Usage. Both e-mail and voice-mail systems increasingly are seen by employers as areas where employers have a right to monitor what is said and transmitted. Information and telecommunications technological advances have become a major issue for employers regarding employee privacy. The use of e-mail and voice mail increases every day, also raising each employer's liability if they improperly monitor or inspect employee electronic communications.

Tracking employee Internet usage is common. Through this monitoring, employers attempt to guard against some employees accessing pornographic or other Web sites that could create problems for employers. Therefore, many employers have purchased software that tracks the Web sites accessed by employees and blocks certain categories and Web sites inappropriate for business use.

Workplace Performance Monitoring and Surveillance

Employers also use workplace searches and surveillance as part of employee performance monitoring. Employers may conduct workplace investigations for theft and other illegal behavior.

Employee Substance Abuse and Employer Drug Testing

The issues of substance abuse and drug testing at work have received a great deal of attention.[5] The Drug-Free Workplace Act requires government contractors to take steps to eliminate employee drug usage. Failure to do so can lead to contract termination. Tobacco and alcohol do not qualify as controlled substances under the act, and off-the-job drug use is not included. Additionally, the U.S. Department of Transportation (DOT) requires regular testing of truck and bus drivers, train crews, mass-transit employees, airline pilots and mechanics, pipeline workers, and licensed sailors.[6]

Disciplinary action of an employee because of substance-abuse problems must be done only in keeping with the due process described in an employer's policy. Unless state or local law prohibits testing, employers have a right to require applicants or employees to submit to a drug test. Random drug testing of current employees may be more controversial, and public agencies must show "probable cause" to conduct drug tests.

HR POLICIES, PROCEDURES, AND RULES

It is useful at this point to consider some guidelines for HR policies, procedures, and rules since they affect employee rights (just discussed) and discipline (discussed next). When a choice among actions is available, **policies** act as general guidelines that focus organizational actions. Policies are general in nature, while procedures and rules are specific to a situation.

Procedures provide for customary methods of handling activities and are more specific than policies. For example, a policy may state that employees will be given vacations. Procedures establish a specific method for authorizing vacation time without disrupting work.

Rules are specific guidelines that regulate and restrict the behavior of individuals. They are similar to procedures in that they guide action and typically allow no discretion in their application. Rules reflect a management decision that action be taken—or not taken—in a given situation. They provide more specific behavioral guidelines than policies.

Employee Handbooks

Employee handbooks give employees a reference source for company policies and rules and can be a positive tool for effective management of human resources. Even smaller organizations can prepare handbooks relatively easily using available computer software. Not having an employee handbook with HR policies spelled out can leave an organization open to costly litigation and out-of-court settlements.

Employee Discipline

The earlier discussion about employee rights provides an appropriate introduction to the topic of employee discipline, because employee rights often are a key issue in disciplinary cases. **Discipline** is a form of training that enforces organizational rules. Those most often affected by the discipline systems in an organization are problem employees. Common disciplinary issues caused by problem employees include absenteeism, tardiness, productivity deficiencies, alcoholism, and insubordination. There are several different approaches to employee discipline.

Positive Discipline Approach. The positive discipline approach builds on the philosophy that violations are actions that usually can be constructively corrected without penalty. In this approach, managers focus on fact-finding and guidance to encourage desirable behaviors, rather than using penalties to discourage undesirable behaviors.

Progressive Discipline Approach. As another approach, progressive discipline incorporates a sequence of steps, each of which becomes progressively more stringent and is designed to change the employee's inappropriate behavior. A typical progressive discipline system, and most progressive discipline procedures use verbal and written reprimands and suspension before resorting to dismissal.

Because of legal concerns, managers must understand discipline and know how to administer it properly. Effective discipline should be aimed at the behavior, not at the employee personally, because the reason for discipline is to improve performance. Discipline can be positively related to performance, which surprises those who feel that discipline can only harm behavior.

Discharge: The Final Disciplinary Step

The final stage in the disciplinary process is discharge or termination. Both the positive and progressive approaches to discipline clearly provide warnings to employees about the seriousness of their performance problems before dismissal occurs. When dismissal occurs, the reasons for the termination should be clearly stated. Finally, throughout the termination discussion the supervisor and others need to remain professional and calm, rather than becoming emotional, apologetic, or making sarcastic or demeaning remarks.[7]

NOTES

1. Jon Grice, "The Cost of Comp," *Occupational Health & Safety*, February 2001, 59–60.
2. "OSHA at 30: Three Decades of Progress in Occupational Safety and Health," *Job Safety & Health Quarterly*, Spring 2001, 23–32.
3. Robert A. Menard, "Talking Dollars and Sense," *Occupational Health & Safety*, February 2001, 62–65.
4. Marlene Piturro, "Workplace Violence," *Strategic Finance*, May 2001, 35–38.
5. Employer Tip Sheet #9, The National Clearinghouse for Alcohol and Drug Information, available at *http://www.health.org/govpubs/workit/ts9.htm*.
6. Michael A. Gips, "Industry Comment Shapes Drug Testing Rule," *Security Management*, March 2001, 18.
7. Sarah Breckenridge and Michele Marchetti, "The Fire Drill." *Smart Money*, October 2001, 141–142.

INTERNET RESEARCH

Occupational Safety and Health Administration This Web site is the OSHA home page. Access to the OSHA library, regulations for compliance, newsroom, and much more can be found here. **http://www.osha.gov/**

Institute for a Drug-Free Workplace This Web site provides employers with information on a drug-free workplace including the state and federal laws regarding drug testing. **http://www.drugfreeworkplace.org/**

SUGGESTED READINGS

Lynne McClure, *Anger and Conflict in the Workplace*, Impact Publications, 2000.

Lisa A. Milam-Perez, *Workplace Safety*, CCH, 2003.

Mark Moran, *The OSHA Recordkeeping Answer Book*, Safety Certified, 2001.

Thomas H. Sawyer, *Employee Services Management*, Sagamore Publishing, 2001.

Chapter 11

Labor Relations

A **union** is a formal association of workers that promotes the interests of its members through collective action. The state and nature of union-management relations varies among countries. In the United States, a complex system of laws, regulations, court decisions, and administrative rulings have established that workers may join unions when they wish to do so. Although fewer workers choose to do so today than before, the mechanisms remain for a resurgence of unions if employees feel they need formal representation to deal with management.

NATURE OF UNIONS

Employers usually would rather not have to deal with unions because they constrain what managers can and cannot do in a number of areas. Generally, union workers receive higher wages and benefits than do non-union workers.[1] Unions *can* be associated with higher productivity, although management must find labor-saving ways of doing work to offset the higher labor costs.

Some employers pursue a strategy of good relations with the unions. Others may choose an aggressive, adversarial approach. Regardless of the employer's strategy, several common factors explain why employees unionize.

Why Employees Unionize

Whether a union targets a group of employees or the employees themselves request union assistance, the union still must win sufficient support from the employees in order to become their legal representative. Research consistently shows that employees join unions for two primary reasons: (1) they are dissatisfied with how they are treated by their employers, and (2) they believe that unions can improve their work situations. If the employees do not receive organizational justice from their employers, they turn to unions for assistance in obtaining what they believe is equitable. The major factors that can trigger unionization are compensation, working environment, management style, and organizational treatment issues.

Union Structure

American labor is represented by many different kinds of unions. But regardless of size and geographical scope, two basic types of unions developed over time. In a **craft union**, members all do one type of work, often using specialized skills and training. Examples include the International Association of Bridge, Structural, and Ornamental Iron Workers, and the American Federation of Television and Radio Artists. An **industrial union** includes many persons working in the same industry or company, regardless of jobs held. The United Food and Commercial Workers, the United Auto Workers, and the American Federation of State, County, and Municipal Employees are examples of industrial unions.

Labor organizations have developed complex organizational structures with multiple levels. The broadest level is the **federation**, which is a group of autonomous national and international unions. A federation allows individual unions to work together and present a more unified front to the public, legislators, and members. The most prominent federation in the United States is the AFL-CIO, which is a confederation of national and international unions.

Union Membership in the United States

The statistics on union membership tell a disheartening story for organized labor in the United States over the past several decades. Unions represented more than 30% of the workforce from 1945 through 1960. But by 2002, unions in the United States represented less than 14% of all civilian workers. When unionized government employees are excluded, unions represent only 9.5% of the private-sector workforce. Even more disheartening for the unions, the actual number of members has declined in most years even though more people are employed than previously. Of the approximately 120 million U.S. workers, only about 16 million belong to a union.[2]

Public-Sector Unionism. An area where unions have had some measure of success is with public-sector employees, particularly with state and local government workers. The government sector (federal, state, and local) is the most highly unionized part of the U.S. workforce.

Unionization of state and local government employees presents some unique problems and challenges. First, some employees work in critical service areas. Allowing police officers, firefighters, and sanitation workers to strike endangers public health and safety. Consequently, more than 30 states have laws prohibiting public employee work stoppages. These laws also identify a variety of ways to resolve negotiation impasses, including arbitration. But unions still give employees in these areas greater security and better ability to influence decisions on wages and benefits.

Although unions in the federal government hold the same basic philosophy as unions in the private sector, they do differ somewhat. Previous Executive Orders and laws established methods of labor-management relations that consider the special circumstances present in the federal government. In the United States, the government sector is the only one to see recent growth and strengthening of unions.

Reasons for Union Decline in the U.S. Several issues are considered to have contributed to the decline of unions: deregulation, foreign competition, a larger number of people looking for jobs, and a general perception by firms that dealing with unions is expensive compared with the non-union alternative. Also, management has taken a much more activist stance against unions than during the previous years of union growth.

To some extent, unions may be a victim of their own successes. Because unions emphasized helping workers obtain higher wages, shorter working hours, job security, and safe-working conditions from their employers, some believe that one cause for the decline of unions has been their success in getting their important issues passed into law for everyone. Therefore, unions are not as necessary for many workers, even though they enjoy the results of past union efforts to influence legislation.

A look at Figure 11.1 reveals that non-governmental union members are heavily concentrated in transportation, utilities, and other "industrial" jobs. Unions also have targeted workers in the technology industry, specifically those

FIGURE 11.1 Union Membership by Industry

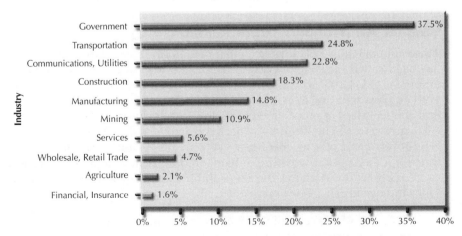

Source: U.S. Department of Labor. Bureau of Labor Statistics.

in the dot.coms such as Amazon.com, Webvan, and other firms. However, the collapse of many dot.coms in 2000–2001 made unionization less likely.[3]

The History of American Unions

The evolution of the union movement in the United States began with early collective efforts by workers to address job concerns and counteract management power. As early as 1794, shoemakers organized a union, picketed, and conducted strikes. However, in those days, unions in the United States received little support from the courts. In 1806, when the shoemaker's union struck for higher wages, a Philadelphia court found union members guilty of engaging in a "criminal conspiracy" to raise wages.

The right to organize workers and engage in collective bargaining offers little value if workers cannot freely exercise it. Historical evidence shows that management consistently has developed practices calculated to prevent workers from using this right. Over a period of many years the federal government has taken action to both hamper unions and protect them.

BASIC LABOR LAW: THE "NATIONAL LABOR CODE"

The economic crises of the early 1930s and the restrictions on workers' ability to organize into unions led to the passage of landmark labor legislation allowing them to do so. Later acts reflected other pressures and issues that required legislative attention. Together, the following three acts, passed over a period of almost 25 years, comprise what has been labeled the "National Labor Code": (1) the Wagner Act, (2) the Taft-Hartley Act, and (3) the Landrum-Griffin Act. Each act was passed to focus on some facet of the relationships between unions and management.

Wagner Act (National Labor Relations Act)

The National Labor Relations Act, more commonly referred to as the Wagner Act, has been called the Magna Carta of labor and was, by anyone's standards, prounion. Passed in 1935, the Wagner Act was an outgrowth of the Great Depression. With employers having to close or cut back their operations, workers were left with little job security. Unions stepped in to provide a feeling of solidarity and strength for many workers. The Wagner Act declared, in effect, that the official policy of the U.S. government was to encourage collective bargaining. Specifically, it established workers' right to organize unhampered by management interference.

To protect union rights, the act prohibited employers from undertaking the following five unfair labor practices:

▶ Interfering with, restraining, or coercing employees in the exercise of their right to organize or to bargain collectively
▶ Dominating or interfering with the formation or administration of any labor organization

▶ Encouraging or discouraging membership in any labor organization by discriminating with regard to hiring, tenure, or conditions of employment

▶ Discharging or otherwise discriminating against an employee because he or she filed charges or gave testimony under the act

▶ Refusing to bargain collectively with representatives of the employees

Another key part of the Wagner Act established the National Labor Relations Board (NLRB) as an independent entity to enforce the provisions of the act. The NLRB administers all provisions of the Wagner Act and subsequent labor relations acts. Primary functions of the NLRB include conducting unionization elections, investigating complaints by employers or unions through its fact-finding process, issuing opinions on its findings, and prosecuting violations in court. The five members of the NLRB serve staggered terms; they are appointed by the President of the United States and confirmed by the U.S. Senate.

Taft-Hartley Act (Labor-Management Relations Act)

The passage in 1947 of the Labor-Management Relations Act, better known as the Taft-Hartley Act, addressed the concerns of many who felt that unions had become too strong. As an attempt to balance the collective bargaining equation, this act was designed to offset the pro-union Wagner Act by limiting union actions; therefore, it was considered to be pro-management and became the second part of the National Labor Code.

The new law amended or qualified in some respect all of the major provisions of the Wagner Act and established an entirely new code of conduct for unions. The Taft-Hartley Act forbade unions from a series of unfair labor practices, much like those prohibited by management. Coercion, discrimination against non-members, refusing to bargain, excessive membership fees, and other practices were not allowed by unions. A 1974 amendment extended coverage of the Taft-Hartley Act to private, non-profit hospitals and nursing homes.

National Emergency Strikes. The Taft-Hartley Act allows the President of the United States to declare that a strike presents a national emergency. A **national emergency strike** is one that would impact an industry or a major part of it in such a way that the national economy would be significantly affected.

Right-to-Work Provision. One specific provision of the Taft-Hartley Act, Section 14(b), deserves special explanation. This section allows states to pass laws that restrict compulsory union membership. Accordingly, some states have passed **right-to-work laws**, which prohibit requiring employees to join unions as a condition of obtaining or continuing employment. The laws were so named because they allow a person the right to work without having to join a union.

Landrum-Griffin Act (Labor-Management Reporting and Disclosure Act)

The third segment of the National Labor Code, the Landrum-Griffin Act, was passed in 1959. A congressional committee investigating the Teamsters Union found corruption in the union. The law was passed to protect the rights of individual union members against such practices. Under the Landrum-Griffin Act, unions are required to have bylaws, make financial reports, and provide union members with a bill of rights. It also appointed the Secretary of Labor to act as a watchdog of union conduct. Because a union is supposed to be a democratic institution in which union members vote on and elect officers and approve labor contracts, the Landrum-Griffin Act was passed in part to ensure that the federal government protects those democratic rights.

In a few instances, union officers have attempted to maintain their jobs by physically harassing or attacking individuals who have tried to oust them from office. In other cases, union officials have "milked" pension fund monies for their own use. Such instances are not typical of most unions, but illustrate the need for legislative oversight to protect individual union members.

Civil Service Reform Act of 1978

Passed as part of the Civil Service Reform Act of 1978, the Federal Service Labor-Management Relations statute made major changes in how the federal government deals with unions. The act also identified areas subject to bargaining. For example, as a result of the law, wages and benefits are not subject to bargaining. Instead, they are set by congressional actions.

The act established the Federal Labor Relations Authority (FLRA) as an independent agency similar to the NLRB. The FLRA, a three-member body appointed on a bipartisan basis, was given authority to oversee and administer union-management relations in the federal government and to investigate unfair practices in union organizing efforts.

THE PROCESS OF UNIONIZING

The process of unionizing an employer may begin in one of two primary ways: (1) union targeting of an industry or company, or (2) employees requesting union representation. In the former case, the local or national union identifies a firm or industry in which it believes unionization can succeed. The logic for targeting is that if the union succeeds in one firm or a portion of the industry, then many other workers in the industry will be more willing to consider unionizing.

The second impetus for union organizing occurs when individual workers in an employer contact a union and express a desire to unionize. The employees themselves—or the union—then may begin to campaign to win support among the other employees.

Employers may make strategic decisions and take aggressive steps to remain non-union. Such a choice is perfectly rational, but may require some specific HR policies and philosophies to accomplish. "Preventative" employee relations may emphasize good morale and loyalty based on concern for employees, competitive wages and benefits, a fair system for dealing with employee complaints, and safe working conditions. Other issues may also play a part in employees' decisions to stay non-union, but if employers adequately address the points just listed, fewer workers are likely to feel the need for a union to represent them.

Once unionizing efforts begin, all activities must conform to the requirements established by applicable labor laws. Both management and the unions must adhere to those requirements, or the results of the effort can be appealed to the NLRB and overturned. With those requirements in mind, the union can embark on the typical union organizing process, as outlined in Figure 11.2.

Organizing Campaign

Like other entities seeking members, a union usually mounts an organized campaign to persuade individuals to support its efforts. This persuasion takes many forms, including personally contacting employees outside of work, mailing materials to employees' homes, inviting employees to attend special meetings away from the company, and publicizing the advantages of union membership. Brochures, leaflets, and circulars can be passed out to employees as they leave work, mailed to their homes, or even attached to their vehicles, as long as they comply with the rules established by laws and the NLRB.

FIGURE 11.2   Typical Unionization Process

Authorization Cards

A **union authorization card** is signed by an employee to designate a union as his or her collective bargaining agent. At least 30% of the employees in the targeted group must sign authorization cards before an election can be called. In reality, the fact that an employee signs an authorization card does not mean that the employee is in favor of a union; it means only that he or she would like the opportunity to vote on having one. Employees who do not want a union still might sign authorization cards because they want management to know they are disgruntled.

Representation Election

An election to determine whether a union will represent the employees is supervised by the NLRB for private-sector organizations and by other legal bodies for public-sector organizations. If two unions are attempting to represent the same employees, the employees will have three choices: union A, union B, or no union.

Unfair Labor Practices. Employers and unions engage in a number of activities before an election. Both the Wagner Act and the Taft-Hartley Act place restrictions on these activities. Various tactics may be used by management representatives in attempting to defeat a unionization effort. Such tactics often begin when union publicity appears or during the distribution of authorization cards. Some employers hire experts who specialize in combating unionization efforts. Using these "union busters," as they are called by unions, appears to enhance employers' chances of winning the representation election. For example, Wal-Mart uses aggressive tactics to avoid unionization by employees.

Election Process. Assuming an election is held, the union need receive only the votes of a *majority of those voting* in the election. For example, if a group of 200 employees is the identified unit, and only 50 people vote, only 50% of the employees voting plus one (in this case, 26) would need to vote yes in order for the union to be named as the representative of all 200 employees. Over the past few years, unions have won representation elections about 50% of the time.[4]

Certification and Decertification

Official certification of a union as the legal representative for employees is given by the NLRB (or by the equivalent body for public-sector organizations). Once certified, the union attempts to negotiate a contract with the employer. The employer *must* bargain, because refusing to bargain with a certified union constitutes an unfair labor practice. Newly certified unions are given up to a year before decertification can be attempted by workers in the bargaining unit.

When members no longer wish to be represented by the union, they can use the election process also. Similar to the unionization process, **decertification** is a process whereby a union is removed as the representative of a group of employees. Employees attempting to oust a union must obtain decertification authorization cards signed by at least 30% of the employees in the bargaining unit before an election may be called. If a majority of those voting in the election want to remove the union, the decertification effort succeeds.

Contract Negotiation (Collective Bargaining)

Collective bargaining, the last step in unionization, is the process whereby representatives of management and workers negotiate over wages, hours, and other terms and conditions of employment. This give-and-take process between representatives of two organizations attempts to establish conditions beneficial to both. It is also a relationship based on relative power.

The power relationship in collective bargaining involves conflict, and the threat of conflict seems necessary to maintain the relationship. But perhaps the most significant aspect of collective bargaining is that it is a continuing relationship that does not end immediately after agreement is reached. Instead, it continues for the life of the labor agreement and beyond. Therefore, the more cooperative the attitude that management takes, the less hostility and conflict with unionized employees carries over to the workplace.[5] However, this cooperation does not mean that the employer gives in to all union demands.

A major concern of union representatives when bargaining is the negotiation of **union security provisions**, which are contract clauses to aid the union in obtaining and retaining members. One union security provision is the *dues checkoff,* which provides for the automatic deduction of union dues from the payroll checks of union members. The dues checkoff makes it much easier for the union to collect its funds; otherwise it must collect dues by billing each member separately.

THE BARGAINING PROCESS

The collective bargaining process consists of a number of stages: preparation, initial demands, negotiations, settlement or impasse, and strikes or lockouts.

Preparation and Initial Demands

Both labor and management representatives spend much time preparing for negotiations. Employer and industry data concerning wages, benefits, working conditions, management and union rights, productivity, and absenteeism are gathered. If the organization argues that it cannot afford to pay what the union is asking, the employer's financial situation and accompanying data become all the more relevant. However, the union must request such information before the employer is obligated to provide it. Typical bargaining includes initial proposals of expectations by both sides. The amount of rancor or calmness exhibited may set the tone for future negotiations between the parties.

Continuing Negotiations

After taking initial positions, each side attempts to determine what the other side values highly so the best bargain can be struck. For example, the union may be asking the employer to pay for dental benefits as part of a package that also includes wage increases and retirement benefits. Provisions in federal law require that both employers and union bargaining representatives negotiate in good faith. In good-faith negotiations, the parties agree to send negotiators who can bargain and make decisions, rather than people who do not have the authority to commit either group to a decision.

Settlement and Contract Agreement

After reaching an initial agreement, the bargaining parties usually return to their respective constituencies to determine if the informal agreement is acceptable. A particularly crucial stage is **ratification** of the labor agreement, which occurs when union members vote to accept the terms of a negotiated agreement. Prior to the ratification vote, the union negotiating team explains the agreement to the union members and presents it for a vote. If the members approve the agreement, it is then formalized into a contract. Figure 11.3 lists typical items in labor agreements.

Bargaining Impasse

Regardless of the structure of the bargaining process, labor and management do not always reach agreement on the issues. If impasse occurs, then the disputes can be taken to conciliation, mediation, or arbitration.

FIGURE 11.3   Typical Items in a Labor Agreement

Labor Agreement

1. Purpose of agreement
2. Nondiscrimination clause
3. Management rights
4. Recognition of the union
5. Wages
6. Incentives
7. Hours of work
8. Vacations
9. Sick leave and leaves of absence
10. Discipline
11. Separation allowance
12. Seniority
13. Bulletin boards
14. Pension and insurance
15. Safety
16. Grievance procedure
17. No-strike or lockout clause
18. Definitions
19. Terms of contract (dates)
20. Appendices

Conciliation and Mediation. When an impasse occurs, an outside party such as the Federal Mediation and Conciliation Service may aid the two deadlocked parties to continue negotiations and arrive at a solution. In **conciliation**, the third party attempts to keep union and management negotiators talking so that they can reach a voluntary settlement, but makes no proposals for solutions. In **mediation**, the third party assists the negotiators in reaching a settlement.

Arbitration. The process of **arbitration** uses a neutral third party to make a decision. It can be conducted by either an individual or a panel of individuals. Arbitration attempts to solve bargaining impasses.

Strikes and Lockouts

If a deadlock cannot be resolved, then an employer may resort to a lockout—or a union may choose to strike. During a **strike**, union members refuse to work in order to put pressure on an employer. Often, the striking union members picket or demonstrate against the employer outside the place of business by carrying placards and signs. In a **lockout**, management shuts down company operations to prevent union members from working. This action may avert possible damage or sabotage to company facilities or injury to employees who continue to work.

Management retains and sometimes uses its ability to simply replace workers who strike. Workers' rights vary depending on the type of strike that occurs. For example, in an economic strike, an employer is free to replace the striking workers. But with an unfair labor practices strike, workers who want their jobs back at the end of the strike must be reinstated.

UNION-MANAGEMENT COOPERATION

The adversarial relationship that naturally exists between unions and management may seem to encourage strikes and lockouts. However, such conflicts are relatively rare. Even more encouraging is the growing recognition on the part of union leaders and employer representatives that cooperation between management and labor unions offers the most sensible route if organizations are going to compete effectively in a global economy.

Cooperation and Joint Efforts

A number of notable examples illustrate successful union-management cooperation. One of the most frequently cited examples is at Saturn Corporation, a part of General Motors. There union-management cooperation was established when the Tennessee plant was built, and it survived a number of challenges and changes for more than a decade.[6] Other firms with successful union-management cooperation include Ford Motor and Boeing, although conflicts in these relationships occasionally arise.

Employee Involvement Program

Suggesting that union-management cooperation or involving employees in making suggestions and decisions could be bad seems a little illogical. Yet some decisions by the NLRB appear to have done just that. Some historical perspective is required to understand the issues that surrounded the decisions.

In the 1930s, when the Wagner Act was written, certain employers would form sham "company unions," coercing workers into joining them in order to keep legitimate unions from organizing the employees. As a result, the Wagner Act contained prohibitions against employer-dominated labor organizations. These prohibitions were enforced, and company unions disappeared. But the growing use of employee involvement programs in organizations today have raised new concerns.

Because of the Wagner Act, many employee involvement programs set up in recent years may be illegal, according to an NLRB decision dealing with Electromation, an Elkhart, Indiana, firm. Electromation used teams of employees to solicit other employees' views about such issues as wages and working conditions. The NLRB labeled them as "labor organizations," according to the Wagner Act in 1935. It further found that the teams were "dominated" by management, which formed the teams, set their goals, and decided how they would operate. The result of this and other decisions forced many employers to rethink and restructure their employee involvement efforts.

GRIEVANCE MANAGEMENT

Unions know that employee dissatisfaction is a potential source of trouble for employers, whether it is expressed or not. Hidden dissatisfaction grows and creates reactions that may be completely out of proportion to the original concerns. Therefore, it is important that dissatisfaction be given an outlet. A **complaint**, which is merely an indication of employee dissatisfaction, is one outlet.

If the employee is represented by a union, and the employee says, "I should have received the job transfer because I have more seniority, which is what the union contract states," and she submits it in writing, then that complaint becomes a grievance. A **grievance** is a complaint formally stated in writing. Management should be concerned with both complaints and grievances, because both indicate potential problems within the workforce. Without a grievance procedure, management may be unable to respond to employee concerns because managers are unaware of them. Therefore, a formal grievance procedure provides a valuable communication tool for the organization.

Grievance Procedures

Grievance procedures are formal communications channels designed to settle grievances as soon as possible after the problem arises. First-line supervisors are usually closest to a problem; however, the supervisor is concerned with many other matters besides one employee's grievance, and may even be the subject of an employee's grievance. So, to receive the appropriate attention, grievances go through a specific process for resolution.

Steps in a Grievance Procedure

Grievance procedures can vary in the number of steps they include. A typical grievance procedure includes the following steps:

1. The employee discusses the grievance with the union steward (the union's representative on the job) and the supervisor.
2. The union steward discusses the grievance with the supervisor's manager.
3. The union grievance committee discusses the grievance with appropriate company managers.
4. The representative of the national union discusses the grievance with designated company executives.
5. The final step may be to use an impartial third party for ultimate disposition of the grievance.

If the grievance remains unsettled, representatives for both sides would continue to meet to resolve the conflict. On rare occasions, a representative from the national union might join the process. Or, a corporate executive from headquarters (if the firm is a large corporation) might be called in to help resolve the grievance. If not solved at this stage, the grievance goes to arbitration.

Grievance arbitration is a means by which a third party settles disputes arising from different interpretations of a labor contract. This process should not be confused with contract or issues arbitration, in which arbitration is used to determine how a contract will be written. The U.S. Supreme Court has ruled that grievance arbitration decisions issued under labor contract provisions are enforceable.[7] The subjects of grievance arbitration include more than 50 different topic areas, with discipline and discharge, safety and health, and security issues being more prevalent.

Global Labor-Management Relations

In some countries, unions either do not exist at all or are relatively weak. Such is the case in China and a number of African countries. In other countries, unions are extremely strong and are closely tied to political parties. For instance, in Italy national strikes occur regularly to protest proposed government policy changes on retirement, pension programs, and regulations regarding dismissal of employees. The strength and nature of unions differ from country to country.

Some countries require that firms have union or worker representatives on their boards of directors. This practice, called **co-determination**, is common in European countries. Differences from country to country in how collective bargaining occurs also are quite noticeable. In the United States, local unions bargain with individual employers to set wages and working conditions. In Australia, unions argue their cases before arbitration tribunals. In Scandanavia, national agreements with associations of employers are the norm. In France and Germany, industry-wide or regional agreements are common. In Japan, local unions bargain but combine at some point to determine national wage patterns.

Another type of employment regulations involves worker consultation requirements. The EU requires that firms with 50 or more employees consult with workers (and their union representatives) before laying off employees, relocating facilities and operations, or engaging in corporate restructuring actions. These regulations apply in all EU countries except the United Kingdom and Ireland, who received exemptions for seven years.

NOTES

1. Barry T. Hirsch and David A. MacPherson, *Union Membership and Earnings Data Book,* (Washington, DC: BNA Plus, 2001).
2. U.S. Department of Labor, Bureau of Labor Statistics, 2002.
3. Katherine Pflegler, "Unions Striking Out in High-Tech Sector," *Omaha World-Herald,* February 4, 2001, 1G; and Nick Wingfield and Yochi J. Dreazen, "Dot.Com Rout Is a Mixed Blessing for Unionizers," *The Wall Street Journal,* January 2, 2001, A9.
4. "Union Organizing," *Bulletin to Management,* December 21, 2000, 405.
5. Gillian Flynn, "When the Unions Come Calling," *Workforce,* November 2000, 82–87.
6. Saul R. Rubinstein, "A Different Kind of Union: Balancing Co-Management and Representation," *Industrial Relations,* 40 (2001), 163–203.
7. *Eastern Associated Coal Co. vs. United Mine Workers of America,* U.S. S. Ct. 99-1038, November 28, 2000.

INTERNET RESEARCH

LaborNet This site describes unions, news, legislation, and upcoming union events. **http://www.labornet.org**

AFL-CIO The AFL-CIO's homepage provides union movement information. **http://www.aflcio.org**

SUGGESTED READINGS

T. O. Collier, *Supervisor's Guide to Labor Relations,* SHRM, 2001.

Court D. Gifford, *Directing of U.S. Labor Organizations,* Bureau of National Affairs, 2003.

William H. Holley, Kenneth M. Jennings, and Roger S. Wolters, *The Labor Relations Process,* 7th ed. South-Western Thomson Learning, 2001.

William W. Osborne, Jr., *Labor Union Law and Regulation,* Bureau of National Affairs, 2003.

Appendix A

Human Resource Certification Institute Test Specifications*

The two levels of certification are the Professional in Human Resources (PHR) and the Senior Professional in Human Resources (SPHR). Two different exams are used for certification testing. PHR questions tend to be at an operational/technical level, whereas SPHR questions tend to be more at the strategic and/or policy level.

Examination questions for both levels cover a wide range of topics. Each multiple choice exam consists of 200 scored questions plus 25 pretest questions for a total of 225 questions. Pretest questions are not counted in the scoring of the examination and are used for statistical purposes only. Each question lists *four possible answers*, only one of which is correct.

ITEM CLASSIFICATION SCHEME

The test specifications identify six functional areas. After each major functional area are the weightings for that area. **The first number in the parentheses is the PHR percentage weighting and the second number is the SPHR percentage weighting.** Within each area *responsibilities* and *knowledge* topics are specified.

* © Human Resource Certification Institute. Used with permission. For more information, go to http://www.hrci.org.

FUNCTIONAL AREA:

01 STRATEGIC MANAGEMENT (12%, 26%)

The processes and activities used to formulate HR objectives, practices, and policies to meet the short- and long-range organizational needs and opportunities, to guide and lead the change process, and to evaluate HR's contributions to organizational effectiveness.

Responsibilities:

Interpret information related to the organization's operations from internal sources, including financial/accounting, marketing, operations, information technology, and individual employees, in order to participate in strategic planning and policy making.

01 Interpret information related to the general business environment, industry practices and developments, and technological developments from external sources (for example, publications, government documents, media, and trade organizations), in order to participate in strategic planning and policy making.

03 Participate as a partner in the organization's strategic planning process.

04 Establish strategic relationships with individuals in the organization, to influence organizational decision-making.

05 Establish relationships/alliances with key individuals in the community and in professional capacities to assist in meeting the organization's strategic needs.

06 Evaluate HR's contribution to organizational effectiveness, including assessment, design, implementation, and evaluation of activities with respect to strategic and organizational measurement in HR objectives. *(** 06 refers to participation in change management)*

07 Provide direction and guidance during changes in organizational processes, operations, planning, intervention, leadership training and culture that balances the expectations and needs of the organization, its employees, and other stakeholders (including customers). *(** 07 refers to participation in change management)*

08 Develop and shape organizational policy related to the organization's management of its human resources.

09 Cultivate leadership and ethical values in self and others through modeling and teaching.

10 Provide information for the organizational budgeting process, including budget development and review.

11 Monitor legislative environment for proposed changes in law and take appropriate action to support, modify, or stop the proposed action (for example, write to a member of Congress, provide expert testimony at a public hearing, lobby legislators).

Knowledge of:

01 lawmaking and administrative regulatory processes

02 internal and external environmental scanning techniques

03 strategic planning process and implementation

04 organizational social responsibility (for example, welfare to work, philanthropy, alliances with community-based organizations)

05 management functions, including planning, organizing, directing, and controlling

06 techniques to sustain creativity and innovation

FUNCTIONAL AREA:

02 WORKFORCE PLANNING AND EMPLOYMENT (26%, 16%)

The processes of planning, developing, implementing, administering, and performing ongoing evaluation of recruiting, hiring, orientation, and organizational exit to ensure that the workforce will meet the organization's goals and objectives.

Responsibilities:

01 Identify staffing requirements to meet the goals and objectives of the organization.

02 Conduct job analyses to write job descriptions and develop job competencies.

03 Identify and document the essential job functions for positions.

04 Establish hiring criteria based on the competencies needed.

05 Assess internal workforce, labor market, and recruitment agencies to determine the availability of qualified applicants.

06 Identify internal and external recruitment methods and implement them within the context of the organization's goals and objectives.

07 Develop strategies to market the organization to potential applicants.

08 Establish selection procedures, including interviewing, testing, and reference and background checking.

09 Implement selection procedures, including interviewing, testing, and reference and background checking.

10 Develop and/or extend employment offers.

11 Perform or administer post-offer employment activities (for example, employment agreements, completion of I-9 verification form, relocation agreements, and medical examinations).

12 Facilitate and/or administer the process by which non-US citizens can legally work in the United States.

13 Design, facilitate, and/or conduct the orientation process, including review of performance standards for new hires and transfers.

14 Evaluate selection and employment processes for effectiveness and implement changes if indicated (for example, employee retention).

15 Develop a succession planning process.

16 Develop and implement the organizational exit process, including unemployment insurance claim responses. *(includes severance, turnover and outplacement)*

17 Develop, implement, manage, and evaluate affirmative action program(s), as may be required.

Knowledge of:

07 federal/state/local employment-related laws (for example, Title VII, ADA, ADEA, Vietnam Veterans, WARN) and regulations (for example, EEOC Uniform Guidelines on Employee Selection Procedures)

08 immigration law (for example, visas, I-9)

09 quantitative analyses required to assess past and future staffing (for example, cost benefit analysis, costs-per-hire, selection ratios, adverse impact)

10 recruitment methods and sources

11 staffing alternatives (for example, telecommuting, outsourcing)

12 planning techniques (for example, succession planning, forecasting)

13 reliability and validity of selection tests/tools/methods

14 use and interpretation of selection tests (for example, psychological/personality, cognitive, and motor/physical assessments)

15 interviewing techniques

16 relocation practices

17 impact of compensation and benefits plans on recruitment and retention

18 international HR and implications of international workforce for workforce planning and employment

19 downsizing and outplacement

20 internal workforce planning and employment policies, practices, and procedures

FUNCTIONAL AREA:

03 HUMAN RESOURCE DEVELOPMENT (15%, 13%)

The processes of ensuring that the skills, knowledge, abilities, and performance of the workforce meet the current and future organizational and individual needs through developing, implementing, and evaluating activities and programs addressing employee training and development, change and performance management, and the unique needs of particular employee groups.

Responsibilities:

01 Conduct needs analyses to identify and establish priorities regarding human resource development activities.

02 Develop training programs.

03 Implement training programs.

04 Evaluate training programs.

05 Develop programs to assess employees' potential for growth and development in the organization.

06 Implement programs to assess employees' potential for growth and development in the organization.

07 Evaluate programs to assess employees' potential for growth and development in the organization.

08 Develop change management programs and activities.

09 Implement change management programs and activities.

10 Evaluate change management programs and activities.

11 Develop performance management programs and procedures.

12 Implement performance management programs and procedures.

13 Evaluate performance management programs and procedures.

14 Develop programs to meet the unique needs of particular employees (for example, work-family programs, diversity programs, outplacement programs, repatriation programs, and fast-track programs).

15 Implement programs to meet the unique needs of particular employees (for example, work-family programs, diversity programs, outplacement programs, repatriation programs, and fast-track programs).

16 Evaluate programs to meet the unique needs of particular employees (for example, work-family programs, diversity programs, outplacement programs, repatriation programs, and fast-track programs).

Knowledge of:

21 applicable international, federal, state, and local laws and regulations regarding copyrights and patents

22 human resource development theories and applications (including career development and leadership development)

23 organizational development theories and applications

24 training methods, programs, and techniques *(design, objectives, methods, etc.)*

25 employee involvement strategies

26 task/process analysis

27 performance appraisal and performance management methods

28 applicable international issues (for example, culture, local management approaches/ practices, societal norms)

29 instructional methods and program delivery *(content, building modules of program, selection of presentation/delivery mechanism)*

30 techniques to assess HRD program effectiveness (for example, satisfaction, learning and job performance of program participants, and organizational outcomes such as turnover and productivity)

FUNCTIONAL AREA:

04 COMPENSATION AND BENEFITS (20%, 16%)

The processes of analyzing, developing, implementing, administering, and performing ongoing evaluation of a total compensation and benefits system for all employee groups consistent with human resource management goals.

Responsibilities:

01 Ensure the compliance of compensation and benefits with applicable federal, state, and local laws. *(includes IRS Rulings, strict definitions of which tend to go more with K-31; applications/calculations/ interpretations of those rulings tend to go more with K-32)*

02 Analyze, develop, implement, and maintain compensation policies and a pay structure consistent with the organization's strategic objectives. *(includes broad definitions and designs)*

03 Analyze and evaluate pay rates based on internal

worth and external market conditions. *(includes wage and salary surveys)*

04 Develop/select and implement a payroll system.

05 Administer payroll functions.

06 Evaluate compensation policies to ensure that they are positioning the organization internally and externally according to the organization's strategic objectives. *(0406 refers to 'tweaking,' 'refinement,' or 'alterations;' turnover issues related to compensation also belong under this responsibility)*

07 Conduct a benefit plan needs assessment and determine/select the plans to be offered, considering the organization's strategic objectives. *(0407 addresses more specific definitions and plan design issues; includes 401K; tends to go more with K-38)*

08 Implement and administer benefit plans. *(addresses more the carrying out the objectives of the benefit plan; tends to go more with K-39)*

09 Evaluate benefits program to ensure that it is positioning the organization internally and externally according to the organization's strategic objectives. *(refers more to evaluation and tweaking of the benefit plan; tends to go more with K-38)*

10 Analyze, select, implement, maintain, and administer executive compensation, stock purchase, stock options, and incentive, and bonus programs. *(includes profit-sharing)*

11 Analyze, develop, select, maintain, and implement expatriate and foreign national compensation and benefit programs.

12 Communicate the compensation and benefits plan and policies to the workforce.

Knowledge of:

31 federal, state, and local compensation and benefit laws (for example, FLSA, ERISA, COBRA)

32 accounting practices related to compensation and benefits (for example, excess group term life, compensatory time)

33 job evaluation methods

34 job pricing and pay structures

35 incentive and variable pay methods

36 executive compensation

37 non-cash compensation methods (for example, stock option plans)

38 benefits needs analysis

39 benefit plans (for example, health insurance, life insurance, pension, education, health club)

40 international compensation laws and practices (for example, expatriate compensation, socialized medicine, mandated retirement)

FUNCTIONAL AREA:

05 EMPLOYEE AND LABOR RELATIONS (21%, 24%)

The processes of analyzing, developing, implementing, administering, and performing ongoing evaluation of the workplace relationship between employer and employee (including the collective bargaining process and union relations), in order to maintain effective relationships and working conditions that balance the employer's needs with the employees' rights in support of the organization's strategic objectives.

Responsibilities:

01 Ensure compliance with all applicable federal, state, and local laws and regulations. *(catch-all responsibility, including NLRB, ADA, FMLA)*

02 Develop and implement employee relations programs that will create a positive organizational culture. *(most of the legal definitions and general definitions)*

03 Promote, monitor, and measure the effectiveness of employee relations activities.

04 Assist in establishing work rules and monitor their application and enforcement to ensure fairness and consistency (for union and non-union environments).

05 Communicate and ensure understanding by employees of laws, regulations, and organizational policies.

06 Resolve employee complaints filed with federal, state, and local agencies involving employment practices. *(formal, legal complaints)*

07 Develop grievance and disciplinary policies and procedures to ensure fairness and consistency.

08 Implement and monitor grievance and disciplinary policies and procedures to ensure fairness and consistency. *(includes investigation)*

09 Respond to union organizing activity.

10 Participate in collective bargaining activities, including contract negotiation and administration.

Knowledge of:

41 applicable federal, state, and local laws affecting employment in union and non-union environments, such as anti-discrimination laws, sexual harassment, labor relations, and privacy

42 techniques for facilitating positive employee relations (for example, small group facilitation, dispute resolution, and labor/management cooperative strategies and programs)

43 employee involvement strategies (for example, alternate work schedules, work teams)

44 individual employment rights issues and practices (for example, employment at will, negligent hiring, defamation, employees' rights to bargain collectively)

45 workplace behavior issues/practices (for example, absenteeism, discipline)

46 methods for assessment of employee attitudes, opinions, and satisfaction (for example, opinion surveys, attitude surveys, focus panels)

47 unfair labor practices

48 the collective bargaining process, strategies, and concepts *(up to and after contract)*

49 public sector labor relations issues and practices

50 expatriation and repatriation issues and practices

51 employee and labor relations for local nationals (i.e., labor relations in other countries)

FUNCTIONAL AREA:

06 OCCUPATIONAL HEALTH, SAFETY, AND SECURITY (6%, 5%)

The processes of analyzing, developing, implementing, administering, and performing ongoing evaluation of programs, practices, and services to promote the physical and mental well-being of individuals in the workplace, and to protect individuals and the workplace from unsafe acts, unsafe working conditions, and violence.

Responsibilities:

01 Ensure compliance with all applicable federal, state, and local workplace health and safety laws and regulations.
02 Determine safety programs needed for the organization.
03 Develop and/or select injury/occupational illness prevention programs.
04 Implement injury/occupational illness prevention programs.
05 Develop and/or select safety training and incentive programs.
06 Implement safety training and incentive programs.
07 Evaluate the effectiveness of safety prevention, training, and incentive programs.
08 Implement workplace injury/occupational illness procedures (for example, worker's compensation, OSHA).
09 Determine health and wellness programs needed for the organization.
10 Develop/select, implement, and evaluate (or make available) health and wellness programs.
11 Develop/select, implement, and evaluate security plans to protect the company from liability.
12 Develop/select, implement, and evaluate security plans to protect employees (for example, injuries resulting from workplace violence).
13 Develop/select, implement, and evaluate incident and emergency response plans (for example, natural disasters, workplace safety threats, evacuation).

Knowledge of:

52 federal, state, and local workplace health and safety laws and regulations (for example, OSHA, Drug-Free Workplace Act, ADA)
53 workplace injury and occupational illness compensation laws and programs (for example, worker's compensation)
54 investigation procedures of workplace safety, health, and security enforcement agencies (for example, OSHA)
55 workplace safety risks
56 workplace security risks (for example, theft, corporate espionage, information systems/technology, and vandalism)
57 potential violent behavior and workplace violence conditions
58 general health and safety practices (for example, fire evacuation, HAZCOM, ergonomic evaluations)
59 incident and emergency response plans
60 internal investigation and surveillance techniques
61 Employee Assistance Programs
62 employee wellness programs
63 issues related to chemical use and dependency (for example, identification of symptoms, drug testing, discipline)

CORE Knowledge Required by HR Professionals

64 needs assessment and analysis
65 third-party contract management, including development of requests for proposals (RFPs)
66 communication strategies
67 documentation requirements
68 adult learning processes
69 motivation concepts and applications
70 training methods
71 leadership concepts and applications
72 project management concepts and applications
73 diversity concepts and applications
74 human relations concepts and applications (for example, interpersonal and organizational behavior)
75 HR ethics and professional standards
76 technology and human resource information systems (HRIS) to support HR activities
77 qualitative and quantitative methods and tools for analysis, interpretation, and decision-making purposes
78 change management
79 liability and risk management
80 job analysis and job description methods
81 employee records management (for example, retention, disposal)
82 the interrelationships among HR activities and programs across functional areas

Appendix B

Major Federal Equal Employment Opportunity Laws and Regulations

Act	Year	Key Provisions
Broad-Based Discrimination		
Title VII, Civil Rights Act of 1964	1964	*Prohibits discrimination in employment on basis of race, color, religion, sex or national origin.*
Executives Orders 11246 and 11375	1965 1967	*Require federal contractors and subcontractors to eliminate employment discrimination and prior discrimination through affirmative action.*
Executive Order 11478	1969	*Prohibits discrimination in the U.S. Postal Service and in the various government agencies on the basis of race, color, religion, sex, national origin, handicap, or age.*
Vietnam-Era Veterans Readjustment Act	1974	*Prohibits discriminations against Vietnam-era veterans by federal contractors and the U.S. government and requires affirmative action.*
Civil Rights Act of 1991	1991	*Overturns several past Supreme Court decisions and changes damage claims provisions.*
Congressional Accountability Act	1995	*Extends EEO and Civil Rights Act provisions to U.S. congressional staff.*
Race/National Origin Discrimination		
Immigration Reform and Control Act	1986 1990 1996	*Establishes penalties for employers who knowingly hire illegal aliens; prohibits employment discrimination on the basis of national origin or citizenship.*

Gender/Sex Discrimination

Equal Pay Act	*1963*	*Requires equal pay for men and women performing substantially the same work.*
Pregnancy Discrimination Act	*1978*	*Prohibits discrimination against women affected by pregnancy, childbirth, or related medical conditions; requires that they be treated as all other employees for employment-related purposes, including benefits.*

Age Discrimination

Age Discrimination in Employment	*1967*	*Prohibits discrimination against persons over age 40 and restricts mandatory retirement requirements, except where age is a bona fide occupational qualification.*
Older Workers Benefit Protection Act of 1990	*1990*	*Prohibits age-based discrimination in early retirement and other benefits plans.*

Disability Discrimination

Vocational Rehabilitation Act	*1973*	*Prohibit employers with federal contracts over $2,500 from discriminating against individuals with disabilities.*
Rehabilitation Act of 1974	*1974*	
Americans with Disabilities Act	*1990*	*Requires employer accommodations for individuals with disabilities.*

Appendix C

Guidelines to Lawful and Unlawful Pre-Employment Inquiries

Subject of Inquiry	It May Not Be Discriminatory to Inquire About	It May Be Discriminatory to Inquire About
1. Name	a. Whether applicant has ever worked under a different name	a. The original name of an applicant whose name has been legally changed b. The ethnic association of applicant's name
2. Age	a. If applicant is over the age of 18 b. If applicant is under the age of 18 or 21 if job related (i.e., selling liquor in retail store)	a. Date of birth b. Date of high school graduation
3. Residence	a. Applicant's place of residence b. Alternate contact information	a. Previous addresses b. Birthplace of applicant or applicant's parents c. Length of current and previous addresses
4. Race or Color		a. Applicant's race or color of applicant's skin
5. National Origin and Ancestry		a. Applicant's lineage, ancestry, national origin, parentage, or nationality b. Nationality of applicant's parents or spouse
6. Sex and Family Composition		a. Sex of applicant b. Marital status c. Dependents of applicant or child-care arrangements d. Who to contact in case of emergency
7. Creed or Religion		a. Applicant's religious affiliation b. Church, parish, mosque, synagogue c. Holidays observed

Source: Developed by Robert L. Mathis, Mathis & Associates, L.L.C., Omaha, NE 68164. All rights reserved. No part of this may be reproduced, in any form or by any means, without written permission from Mathis & Associates.

Subject of Inquiry	It May Not Be Discriminatory to Inquire About	It May Be Discriminatory to Inquire About
8. Citizenship	a. Whether the applicant is a U.S. citizen or has current permit/visa to work in U.S.	a. Whether applicant is a citizen of a country other than the U.S. b. Date of citizenship
9. Language	a. Language applicant speaks and/or writes fluently, if job related	a. Applicant's native tongue b. Language commonly used at home
10. References	a. Names of persons willing to provide professional and/or character references for applicant b. Previous work contacts	a. Name of applicant's religious leader b. Political affiliation and contacts
11. Relatives	a. Names of relatives already employed by the employer	a. Name and/or address of any relative of applicant b. Whom to contact in case of emergency
12. Organizations	a. Applicant's membership in any professional, service, or trade organization	a. All clubs or social organizations to which applicant belongs
13. Arrest Record and Convictions	a. Convictions, if related to job performance (disclaimer should accompany)	a. Number and kinds of arrests b. Convictions unless related to job performance
14. Photographs		a. Photograph with application, with resume, or before hiring
15. Height and Weight		a. Any inquiry into height and weight of applicant except where a BFOQ
16. Physical Limitations	a. Whether applicant has the ability to perform job-related functions with or without accommodation	a. The nature or severity of an illness or person's physical condition b. Whether applicant has ever filed workers' compensation claim c. Any recent or past operations or surgery and dates
17. Education	a. Training applicant has received if related to the job b. Highest level of education attained, if validated that having certain educational background (e.g., high school diploma or college degree) is necessary to perform the specific job	a. Date of high school graduation
18. Military	a. Branch of the military applicant served in and ranks attained b. Type of education or training received in military	a. Details on military service records
19. Financial Status		a. Applicant's debts or assets b. Garnishments

Appendix D

Sample Job Description and Specifications

JOB TITLE: Compensation Manager	**JOB CODE:** _____
SUPERVISOR'S TITLE: Vice President of Human Resources	**GRADE:** _____
DEPARTMENT: Human Resources	**FLSA STATUS:** Exempt
	EEOC CLASS: O/M

General Summary: Responsible for the design and administration of all cash compensation programs, ensures proper consideration of the relationship of compensation to performance of each employee, and provides consultation on compensation administration to managers and supervisors.

Essential Duties and Responsibilities:
1. Prepares and maintains job descriptions for all jobs and periodically reviews and updates them. Responds to questions from employees and supervisors regarding job descriptions. (25%)
2. Ensures that Company compensation rates are in line with pay structures. Obtains or conducts pay surveys as necessary and presents recommendations on pay structures on an annual basis. (20%)
3. Develops and administers the performance appraisal program and monitors the use of the performance appraisal instruments to ensure the integrity of the system and its proper use. (20%)
4. Directs the job evaluation process by coordinating committee activities and resolves disputes over job values. Conducts initial evaluation of new jobs prior to hiring and assigns jobs to pay ranges. (15%)
5. Researches and provides recommendations on executive compensation issues. Assists in the development and oversees the administration of all annual bonus payments for senior managers and executives. (15%)
6. Coordinates the development of an integrated HR information system and interfaces with the Management Information Systems Department to achieve departmental goals for information needs. (5%)
7. Performs related duties as assigned or as the situation dictates.

Required Knowledge, Skills, and Abilities:
1. Knowledge of compensation and HR management practices and approaches.
2. Knowledge of effective job analysis methods and survey development and interpretation practices and principles.

3. Knowledge of performance management program design and administration.
4. Knowledge of federal and state wage and hour regulations.
5. Skill in writing job descriptions, memorandums, letters, and proposals.
6. Skill in use of word processing, spreadsheet, and database software.
7. Ability to make presentations to groups on compensation policies and practices.
8. Ability to plan and prioritize work.

Education and Experience:
This position requires the equivalent of a college degree in Business Administration, Psychology, or a related field plus 3–5 years experience in HR management, 2–3 of which should include compensation administration experience. An advanced degree in Industrial Psychology, Business Administration, or HR Management is preferred, but not required.

Physical Requirements	Rarely (0–12%)	Occasionally (12–33%)	Frequently (34–66%)	Regularly (67–100%)
Seeing: Must be able to read reports and use computer				X
Hearing: Must be able to hear well enough to communicate with coworkers				X
Standing/Walking	X			
Climbing/Stooping/Kneeling	X			
Lifting/Pulling/Pushing	X			
Fingering/Grasping/Feeling: Must be able to write, type, and use phone system				X

Working Conditions: Normal office working conditions with the absence of disagreeable elements.

Note: The statements herein are intended to describe the general nature and level of work being performed by employees, and are not to be construed as an exhaustive list of responsibilities, duties, and skills required of personnel so classified. Furthermore, they do not establish a contract for employment and are subject to change at the discretion of the employer.

Glossary

Affirmative action Process in which employers identify problem areas, set goals, and take positive steps to enhance opportunities for protected-class members.

Affirmative action plan (AAP) Formal document that an employer compiles annually for submission to enforcement agencies.

Assessment center A collection of instruments and exercises designed to diagnose individuals' development needs.

Availability analysis An analysis that identifies the number of protected-class members available to work in the appropriate labor markets in given jobs.

Balance sheet approach Compensation package that equalizes cost differences between international assignments and those in the home country.

Bargaining unit Employees eligible to select a single union to represent and bargain collectively for them.

Base pay The basic compensation an employee receives, usually as a wage or salary.

Behavior modeling Copying someone else's behavior.

Behavioral interview Interview in which applicants give specific examples of how they have performed a certain task or handled a problem in the past.

Behavioral rating approach Assesses an employee's behaviors instead of other characteristics.

Benchmark job Job found in many organizations and performed by several individuals who have similar duties that are relatively stable and require similar KSAs.

Benchmarking Comparing specific measures of performance against data on those measures in other "best practice" organizations.

Benefit An indirect reward given to an employee or group of employees as a part of organizational membership.

Benefits needs analysis A comprehensive look at all aspects of benefits.

Bona fide occupational qualification (BFOQ) Characteristic providing a legitimate reason why an employer can exclude persons on otherwise illegal bases of consideration.

Bonus A one-time payment that does not become part of the employee's base pay.

Broadbanding Practice of using fewer pay grades having broader ranges than in traditional compensation systems.

Business agent A full-time union official who operates the union office and assists union members.

Business necessity A practice necessary for safe and efficient organizational operations.

Career The series of work-related positions a person occupies throughout life.

Central tendency error Rating all employees in a narrow range in the middle of the rating scale.

Checklist Performance appraisal tool that uses a list of statements or words that are checked by raters.

Closed shop A firm that requires individuals to join a union before they can be hired.

Coaching Training and feedback given to employees by immediate supervisors.

Co-determination A practice whereby union or worker representatives are given positions on a company's board of directors.

Cognitive ability tests Tests that measure an individual's thinking, memory, reasoning, and verbal and mathematical abilities.

Collective bargaining Process whereby representatives of management and workers negotiate over wages, hours, and other terms and conditions of employment.

Commission Compensation computed as a percentage of sales in units or dollars.

Compa-ratio Pay level divided by the midpoint of the pay range.

Compensable factor Identifies a job value commonly present throughout a group of jobs.

Compensation committee A subgroup of the board of directors composed of directors who are not officers of the firm.

Compensatory time off Hours given in lieu of payment for extra time worked.

Competencies Basic characteristics that can be linked to enhanced performance by individuals or teams.

Complaint Indication of employee dissatisfaction.

Compressed workweek One in which a full week's work is accomplished in fewer than five days.

Conciliation Process by which a third party attempts to keep union and management negotiators talking so that they can reach a voluntary settlement.

Concurrent validity Measured when an employer tests current employees and correlates the scores with their performance ratings.

Construct validity Validity showing a relationship between an abstract characteristic and job performance.

Constructive discharge Occurs when an employer deliberately makes conditions intolerable in an attempt to get an employee to quit.

Content validity Validity measured by use of a logical, nonstatistical method to identify the KSAs and other characteristics necessary to perform a job.

Contractual rights Rights based on a specific contractual agreement between employer and employee.

Contrast error Tendency to rate people relative to others rather than against performance standards.

Contributory plan Pension plan in which the money for pension benefits is paid in by both employees and employers.

Co-Payment Employee's payment of a portion of the cost of both insurance premiums and medical care.

Core competency A unique capability that creates high value and that differentiates the organization from its competition.

Correlation coefficient Index number giving the relationship between a predictor and a criterion variable.

Cost-benefit analysis Comparison of costs and benefits associated with training.

Craft union One whose members do one type of work, often using specialized skills and training.

Criterion-related validity Validity measured by a procedure that uses a test as the predictor of how well an individual will perform on the job.

Culture Societal forces affecting the values, beliefs, and actions of a distinct group of people.

Cumulative trauma disorders (CTDs) Muscle and skeletal injuries that occur when workers repetitively use the same muscles to perform tasks.

Decertification Process whereby a union is removed as the representative of a group of employees.

Defined-benefit plan One in which an employee is promised a pension amount based on age and service.

Defined-contribution plan One in which the employer makes an annual payment to an employee's pension account.

Development Efforts to improve employees' ability to handle a variety of assignments.

Differential piece-rate system A system in which employees are paid one piece-rate wage for units produced up to a standard output and a higher piece-rate wage for units produced over the standard.

Disabled person Someone who has a physical or mental impairment that substantially limits life activities, who has a record of such an impairment, or who is regarded as having such an impairment.

Discipline Form of training that enforces organizational rules.

Disparate impact Occurs when substantial underrepresentation of protected-class members results from employment decisions that work to their disadvantage.

Disparate treatment Situation that exists when protected-class members are treated differently from others.

Distributive justice The perceived fairness in the distribution of outcomes.

Diversity The differences among people.

Draw An amount advanced from and repaid to future commissions earned by the employee.

Due process Means used for individuals to explain and defend their actions against charges or discipline.

Duty A larger work segment composed of several tasks that are performed by an individual.

Economic value added (EVA) A firm's net operating profit after the cost of capital is deducted.

e-learning The use of the Internet or an organizational intranet to conduct training on-line.

Employee assistance program One that provides counseling and other help to employees having emotional, physical, or other personal problems.

Employee stock ownership plan (ESOP) A plan whereby employees gain stock ownership in the organization for which they work.

Employment-at-will (EAW) A common law doctrine stating that employers have the right to hire, fire, demote, or promote whomever they choose, unless there is a law or contract to the contrary.

Employment contract Agreement that formally outlines the details of employment.

Employment "test" Any employment procedure used as the basis for making an employment-related decision.

Environmental scanning Process of studying the environment of the organization to pinpoint opportunities and threats.

Encapsulated development Situation in which an individual learns new methods and ideas in a development course and returns to a work unit that is still bound by old attitudes and methods.

Equal employment opportunity (EEO) Individuals should have equal treatment in all employment-related actions.

Equity The perceived fairness of what the person does compared with what the person receives.

Ergonomics The study and design of the work environment to address physiological and physical demands on individuals.

Essential job functions Fundamental duties of a job.

Exempt employees Employees to whom employers are not required to pay overtime under the Fair Labor Standards Act.

Exit interview An interview in which individuals are asked to identify reasons for leaving the organization.

Expatriate An employee, working in an operation, who is not a citizen of the country in which the operation is located, but is a citizen of the country of the headquarters organization.

Expatriation Preparing and sending global employees to their foreign assignments.

Extranet An Internet-linked network that allows employees access to information provided by external entities.

Federation Group of autonomous national and international unions.

Feedback The amount of information received about how well or how poorly one has performed.

Flexible benefits plan One that allows employees to select the benefits they prefer from groups of benefits established by the employer.

Flexible spending account Account that allows employees to contribute pretax dollars to buy additional benefits.

Flexible staffing Use of recruiting sources and workers who are not traditional employees.

Flextime Scheduling arrangement in which employees work a set number of hours per day but vary starting and ending times.

Forced distribution Performance appraisal method in which ratings of employees' performance are distributed along a bell-shaped curve.

Forecasting Use of information from the past and present to identify expected future conditions.

401(k) plan An agreement in which a percentage of an employee's pay is withheld and invested in a tax-deferred account.

4/5ths rule Rule stating that discrimination generally is considered to occur if the selection rate for a protected group is less than 80% (4/5ths) of the selection rate for the majority group or less than 80% of the group's representation in the relevant labor market.

Gainsharing The sharing with employees of greater-than-expected gains in profits and/or productivity.

Garnishment A court action in which a portion of an employee's wages is set aside to pay a debt owed a creditor.

Glass ceiling Discriminatory practices that have prevented women and other protected-class members from advancing to executive-level jobs.

Global organization One having corporate units in a number of countries integrated to operate worldwide.

Golden parachute A severance benefit that provides protection and security to executives in the event that they lose their jobs or their firms are acquired by other firms.

Graphic rating scale A scale that allows the rater to mark an em-ployee's performance on a continuum.

Green-circled employee An incumbent who is paid below the range set for the job.

Grievance Complaint formally stated in writing.

Grievance arbitration Means by which a third party settles disputes arising from different interpretations of a labor contract.

Grievance procedures Formal channels of communications used to resolve grievances.

Halo effect Rating a person high on all items because of performance in one area.

Health A general state of physical, mental, and emotional well-being.

Health maintenance organization (HMO) Managed care plan that provides services for a fixed period on a prepaid basis.

Health promotion A supportive approach to facilitate and encourage employees to enhance healthy actions and lifestyles.

Health promotion A supportive approach to facilitate and encourage employees to enhance healthy actions and lifestyles.

Host-country national An employee working for a firm in an operation who is a citizen of the country where the operation is located, but where the headquarters for the firm are in another country.

Hostile environment Sexual harassment where an individual's work performance or psychological well-being is unreasonably affected by intimidating or offensive working conditions.

HR audit A formal research effort that evaluates the current state of HR management in an organization.

HR generalist A person with responsibility for performing a variety of HR activities.

HR research The analysis of data from HR records to determine the effectiveness of past and present HR practices.

HR specialist A person with in-depth knowledge and expertise in a limited area of HR.

Human Resource (HR) management The design of formal systems in an organization to ensure effective and efficient use of human talent to accomplish organizational goals.

HR strategies Means used to anticipate and manage the supply of and demand for human resources.

Human resource information system (HRIS) An integrated system designed providing information used in HR decision making.

Human resource (HR) management The design of formal systems in an organization to ensure effective and efficient use of human talent to accomplish organizational goals.

Human resource (HR) planning Process of analyzing and identifying the need for and availability of human resources so that the organization can meet its objectives.

Illegal issues Collective bargaining issues that would require either party to take illegal action.

Immediate confirmation The concept that people learn best if reinforcement and feedback is given after training.

Importing and exporting Selling and buying goods and services with organizations in other countries.

Independent contractors Workers who perform specific services on a contract basis.

Individual-centered career planning Career planning that focuses on individuals' careers rather than on organizational needs.

Individualism Dimension of culture that refers to the extent to which people in a country prefer to act as individuals instead of members of groups.

Individual retirement account (IRA) A special account in which an employee can set aside funds that will not be taxed until the employee retires.

Industrial union One that includes many persons working in the same industry or company, regardless of jobs held.

Informal training Training that occurs through interactions and feedback among employees.

Integrated disability management programs A benefit that combines disability insurance programs and efforts to reduce workers' compensation claims.

Intranet An organizational network that operates over the Internet.

Job Grouping of tasks, duties, and responsibilities that constitutes the total work assignment for employees.

Job analysis Systematic way to gather and analyze information about the content, context, and the human requirements of jobs.

Job criteria Important elements in a given job.

Job description Identification of the tasks, duties, and responsibilities of a job.

Job design Organizing tasks, duties, and responsibilities into a productive unit of work.

Job enlargement Broadening the scope of a job by expanding the number of different tasks to be performed.

Job enrichment Increasing the depth of a job by adding the responsibility for planning, organizing, controlling, and evaluating the job.

Job evaluation The systematic determination of the relative worth of jobs within an organization.

Job posting A system in which the employer provides notices of job openings and employees respond to apply.

Job rotation The process of shifting a person from job to job.

Job satisfaction A positive emotional state resulting from evaluating one's job experience.

Job specifications The knowledge, skills, and abilities (KSAs) an individual needs to perform a job satisfactorily.

Just cause Reasonable justification for taking employment-related actions.

Keogh plan A type of individualized pension plan for self-employed individuals.

Labor force population All individuals who are available for selection if all possible recruitment strategies are used.

Labor markets The external supply pool from which organizations attract employees.

Lockout Shutdown of company operations undertaken by management to prevent union members from working.

Lock out/tag out regulations Requirements that locks and tags be used to make equipment inoperative for repair or adjustment.

Long-term orientation Dimension of culture that refers to values people hold that emphasize the future, as opposed to short-term values focusing on the present and the past.

Lump-sum increase (LSI) A one-time payment of all or part of a yearly pay increase.

Managed care Approaches that monitor and reduce medical costs using restrictions and market system alternatives.

Marginal functions Duties that are part of a job but are incidental or ancillary to the purpose and nature of a job.

Management by objectives (MBO) Specifies the performance goals that an individual and her or his manager agree to try to attain within an appropriate length of time.

Management rights Those rights reserved to the employer to manage, direct, and control its business.

Mandated benefits Ones that employers in the United States must provide to employees by law.

Mandatory issues Collective bargaining issues identified specifically by labor laws or court decisions as subject to bargaining.

Market line The line on a graph showing the relationship between job value, as determined by job evaluation points and pay survey rates.

Masculinity/femininity Dimension of cultures that refers to the degree to which "masculine" values prevail over "feminine" values.

Massed practice The performance of all of the practice at once.

Maturity curve Curve that depicts the relationship between experience and pay rates.

Mediation Process by which a third party assists negotiators in reaching a settlement.

Mentoring A relationship in which experienced managers aid individuals in the earlier stages of their careers.

Motivation The desire within a person causing that person to act.

Multinational enterprise (MNE) An organization with operating units located in foreign countries.

National emergency strike A strike that would impact the national economy significantly.

Non-compete agreement Agreement that prohibits an individual who leaves the organization from competing with the employer in the same line of business for a specified period of time.

Non-contributory plan Pension plan in which all the funds for pension benefits are provided by the employer.

Nondirective interview Interview that uses questions that are developed from the answers to previous questions.

Non-exempt employees Employees who must be paid overtime under the Fair Labor Standards Act.

Ombudsman Person outside the normal chain of command who acts as a problem solver for both management and employees.

Open shop Workers are not required to join or pay dues to unions.

Organization-centered career planning Career planning that focuses on jobs and on identifying career paths that provide for the logical progression of people between jobs in an organization.

Organizational commitment The degree to which employees believe in and accept organizational goals and desire to remain with the organization.

Organizational culture The shared values and beliefs of a workforce.

Orientation The planned introduction of new employees to their jobs, co-workers, and the organization.

Paid time-off plan Plan that combines all sick leave, vacation time, and holidays into a total number of hours or days that employees can take off with pay.

Panel interview Interview in which several interviewers interview the candidate at the same time.

Pay compression Situation in which pay differences among individuals with different levels of experience and performance in the organization becomes small.

Pay equity Similarity in pay for jobs requiring comparable levels of knowledge, skill, and ability, even if actual job duties differ significantly.

Pay grade A grouping of individual jobs having approximately the same job worth.

Pay survey A collection of data on compensation rates for workers performing similar jobs in other organizations.

Peer review panel A panel of employees hears appeals from disciplined employees and makes recommendations or decisions.

Pension plans Retirement benefits established and funded by employers and employees.

Performance What an employee does or does not do.

Performance appraisal The process of evaluating how well employees perform their jobs when compared to a set of standards, and then communicating that information to employees.

Performance consulting A process in which a trainer and the organizational client work together to boost workplace performance in support of business goals.

Performance management system Processes used to identify, encourage, measure, evaluate, improve, and reward employee performance.

Performance standards Indicators of what the job accomplishes and how performance is measured in key areas of the job description.

Permissive issues Collective bargaining issues that are not mandatory but relate to certain jobs.

Perquisites (perks) Special benefits—usually noncash items—for executives.

Person-job fit Matching the KSAs of people with the characteristics of jobs.

Person-organization fit The congruence between individuals and organizational factors.

Phased retirement Approach in which employees reduce their workloads and pay.

Physical ability tests Tests that measure individual abilities such as strength, endurance, and muscular movement.

Piece-rate system A pay system in which wages are determined by multiplying the number of units produced by the piece rate for one unit.

Placement Fitting a person to the right job.

Policies General guidelines that focus organizational actions.

Portability A pension plan feature that allows employees to move their pension benefits from one employer to another.

Power distance Dimension of culture that refers to the inequality among the people of a nation.

Predictive validity Measured when test results of applicants are compared with subsequent job performance.

Preferred provider organization (PPO) A health-care provider that contracts with an employer group to provide health-care services to employees at a competitive rate.

Primacy effect Information received first gets the most weight.

Primary research Research method in which data are gathered firsthand for the specific project being conducted.

Procedural justice The perceived fairness of the process and procedures used to make decisions about employees.

Procedures Customary methods of handling activities.

Production cells Groupings of workers who produce entire products or components.

Productivity A measure of the quantity and quality of work done, considering the cost of the resources used.

Profit sharing A system to distribute a portion of the profits of the organization to employees.

Protected class Individuals within a group identified for protection under equal employment laws and regulation.

Psychological contract The unwritten expectations employees and employers have about the nature of their work relationships.

Psychomotor tests Tests that measure dexterity, hand-eye coordination, arm-hand steadiness, and other factors.

Quality circle Small group of employees who monitor productivity and quality and suggest solutions to problems.

Quid pro quo Sexual harassment in which employment outcomes are linked to the individual granting sexual favors.

Ranking Listing of all employees from highest to lowest in performance.

Rater bias Error that occurs when a rater's values or prejudices distort the rating.

Ratification Process by which union members vote to accept the terms of a negotiated labor agreement.

Realistic job preview (RJP) The process through which a job applicant receives an accurate picture of a job.

Recency effect Error in which the rater gives greater weight to recent events when appraising an individual's performance.

Reasonable accommodation A modification or adjustment to a job or work environment for a qualified individual with a disability.

Recruiting The process of generating a pool of qualified applicants for organizational jobs.

Red-circled employee An incumbent who is paid above the range set for the job.

Reinforcement People tend to repeat responses that give them some type of positive reward and avoid actions associated with negative consequences.

Reliability Consistency with which a test measures an item.

Repatriation Planning, training, and reassignment of global employees to their home countries.

Responsibilities Obligations to perform certain tasks and duties.

Retaliation Punitive actions taken by employers against individuals who exercise their legal rights.

Return on investment (ROI) Calculation showing the value of expenditures for HR activities.

Reverse discrimination When a person is denied an opportunity because of preferences given to protected-class individuals who may be less qualified.

Right to privacy Defined for individuals as the freedom from unauthorized and unreasonable intrusion into their personal affairs.

Rights That which belongs to a person by law, nature, or tradition.

Right-to-sue letter A letter issued by the EEOC that notifies a complainant that he or she has 90 days in which to file a personal suit in federal court.

Right-to-work laws State laws that prohibit requiring employees to join unions as a condition of obtaining or continuing employment.

Rules Specific guidelines that regulate and restrict the behavior of individuals.

Sabbatical leave Paid time off the job to develop and rejuvenate oneself.

Safety Condition in which the physical well-being of people is protected.

Salaries Consistent payments made each period regardless of number of hours worked.

Salting Practice in which unions hire and pay people to apply for jobs at certain companies.

Secondary research Research method using data already gathered by others and reported in books, articles in professional journals, or other sources.

Security Protection of employees and organizational facilities.

Security audit A comprehensive review of organizational security.

Selection Process of choosing individuals who have needed qualifications to fill jobs in an organization.

Selection criterion Characteristic that a person must have to do a job successfully.

Selection rate The percentage hired from a given group of candidates.

Self-directed work team One composed of individuals assigned a cluster of tasks, duties, and responsibilities to be accomplished.

Self-efficacy A person's belief that he/she can successfully learn the training program content.

Seniority Time spent in the organization or on a particular job.

Separation agreement Agreement in which a terminated employee agrees not to sue the employer in exchange for specified benefits.

Serious health condition A health condition requiring inpatient, hospital, hospice, or residential medical care or continuing physician care.

Severance pay A security benefit voluntarily offered by employers to employees who lose their jobs.

Sexual harassment Actions that are sexually directed, are unwanted, and subject the worker to adverse employment conditions or create a hostile work environment.

Shamrock team One composed of a core of members, resource experts who join the team as appropriate, and part-time/temporary members as needed.

Simulation A development technique that requires participants to analyze a situation and decide the best course of action based on the data given.

Situational interview A structured interview composed of questions about how applicants might handle specific job situations.

Skill variety The extent to which the work requires several different activities for successful completion.

Spaced practice Several practice sessions spaced over a period of hours or days.

Special-purpose team Organizational team formed to address specific problems, improve work processes, and enhance product and service quality.

Statutory rights Rights based on laws.

Stock option A plan that gives an individual the right to buy stock in a company, usually at a fixed price for a period of time.

Straight piece-rate system A pay system in which wages are determined by multiplying the number of units produced by the piece rate for one unit.

Strategic Human Resource Management (SHRM) Organizational use of employees to gain or keep a competitive advantage against competitors.

Stress interview Interview designed to create anxiety and put pressure on an applicant to see how the person responds.

Strike Work stoppage in which union members refuse to work in order to put pressure on an employer.

Structured interview Interview that uses a set of standardized questions asked of all job applicants.

Substance abuse The use of illicit substances or the misuse of controlled substances, alcohol, or other drugs.

Succession planning Process of identifying a longer-term plan for the orderly replacement of key employees.

Suggestion system A formal method of obtaining employee input and upward communication.

Task A distinct, identifiable work activity composed of motions.

Task identity The extent to which the job includes a "whole" identifiable unit of work that is carried out from start to finish and that results in a visible outcome.

Task significance The impact the job has on other people.

Tax equalization plan Compensation plan used to protect expatriates from negative tax consequences.

Team interview Interview in which applicants are interviewed by the team members with whom they will work.

Telecommuting Process of going to work via electronic computing and telecommunications equipment.

Third-country national A citizen of one country, working in a second country, and employed by an organization headquartered in a third country.

Training A process whereby people acquire capabilities to aid in the achievement of organizational goals.

Transition stay bonus Extra payment for employees whose jobs are being eliminated, thereby motivating them to remain with the organization for a period of time.

Turnover Process in which employees leave the organization and have to be replaced.

Uncertainty avoidance Dimension of culture that refers to the preference of people in a country for structured rather than unstructured situations.

Undue hardship Significant difficulty or expense imposed on an employer when making an accommodation for individuals with disabilities.

Union A formal association of workers that promotes the interests of its members through collective action.

Union authorization card Card signed by an employee to designate a union as his or her collective bargaining agent.

Union security provision Contract clauses to aid the union in obtaining and retaining members.

Union steward An employee elected to serve as the first-line representative of unionized workers.

Unit labor cost Computed by dividing the average cost of workers by their average levels of output.

Utility analysis Analysis in which economic or other statistical models are built to identify the costs and benefits associated with specific HR activities.

Utilization analysis An analysis that identifies the number of protected-class members employed and the types of jobs they hold in an organization.

Utilization review An audit and review of the services and costs billed by health-care providers.

Validity Extent to which a test actually measures what it says it measures.

Variable pay Type of compensation linked to individual, team, or organizational performance.

Vesting The right of employees to receive benefits from their pension plans.

Wages Payments directly calculated on the amount of time worked.

Wellness programs Programs designed to maintain or improve employee health before problems arise.

Well-pay Extra pay for not taking sick leave.

Whistle-blowers Individuals who report real or perceived wrongs committed by their employers.

Work Effort directed toward producing or accomplishing results.

Workflow analysis A study of the way work (inputs, activities, and outputs) moves through an organization.

Work sample tests Tests that require an applicant to perform a simulated job task.

Workers' compensation Benefits provided to persons injured on the job.

Wrongful discharge Occurs when an employer terminates an individual's employment for reasons that are improper or illegal.

Yield ratios A comparison of the number of applicants at one stage of the recruiting process to the number at the next stage.

Index

Note: Page numbers in *italics* refer to illustrations

Z